Designing Effective Assessment

Principles and Profiles of Good Practice

Trudy W. Banta, Elizabeth A. Jones,
Karen E. Black

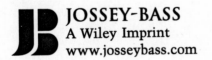

JOSSEY-BASS
A Wiley Imprint
www.josseybass.com

Published by Jossey-Bass
A Wiley Imprint
989 Market Street, San Francisco, CA 94103-1741—www.josseybass.com

Jossey-Bass books and products are available through most bookstores. To contact Jossey-Bass directly call our Customer Care Department within the U.S. at 800-956-7739, outside the U.S. at 317-572-3986, or fax 317-572-4002.

Jossey-Bass also publishes its books in a variety of electronic formats. Some content that appears in print may not be available in electronic books.

Library of Congress Cataloging-in-Publication Data

Banta, Trudy W.
  Designing effective assessment : principles and profiles of good practice / Trudy W. Banta, Elizabeth A. Jones, Karen E. Black.
      p. cm.
  Includes bibliographical references and index.
  ISBN 978-0-470-39334-5 (pbk.)
  1. Universities and colleges—United States—Examinations. 2. Education, Higher—United States—Evaluation. 3. Educational tests and measurements—United States. 4. Education, Higher—United States—Evaluation—Case studies. I. Jones, Elizabeth A. II. Black, Karen E. III. Title.
  LB2366.2.B36 2009
  378'.01—dc22

                                                                                    2009009809

10 9 8 7 6 5 4 3

THE JOSSEY-BASS

HIGHER AND ADULT EDUCATION SERIES

To
Holly, Logan, and T. J.
Father, Mother, and Debbie
Marie, Mary, Earl, Joe, Mary Anne, Beth, Ryan,
Brett, Claire, and Moses

And special thanks to
Shirley Yorger

CONTENTS

RESOURCES

PREFACE

"Please send me some examples of assessment in general education." "I need examples of assessment in engineering and business." "How can we encourage faculty to engage in assessment?" "Can you name ten institutions that are doing good work in assessment?" These are the questions colleagues around the globe send us via e-mail or ask us at conferences or during campus visits. These are the questions that motivated the three authors of this book to develop its content on outcomes assessment in higher education.

Two of us—Karen Black and Trudy Banta—were involved in a similar project in the mid-1990s. With colleagues Jon P. Lund and Frances W. Oblander, we edited *Assessment in Practice: Putting Principles to Work on College Campuses* (Banta, Lund, Black, & Oblander, 1996). That book began with chapters on each of ten principles of good practice that had emanated from assessment experience prior to 1995 and continued with a section containing 86 short case studies of campus assessment practice categorized by the focus of assessment in each, including general education, student development, or classroom assessment. The principles and the cases in that 1996 publication are as relevant and useful today as they were then. In fact, two of us are still using the book as a reference and some of the cases as examples in the courses we teach for students enrolled in doctoral programs in higher education. Nevertheless, we decided that a new book organized similarly would give us even more examples to share when we are asked questions like those noted earlier.

First we posted a request on the ASSESS listserv for brief profiles of good practice in assessment. In addition, we sent some 800 e-mail requests to individuals who had contributed to *Assessment in Practice*, or to the bimonthly *Assessment Update*, or who had presented at the Assessment Institute in Indianapolis in recent years. We received approximately 180 expressions of interest in contributing a profile. We then wrote to these 180 individuals and asked them to prepare a 1,500-word profile using an outline we provided.

The outline we used for case studies for *Assessment in Practice* contained just four headings to guide authors in developing their narratives: Background and Purpose (of the Assessment Activity), Method, Findings and Their Use, and Success Factors. Now that more than a decade has passed, we wanted to know if the use of our findings had had a noticeable or measurable effect on practice, and more important, on student learning and success. We also were interested in details such as the years of implementation, and the cost of the assessment initiatives. Therefore, our outline for authors of profiles for this book contains the following headings: Background and Purpose(s) of Assessment, Assessment Method(s) and Year(s) of Implementation, Required Resources, Findings, Use of Findings, Impact of Using the Findings, Success Factors, and Relevant Institutional Web Sites Pertaining to This Assessment Practice.

We were surprised and pleased that a large proportion of the early expressions of interest we received led to the development of full profiles. By our deadline we had received 146 of these. After reviewing them we wrote Part One of this volume, illustrating the principles of good practice in assessment that we consider essential with examples from some of the 146 profiles. We used as the primary reference for the principles a section titled, "Characteristics of Effective Outcomes Assessment" in *Building a Scholarship of Assessment* (Banta & Associates, 2002). That listing was based on work by Hutchings (1993); Banta and Associates (1993); Banta et al. (1996); American Productivity and Quality Center (1998); and Jones, Voorhees, and Paulson (2002).

For Part Two of this volume we selected for inclusion in their entirety 49 of the most fully developed of the profiles we had received. As in *Assessment in Practice*, we placed each of the profiles in a category based on its primary focus, such as general education, academic major, or program review. The profiles in each category are preceded by a narrative that explains their most important features.

Initially we were quite frustrated by the fact that although we had received so many good profiles, we were able to use only a third of them due to space limitations. But then, after securing permission, we decided to list in Resource A all of the institutions and authors from the collection of 146 profiles. In almost every case we have provided a Web site that may be consulted for further information about the assessment practices under way at the institution identified. In Resource B all the profiles are categorized to make it easier for readers to find the type of assessment (general education or graduate programs) they seek. Resource C presents a list of institutions by Carnegie Classification for the 49 profiles used in their entirety. Resource D contains the titles of the authors of the 49 full profiles.

The institutional profiles of assessment practice that we received represent a range of public and private institutions, from community colleges to research universities. Representation is also national in scope: profiles were received from institutions in California and Massachusetts, Florida and Oregon, and many states in between. As is clear from reading the "Background and Purpose" sections of the profiles, accreditation, both regional and disciplinary, has been a major driving force behind assessment at many of these institutions. State requirements for public institutions also played a role in some of the examples.

As we know so well, state and national legislators and federal policy makers are calling on colleges and universities to furnish concrete evidence of their accountability. Many of our constituents believe that standardized test scores will provide the evidence of student learning that is needed, and tests of generic skills such as writing and critical thinking are being suggested as the sources of such evidence. The profiles we have reviewed will disappoint decision makers in this regard. In almost all cases where standardized tests of generic skills have been used at these institutions, the test scores are not being reported as a single source of evidence of student learning. Faculty who have studied the scores over several years with the intention of using them to provide direction for improvements have determined that test scores alone are not adequate to the task of defining what students learn in college, nor are they illuminating and dependable guides for making decisions about improvements in curriculum and methods of instruction that will enhance student learning. Where standardized tests of generic skills have been tried, in most cases they have been supplemented with indirect measures such as questionnaires and focus groups and/or faculty-developed direct measures such as classroom tests or capstone projects.

Few of these assessment profiles contain the kind of quantitative data that could be reported simply and grasped easily by external audiences. Moreover, the information in the section "Impact of Using Findings" is seldom expressed in measurable terms. But we have assembled a wealth of information we can use to respond to that oft-asked question of how to engage faculty in assessment. And the evidence of student learning, engagement, and satisfaction that has been amassed has, in fact, been used to add courses and other learning experiences to the curriculum, to educate faculty about better ways to teach, and to improve student support services such as advising. Faculty time and administrative leadership are the chief resources identified as critical to the success of assessment initiatives.

We sincerely hope that this book will be regarded by faculty, staff, and administrators as the rich resource of principles and profiles of good assessment practice that we envision.

September 2008   Trudy W. Banta
                                                                    Elizabeth A. Jones
                                                                    Karen E. Black

THE AUTHORS

Trudy W. Banta is professor of higher education and senior advisor to the chancellor for academic planning and evaluation at Indiana University–Purdue University Indianapolis. She has developed and coordinated 21 national conferences and 15 international conferences on the topic of assessing quality in higher education. She has consulted with faculty and administrators in 46 states, Puerto Rico, South Africa, and the United Arab Emirates and has by invitation addressed national conferences on outcomes assessment in Canada, China, England, France, Germany, Spain, and Scotland. Dr. Banta has edited 15 published volumes on assessment, contributed 26 chapters to published works, and written more than 200 articles and reports. She is the founding editor of *Assessment Update*, a bimonthly periodical published since 1989. She has been recognized for her work by the American Association for Higher Education, American College Personnel Association, American Productivity and Quality Center, Association for Institutional Research, National Council on Measurement in Education, and National Consortium for Continuous Improvement in Higher Education.

Elizabeth A. Jones is professor of higher education leadership at West Virginia University (WVU). She has conducted assessment research supported by the National Postsecondary Education Cooperative that resulted in the publication of two books.

She served as the principal investigator of a general education assessment project supported by the Fund for the Improvement of Postsecondary Education.

She has chaired the general education assessment committee at WVU and offered numerous professional development seminars to both student affairs staff and faculty members. Dr. Jones has published numerous articles pertaining to assessment and has presented at national conferences. She is currently the editor of the *Journal of General Education* published by the Pennsylvania State University Press.

Karen E. Black is director of program review at Indiana University–Purdue University Indianapolis where she teaches in the organizational leadership and supervision department and is an adjunct faculty member in University College. She is managing editor of *Assessment Update*.

Designing Effective Assessment

PART ONE

PRINCIPLES OF GOOD PRACTICE IN OUTCOMES ASSESSMENT

We introduce this volume with a set of principles for good practice in assessing the outcomes of higher education that have been drawn from several sources, principally from the "characteristics of effective outcomes assessment" in *Building a Scholarship of Assessment* (Banta & Associates, 2002, pp. 262–263). This collection of principles is by no means exhaustive, but it covers many of the components considered by practitioners to be essential to good practice. The principles are presented in three groups, each associated with a phase of assessment: first planning, then implementing, and finally improving and sustaining assessment initiatives. Current literature is cited in providing a foundation for the principles, and brief excerpts from some of the 146 profiles submitted for this book are used to illustrate them.

In Chapter 1, "Planning Effective Assessment," we present the following principles as essential:

- Engaging stakeholders
- Connecting assessment to valued goals and processes
- Creating a written plan
- Timing assessment
- Building a culture based on evidence

In Chapter 2, "Implementing Effective Assessment," these principles are identified and discussed:

- Providing leadership
- Creating faculty and staff development opportunities
- Assessing processes as well as outcomes
- Communicating and using assessment findings

In Chapter 3, "Improving and Sustaining Effective Assessment," the following principles are described and illustrated:

- Providing credible evidence of learning to multiple stakeholders
- Reviewing assessment reports
- Ensuring use of assessment results
- Evaluating the assessment process

CHAPTER ONE

PLANNING EFFECTIVE ASSESSMENT

Effective assessment doesn't just happen. It emerges over time as an outcome of thoughtful planning, and in the spirit of continuous improvement, it evolves as reflection on the processes of implementing and sustaining assessment suggests modifications.

Engaging Stakeholders

A first step in planning is to identify and engage appropriate stakeholders. Faculty members, academic administrators, and student affairs professionals must play principal roles in setting the course for assessment, but students can contribute ideas and so can trustees, employers, and other community representatives. We expect faculty to set broad learning outcomes for general education and more specific outcomes for academic majors. Trustees of an institution, employers, and other community representatives can review drafts of these outcomes and offer suggestions for revision based on their perspectives regarding community needs. Student affairs professionals can comment on the outcomes and devise their own complementary outcomes based on plans to extend learning into campus environments beyond the classroom. Students have the ability to translate the language of the academy, where necessary, into terms that their peers will understand. Students also can help to design data-gathering strategies and instruments as assessment moves from the planning phase to implementation. Finally, regional accreditors and national disciplinary and professional organizations contribute ideas for the planning phase of assessment. They often set standards for assessing student learning and provide resources in the form of written materials and workshops at their periodic meetings.

Connecting Assessment to Valued Goals and Processes

Connecting assessment to institution-wide strategic planning is a way to increase the perceived value of assessment. Assessment may be viewed as the mechanism for gauging progress on every aspect of an institution's plan. In the planning process the need to demonstrate accountability for student learning may become a mechanism for ensuring that student learning outcomes, and their assessment, are included in the institutional plan. However assessment is used, plans to carry it out must be based on clear, explicit goals.

Since 1992 assessment of progress has been one of the chief mechanisms for shaping three strategic plans at Pace University (Barbara Pennipede and Joseph Morreale, see Resource A, p. 289). In 1997 the success of the first 5-year plan was assessed via a survey of the 15 administrators and 10 faculty leaders who had been responsible for implementing the plan. In 2001, in addition to interviews with the principal implementers, other faculty, staff, and students, as well as trustees, were questioned in focus groups and open meetings and via e-mail.

By 2003 the Pace president had decided that assessment of progress on the plan needed to occur more often—annually rather than every fifth year. Pace faculty and staff developed a strategic plan assessment grid, and data such as student performance on licensing exams, participation in key campus programs, and responses to the UCLA freshman survey were entered in appropriate cells of the grid to be monitored over time.

Likewise, at Iona College 25 dashboard indicators are used to track progress on all elements of Iona's mission (Warren Rosenberg, see p. 262). Iona's Key Performance Indicators, which are called KPIs, include statistics supplied by the institutional research office on such measures as diversity of the faculty and student body (percentages of females and nonwhite constituents), 6-year graduation rates, and percentage of graduates completing internships. Student responses to relevant items on the National Survey of Student Engagement (NSSE) are used in monitoring progress toward the mission element stated "Iona College graduates will be sought after because they will be skilled decision-makers . . . independent thinkers . . . lifelong learners . . . adaptable to new information and technologies."

According to Thomas P. Judd and Bruce Keith (see p. 46), "the overarching academic goal" that supports the mission of the U.S. Military Academy is this: "Graduates anticipate and respond effectively to the uncertainties of a changing technological, social, political, and economic world." This broad goal is implemented through ten more specific goals such as ensuring that graduates can think and act creatively, recognize moral issues and apply ethical considerations in decision making, understand human behavior, and be proficient in the fundamentals of engineering and information technology. Each of these goals yields clear, explicit statements of student outcomes. Faculty at West Point set performance standards for each outcome and apply rubrics in assessing student work. The ten goals provide guidance for the development of 30 core courses that are taken by all students at the Military Academy.

Outcomes assessment cannot be undertaken solely for its own sake. Assessment that spins in its own orbit, not intersecting with other processes that are valued in the academy, will surely fail the test of relevance once it is applied by decision makers. Assessment will become relevant in the eyes of faculty and administrators when it becomes a part of the following: strategic planning for programs and the institution; implementation of new academic and student affairs programs; making decisions about the competence of students; comprehensive program (peer) review; faculty and professional staff development; and/or faculty and staff reward and recognition systems.

Creating a Written Plan

As Suskie (2004, p. 57) puts it, planning for assessment requires "written guidance on who does what when." Which academic programs and student support or administrative units will be assessing which aspects of student learning or components of their programs each year? Who will be responsible for each assessment activity?

A matrix can be helpful in charting progress. As illustrated in Table 1.1, we first set a broad goal or learning outcome in which we are interested, then develop aspects of the goal in the form of specific measurable objectives. A third consideration is where the objective will be taught and learned. Then how will the objective be assessed? What are the assessment findings, and how should they be interpreted and reported? How are the findings used to improve processes, and what impact do the improvements have on achieving progress toward the original goal? Since 1998, a matrix similar to that in Table 1.1 has been used in assessment planning and reporting by faculty and staff in individual departments and offices at Indiana University–Purdue University Indianapolis (see www.planning.iupui.edu/64.html#07).

TABLE 1.1. PLANNING FOR LEARNING AND ASSESSMENT.

1. What general outcome are you seeking?	2. How would you know it (the outcome) if you saw it? (What will the student know or be able to do?)	3. How will you help students learn it? (in class or out of class)	4. How could you measure each of the desired behaviors listed in #2?	5. What are the assessment findings?	6. What improvements have been made based on assessment findings?	7. What has been the impact of improvements?

Walvoord (2004) has provided a useful set of standards for judging an effective assessment plan. She envisions the plan as a written document that

1. embeds assessment in high-stakes and high-energy processes.
2. considers audiences and purposes.
3. arranges oversight and resources.
4. articulates learning goals.
5. incorporates an assessment audit of measures already in place and how the data are used in decision making.
6. includes steps for improving the assessment process.
7. includes steps designed to improve student learning. (p. 11)

The assessment plan at St. Norbert College embodies these standards. It was developed with support from a Title III Strengthening Institutions Grant after insufficient progress in implementing assessment was identified as "an urgent institutional need" (Robert A. Rutter, see Resource A, p. 290). College administrators established the Office of Institutional Effectiveness and the assessment committee was expanded to include campuswide representation. The assessment committee produced the "Plan for Assessing Student Learning Outcomes at St. Norbert College," which was subsequently endorsed by every division of the college as well as the Student Government Association. The institution's mission statement was revised to include student learning outcomes, a comprehensive review of the general education program resulted in a continuous evaluation process that repeats on a four-year cycle, and a rigorous program review process was implemented for academic units. As a result of assessing learning outcomes in general education and major fields, general education course offerings in some areas have been refocused, major and minor programs have been reviewed and improved, a few programs have been terminated, new strategies to support and retain students have been implemented, and a student competence model in student life has been developed.

Timing Assessment

Timing is a crucial aspect of planning for assessment. Ideally, assessment is built into strategic planning for an institution or department and is a component of any new program as it is being conceived. If assessment must be added to a program or event that is already under way, time is needed to convince the initiative's developers of the value of assessment for improving and sustaining their efforts. Finally, because effective assessment requires the use of multiple methods, it is not usually resource-efficient to implement every method right away or even every year. A comprehensive assessment plan will include a schedule for implementing each data-gathering method at least once over a period of three to five years.

At the University of Houston main campus every academic and administrative unit must submit an institutional effectiveness plan each year. Institutional research staff assist faculty with program reviews, surveys, and data analysis. Part-time and full-time assessment professionals are embedded in the colleges to provide day-to-day support. Libby Barlow (see Resource A, p. 293) describes the evolution of the current plan as slow, but asserts that "genuine assessment ... takes time to take root. Higher education is a slow ship to turn ... so pushing faster than faculty are willing to go will inevitably cause backlash and be counterproductive. Time has allowed us to go through several structures to discover what would work."

Building a Culture Based on Evidence

Outcomes assessment can be sustained only if planning and implementation take place in an atmosphere of trust and within a culture that encourages the use of evidence in decision making. Bresciani (2006) notes the following characteristics of such an environment:

1. Key institutional leaders must demonstrate that they genuinely care about student learning issues.
2. Leaders must create a culture of trust and integrity through consistent actions that demonstrate a commitment to ethical and evidence-based decision-making.
3. Connections must be established between formative and summative assessment and between assessment for improvement and assessment for accountability.
4. Curriculum design, pedagogy, and faculty development must be connected to delivery and evaluation of student learning.
5. Faculty research and teaching must be connected so that they complement each other in practice and in the campus reward structure. (pp. 144–146)

At Agnes Scott College the faculty-staff Committee on Assessing Institutional Effectiveness recommended that the president integrate a report on assessment activities in the template for annual reports that all academic and administrative units must submit. Laura Palucki Blake (see Resource A, p. 280) believes this integration of assessment in a report long expected of each unit helps to create a positive culture for assessment. If the president expects it, assessment must be important. Moreover, because each vice president sees the reports from his or her units, assessment evidence takes on added importance in decision making at Agnes Scott.

In subsequent sections of this volume we will describe additional characteristics of the culture in which assessment can thrive.

CHAPTER TWO

IMPLEMENTING EFFECTIVE ASSESSMENT

The most carefully crafted plans will not produce desired results if not implemented in good faith by appropriate people who have the proper knowledge and skills and who are supported by organizational leaders. Assessment scholars (Walvoord, 2004; Suskie, 2004; Palomba & Banta, 1999) have written entire books on specific ways to conduct assessment. Each has offered sound general and step-by-step advice. These authors provide evidence that key principles undergirding successful implementation include providing knowledgeable and effective leadership, with opportunities for faculty and staff development; emphasizing that assessment is essential to learning, and therefore everyone's responsibility; educating faculty and staff about good assessment practices; providing sufficient resources to support assessment; and devolving responsibility for assessment to the unit level. We expand on several of these principles in the paragraphs below.

Providing Leadership

Leadership at all levels is critical for successful assessment programs (Maki, 2004; Suskie, 2004; Peterson & Vaughn, 2002). Academic leaders—including presidents, provosts, deans, department chairs, and leaders in student affairs—must be public advocates for assessment and provide appropriate leadership as well as support for the faculty and staff closest to the assessment process. Through public and private statements and actions, these leaders can enhance the likelihood that the assessment process will be valued and sustained. Such leaders often foster innovations by providing meaningful incentives for participants. Leaders should clearly articulate the need for and importance of a credible and sustainable student outcomes assessment process, but faculty and staff also must commit time and talent to the process.

The task of revitalizing a dormant assessment process at the University of Central Florida has been successful first and foremost because of the commitment and support of the president and senior administrators. The president's sustained attention to the question of how the institution can do better has produced a stronger assessment program and ultimately led to external validation through successful accreditation visits (Julia Pet-Armacost and Robert L. Armacost, see Resource A, p. 293).

Empowering Faculty and Staff to Assume Leadership Roles for Assessment

Faculty and staff routinely take on campuswide and department-level leadership roles—for example, by leading assessment committees or by joining formal or informal research or practitioner groups to discuss and analyze data and to encourage and offer support for their colleagues. Faculty are involved in the design and implementation of student learning activities and the curriculum and thus are the most knowledgeable about goals for student learning in these areas. Likewise, student affairs professionals and advisors are the experts in setting student learning goals for campus activities and advising. All of these individuals must play critical leadership roles in assessing the outcomes of these activities at both the campus level and within colleges, schools, divisions, and departments.

Although leadership is imperative at all levels, assessment has the most impact when responsibility for carrying out assessment resides primarily at the unit level. Because unit faculty and staff have developed the goals for student learning, they must assess student achievement of those goals. The learning that takes place in the process of assessing the degree to which goals are achieved is most useful at the unit level where the principals can take that understanding and apply it in improving curriculum and instruction. Receiving a report from a central office is informative, but results take on new meaning when the persons responsible for the program or process engage in assessment design, implementation, and analysis. And regardless of who collects and analyzes the data, actions based on assessment findings must be taken at the unit level. If individuals in a unit are to embrace the responsibility for taking the action, they must own the assessment process.

Central assessment or institutional research offices can provide leadership by not only collecting and analyzing data and reporting results but also by leading processes. In addition, many academic units such as colleges of business or colleges of education have full-time staff members or faculty members serving as the full-time assessment leader. At St. Cloud State University, the Assessment Peer Consulting Program that trains peer consultants to assist units engaged in assessment is led by staff in the Assessment Office (James Sherohman, see Resource A, p. 290). Based on the strengths of the consultants and the nature of the request, staff assign two campus consultants to assist each unit seeking help with an assessment process. When the work is finished, the requesting unit provides an evaluation of the facilitation process. Sherohman reports that this process has strengthened individual unit assessment processes and has resulted in greater assessment capacity throughout the campus.

Ownership by faculty and staff participating in learning communities such as the Hocking College's Success Skills Integration project has been enhanced by their participation in the process as they struggle to find suitable metrics for measuring student learning in general education courses. As a result of this struggle, faculty are looking for more varied learning opportunities for students. Success of long-term faculty and staff initiatives in general education such as the one at Hocking is attributed to the key roles these individuals have played in developing, implementing, and assessing the program (Judith Maxson and Bonnie Allen Smith, see p. 258).

Providing Sufficient Resources

In a national survey of institution leaders and an extensive literature review, Peterson, Einarson, Augustine, and Vaughan (1999) report that assessment proponents argue for the commitment of resources to assessment initiatives. Authors of this comprehensive study of nearly 1,400 responses (from approximately 2,500 questionnaires distributed) from institutions across the country reported that 49 percent of institutions had established budget allocations "to support their student assessment activities" (p. 94). However, the commitment varied greatly by institution type. Baccalaureate institutions were the most likely to have explicit budget allocations, and research universities the least likely to do so.

In addition to the traditional budget allocations for staff time and relevant materials, leaders must provide resources for developing appropriate methods, giving faculty and staff opportunities to hone their assessment skills, and rewarding those who engage in assessment, whether that be through the traditional promotion and tenure process and staff advancement or through other means, such as assessment grants or awards. Faculty and staff can contribute to the resource base by competing for external grants or awards.

Obtaining external grants has proven to be a useful way to launch an assessment program, but sustaining the program with soft money is risky and should be viewed as a temporary measure. According to Robert A. Rutter (see Resource A, p. 290) federal grants such as the Title III funding received by faculty at St. Norbert College can provide interim support until permanent resources are available for infrastructure. In addition, such funds can be used for faculty development in the form of conference attendance. Partly as a result of what faculty have learned at national meetings, the assessment activity at St. Norbert has matured, as evidenced, for example, by the revisioning of the general education program and its assessment.

A grant from the Bush Foundation was used to fund a longitudinal study at the University of North Dakota. Kelsch and Hawthorne (see Resource A, p. 294) report that these funds were used to provide stipends to individuals to interview students and transcribe their comments, then participate in data analysis days during which faculty considered implications of the data and planned the next year's interviews. During the interviews, students were asked how they experienced the general education curriculum and their learning. Faculty were assigned 10 to 12 students each to interview and were paid $1,000 to $1,500 per year; student participants were given $25 per interview.

Educating Faculty and Staff about Good Assessment Practices

To help faculty and staff understand the potential range of effective assessment practices and how to implement them, many colleges and universities offer special programming through a center for teaching and learning or a faculty-staff development office. Though most of the profiles addressing professional development in this book are focused on academic affairs, it is crucial to provide similar programming for student affairs leaders and staff. Such programming can be designed as an integrated set of learning experiences that take place over several semesters. Aloi, Green, and Jones (2007) discuss the specific nature of six professional development seminars that were offered to all student affairs leaders and staff at West Virginia University. These seminars helped student affairs units develop learner-centered assessment plans. A significant challenge to leaders of professional development initiatives that involve planning and implementing assessment processes is in sustaining the programs' effectiveness. Research suggests that one-time single session workshops or interventions often have little effect on behavior (Licklider, Schnelker, & Fulton, 1997).

Creating development opportunities for instructors is difficult without knowing what types of help faculty need to assess student outcomes. At Widener University, a special task force was appointed to develop and conduct a survey of faculty needs. The results indicated that the following areas needed attention: "developing student-centered learning outcomes, creating assessment criteria, reporting results, and using results to improve teaching and learning" (Brigitte Valesey, see p. 128).

Needs assessments like the one used at Widener can help academic leaders identify which assessment topics need attention and suggest how to offer educational opportunities for faculty. Topics with which most faculty need assistance include how to write student-centered learning outcomes, how to choose the best assessment methods, and how to interpret and use the results of assessment to make targeted improvements.

Faculty learning communities provide an example of a more sustained initiative that may have a greater impact on instructors. In learning communities, instructors typically work together for a semester or more on a specific project. At Texas Christian University, several campus units provided funding to support the creation of six faculty learning communities (FLCs), each representing a part of the core general education curriculum. The FLCS are designed to: "(1) create and maintain appropriate assessment strategies for the category, (2) share the results of the assessment process with faculty who teach in that category, and (3) enhance discussion on teaching within that particular core category" (Catherine Wehlburg, see p. 114).

Ideally faculty development opportunities are provided during the entire assessment cycle—from the very beginning as plans are developed, through the implementation of assessment and interpretation of results, to understanding how to use the results to make improvements.

Faculty members at the University of Northern Iowa conceptualized a professional development plan that addressed the entire assessment process. Developing clear and measurable learning outcomes is an essential early step in the assessment process. The linkages between program-level learning outcomes and individual course-level outcomes can then be gleaned through curriculum maps that identify gaps and redundancies in the program and improve the articulation of outcomes across all program segments. Faculty initially were offered curriculum mapping workshops "to identify gaps and redundancies in the program and improve the articulation of program outcomes across all segments" (Barry Wilson, see p. 111). These workshops focused "primarily on articulating learning outcomes for teaching candidates in the areas of diversity, assessment of learning, and classroom management, which had been identified as in need of improvement in a recent accreditation visit." A second series of workshops at Northern Iowa oriented faculty to assessing student learning outcomes at the course level. In the final wave of professional development, the provost cancelled classes for an entire day so that faculty and administrators could devote time to the study and interpretation of data, and then develop action plans for change.

Joanne M. Crossman tells us that faculty at Johnson and Wales University use multiple approaches to professional development in the Master's of Business Administration program (see p. 243). Senior faculty formally mentor full-time and adjunct instructors, helping them understand how to teach courses and measure student learning in alignment with program learning outcomes. Faculty can participate in workshops to assist in designing and using rubrics and consistently applying the criteria to increase interrater reliability. In addition, faculty create portfolios to document their assignments and rubrics. The rubrics make faculty intentions very explicit and public so that students gain a better understanding of key expectations for individual courses.

Cognitive peer coaching is another strategy wherein faculty colleagues form pairs to improve instruction and assessment over a sustained period of time. Each pair enters into a formal written contract in which partners agree how they will help each other. Faculty at Southern Illinois University-Edwardsville have used this approach and have engaged in: "direct observation of class meetings (including pre- and post-observation meetings); Group Instructional Feedback Techniques (GIFTs, including pre- and post-GIFT meetings); review of syllabi, assignments, exams, and other course materials, with special attention paid to relevance to course objectives; and review of student work samples and grading policies" (Andy Pomerantz and Victoria Scott, see Resource A, p. 291).

The preparation and education of faculty and staff to consider and plan assessment is a crucial element of the process of implementing assessment (Jones, 2002). As leaders thoughtfully plan and develop a series of ongoing professional development learning experiences, participating instructors and staff learn how to conceptualize new ideas and receive constructive feedback from their peers regarding needed improvements.

Assessing Processes as Well as Outcomes

If the processes that lead to the outcomes of student learning are not examined, one cannot truly improve those outcomes. Measuring a desired outcome will do little to improve it without a look at the processes that led to the outcome. As Banta (Banta & Associates, 2002) has reminded us, "a test score alone will not help us improve student learning" (p. 273). What students and faculty *do* makes a difference. Thus, student engagement has been described as a key to student success (Kuh, Kinzie, Schuh, Whitt, & Associates, 2005). Student engagement is commonly assessed using surveys such as the College Student Experiences Questionnaire, and more recently the National Survey of Student Engagement (NSSE), as well as locally developed instruments.

Faculty and staff at North Carolina State University developed the First Year College Student Experiences Survey (SES) to assess involvement by asking students about the types of organizations in which they are involved; the amount of time they spend on certain types of activities; how often they use specific campus resources; and interactions with faculty, peers, and residence hall peer mentors (Kim Outing and Karen Hauschild, see p. 180). Faculty support, shown by willingness to administer the survey in the classroom, and the brevity and online availability of the survey instrument contributed to the success of this practice and ultimately to an expansion of first-year programming.

Both a national survey and a locally developed survey were employed to gauge the level of student engagement at Ohio University (Joni Y. Wadley and Michael Williford, see Resource A, p. 288). NSSE responses revealed that freshman students were less engaged than their peers at other universities. Discussions stimulated by presentations of the NSSE data to deans, chairpersons, and faculty led to the realization that there was not a common learning or engagement experience for first-year students. Further, a locally developed faculty engagement instrument provided insights into instructional issues and faculty practices that contributed to student engagement or the level thereof. A resulting two-year study of the first-year experience produced 33 recommendations of which 17 have been successfully implemented. Another important development is that additional resources have been put into first-year programs, including the establishment of an office that focuses on student success in the first year.

In 1991 Pascarella and Terenzini reviewed over 2,600 studies on the influence of college on students (Pascarella & Terenzini, 1991) and again in 2005 they reviewed some 2,500 studies that had been conducted since the 1991 publication (Pascarella & Terenzini, 2005). Evident in both reviews is the important influence that teacher behavior has on student learning. Specifically, faculty organization and preparation have a positive influence on student learning. These studies confirm the notion that process, or how we arrive at an outcome, is essential to good results.

Consistent with the concept that process is critical to outcomes, faculty at many institutions pay attention to techniques that are found to improve student learning. Medical and dental schools in the United States and Canada have for many years used problem-based learning (PBL). According to Natascha van Hattum-Janssen (see Resource A, p. 289) the University of Minho in Portugal employs a similar process called project-led education (PLE) in engineering courses. In this process, faculty act as tutors for teams of students who work on problems they will face as they enter the profession to produce a model, report, or other such product.

The pervasiveness of PLE at the University of Minho has led faculty to rethink and redesign the faculty evaluation process. Because the role of the faculty member now resembles that of a facilitator rather than "sage on the stage," older faculty evaluation forms are not useful in understanding the success of this more student-centered process. Older forms ask questions about students' expectations and perceptions of the instructor. Scales in a newer version assess faculty knowledge of the subject, faculty attitudes toward the PLE process, success of the project, student critical thinking and problem-solving skills, student attitude toward team work, and student perceptions of their learning. Results from the new instrument have helped instructors reflect on their areas of strength as well as the overall PLE process and the relatively new role of facilitator. Instructors have widely varying interpretations of the tutoring or facilitating role that the faculty member plays. This finding has suggested the need for more training for faculty in an effort to close this gap and to improve the process.

Although classroom processes are critical to student learning, equally important is the assessment process itself. Assessing and reporting results may serendipitously coincide with improved student learning but can coincide equally with no improvements if the process itself is not viewed as sound or indeed is *not* sound. Continuously reviewing and exploring new ways to assess student learning is critical. During the evaluation process at St. Mary's College of Maryland, members of the Core Curriculum Implementation Committee recognized the need to develop coherence between, and to evaluate, the various missions of the college, the core curriculum, and the assessment process itself. Click, Coughlin, O'Sullivan, Stover, and Nutt Williams (see p. 176) stress that these connections are necessary for the success of the core curriculum. Indeed this kind of strong linkage is vital to any successful program.

Communicating and Using Assessment Findings

One of the tenets of good research has always been that results should be communicated and vetted so that the research can benefit others as they pursue similar studies. Those assessing student learning should be held to the same standards and provided the opportunities to learn from colleagues engaged in this process. March (2006) reminds us of the importance of communicating the results of assessment but points out that this step is often considered last and is frequently ignored.

For many years now, assessment practitioners and researchers have pleaded with faculty and staff to ensure that assessment is an ongoing process that communicates to faculty and staff about the learning outcomes and the educational processes on campus and how well they are working to improve student learning and development. Those charged with compiling assessment results at the campus level must find ways to share information about findings that can help to improve teaching and programming processes with those teaching and/or designing and carrying out programs at the unit level.

Assessment leaders at the United States Military Academy describe what they fondly call "state of the union addresses" where course directors give updates on the assessment of the core mathematics courses and the relationship of findings to program goals (Graves and Heidenberg; see Resource A, p. 293). In years past these reports were done only in traditional print form. Though these conversations are not mandatory for faculty, the audience for the state of the union briefings has grown steadily. They have proved to be a useful communication mechanism for course directors to share information about program strengths, issues and concerns, new initiatives, and, most important, about student learning. Many more faculty are hearing about best practices and improvement ideas through these informal conversations.

Likewise, after instituting a new assessment program at Florida A&M University, Uche O. Ohia (see p. 83) reports that the success of this new approach has led to its becoming an accepted framework for linking assessment results to planning and budgeting. Instrumental in the success of this initiative has been the open and consistent communication about the process, the results, and best practices to deans, directors, chairpersons, and vice presidents through orientations, newsletters, roundtable discussions, and the usual printed progress reports.

These first two chapters of Part One describe characteristics of successful assessment initiatives through their planning and implementing phases. In the third chapter we explore ways to improve and sustain assessment programs. We provide examples of successful efforts to review and use assessment results as well as to evaluate the assessment process itself and the outcomes this process seeks to improve.

CHAPTER THREE

IMPROVING AND SUSTAINING EFFECTIVE ASSESSMENT

Many college and university faculty and staff have developed and implemented assessment plans. In this section, we initially review how faculty and staff can provide credible evidence of student learning to relevant internal and external stakeholders. We also examine how academic leaders and those engaged in assessment can use the information gleaned from various assessments to make targeted improvements. Such improvements can include making changes to the overall curriculum or academic program, revising individual courses, or adding new services with additional funding to address students' needs. A formal review of assessment reports can reveal trends or patterns in how faculty and staff are using assessment results to make enhancements. Finally, the formal assessment plan should be evaluated as it is implemented so that appropriate changes can be made to strengthen the assessment measures or the assessment process itself. If assessments yield meaningful results that faculty and staff can use to identify necessary changes, there is greater likelihood that the overall assessment process will be sustained over time.

Providing Credible Evidence of Learning to Multiple Stakeholders

Many faculty and staff members collect relevant and meaningful assessment information pertaining to their students. Often they use multiple assessments over a period to time to determine how well their students have mastered their intended learning outcomes. As Maki (2004) notes, multiple assessment methods are crucial for the following reasons. They

- provide students with multiple opportunities to demonstrate their learning that some may not have been able to show within only timed, multiple choice tests;
- reduce narrow interpretations of student performance based on the limitations often inherent in one particular method;
- contribute to comprehensive interpretations of student achievement at the institution, program, and course levels;
- value the diverse ways in which students learn; and
- value the multiple dimensions of student learning and development (p. 86–87).

Though some assessment leaders may be tempted to rely mainly or solely on indirect methods (those that capture students' perceptions of their learning and the campus environment), this approach does not generate enough meaningful information. Most assessment plans incorporate a combination of indirect assessments and direct assessments (those that provide a direct understanding of what students have learned). According to Thomas P. Judd and Bruce Keith (p. 46), the United States Military Academy (USMA) is an example of an institution that draws on course-embedded assignments (including projects, papers, and tests) to gather direct evidence of student learning in relation to the USMA's ten specific academic goals. Faculty also survey students at least three times and conduct focus groups with graduates' employers. Judd and Keith report that the results gleaned from these multiple assessment methods provide a comprehensive picture of student achievement and development.

A major challenge is to provide evidence of student learning that is credible and meaningful to a variety of stakeholders, including professional and regional accreditors who have explicit standards related to assessment. Most professional accrediting organizations expect faculty within accredited academic programs to demonstrate accountability regarding student performance on a continuous basis. Accreditors want evidence that faculty and staff "identify the knowledge and skills required of all students receiving a degree and determine in advance the level of student performance that will be acceptable" (Diamond, 2008, p. 19).

As faculty and staff review the potential range of instruments and assessments to measure student learning, there are numerous factors to consider. First, validity should be examined to determine "the degree to which evidence supports the interpretation of test scores" (Millett, Payne, Dwyer, Stickler, & Alexiou, 2008, p. 5). A valid method provides a direct and accurate assessment of the learning described in program- or course-level outcomes statements (Maki,

2004). Reliability should also be examined to answer "questions about the consistency and stability of [student] scores" (Millett et al., 2008, p. 8). As faculty members increasingly rely on applying rubrics to student work, interrater reliability becomes another matter to address. Although multiple raters may use the same rubric to assess student work, assessment leaders should carefully determine how consistently individual assessors are judging student work. The goal is to have a high level of consistency among different raters. Validity and reliability are very important to address in a formal manner and on a regular basis in order to provide the most credible evidence of student learning.

Other factors that may affect major decisions about the best assessment methods include the amount of time required for students to complete the assessment, the degree of motivation that students will have to produce their best work, and the cost of purchasing commercial instruments or the amount of time needed to develop assessments.

Administrators and staff should continuously collect information about student performance in relation to the program outcomes established by faculty members and use that information to improve their programs. Teacher education is an example of a field that is influenced by professional accreditation and state-level requirements as well as expectations set forth by university or college faculty.

At Alverno College, faculty have created an assessment system that documents student learning and provides feedback to faculty that they use to improve their teaching and the curriculum (Lake, Hart, Rickards, and Rogers, see pp. 100). The faculty members continually discuss how teacher candidates are performing on their portfolio assessments and then incorporate appropriate changes. Such reforms include modifications to the portfolio requirements as well as curricular program elements, including expanding a one-credit field course to a two-credit course with a focus on assessment. Individual students receive in-depth feedback regarding their performance and their readiness for student teaching. This assessment information is also used for accountability purposes and for dialogue with other external stakeholders. Faculty select a range of student portfolios for external review by the Wisconsin Department of Public Instruction and the National Council for Accreditation of Teacher Education.

The use of electronic portfolios to document student learning in conjunction with rubrics for judging the quality of student work is increasing at many colleges and universities (Diller & Phelps, 2008). The example drawn from Alverno College clearly demonstrates that the results from assessments of student learning can be used for improvement purposes as well as to satisfy the external accountability requirements set forth by a professional accreditor and a state department of education.

The federal government and legislators may impose standardized tests on colleges and universities with the intention of collecting data in ways that allow state comparisons (Malandra, 2008). The United States Department of Education (2006, p. 4) has called on higher education to become "more transparent about cost, price, and student success outcomes," and more "willing to share this information with students and parents." Such transparency does not need to rely solely or mainly on standardized tests. The Alverno College illustration is instructive because students and faculty benefit from a locally designed approach to assessment. Using portfolios, students can understand more fully the criteria by which their progress and work will be judged, and they have the opportunity to see and reflect on the progress they make in addressing key program learning goals. Faculty benefit because their rubrics clearly define the specific expectations they are using to assess student progress and learning. Analysis of the results of applying the rubrics then helps faculty identify where improvements need to be made. Ultimately the faculty may be more committed to the entire assessment process because they have created it. As Banta (2007, p. 12) notes, "the most authentic assessment will be achieved through electronic portfolios for which students themselves develop the content."

Reviewing Assessment Reports

College and university administrators typically require undergraduate program faculty to document the results of their assessments on a regular basis. Ideally, as faculty and administrators collect these reports, they will review them and provide feedback to each other and to administrators about the quality of implemented assessment plans. They also will offer constructive insights about areas that could be strengthened in the future. Institutional leaders can review all of the assessment reports to determine trends across programs and services in terms of successes and challenges. Such information can be used to refine current professional development initiatives. If faculty and staff seriously consider and address the feedback, the overall assessment process can be enhanced.

At the College of Wooster, Theresa Ford and John G. Neuhoff (see Resource A, p. 291) report that the Assessment Committee developed Guidelines for Assessment to assist academic departments and programs as they developed their assessment plans. These guidelines included a detailed schedule for departments and programs to develop student learning outcomes and identify direct and indirect measures of assessment, and set deadlines for the Assessment Committee to provide feedback to departments and programs.

Upon their formal review of assessment reports, Assessment Committee members discovered that, with the exception of three departments, all departments and programs had designed fully integrated assessment plans. In addition, faculty in most departments used multiple assessment methods and decided to assess student learning directly through the Senior Independent Study, Wooster's capstone experience. The Assessment Committee found that there were explicit examples of programs using the assessment results to make changes in pedagogy or in the curriculum, including adjustments to the sequencing of courses to provide more direct opportunities within courses for students to master a particular goal. They also found that as program faculty gained experience with certain assessments, they used the resulting information to target refinements to the plan itself, including changing assessment measures or eliminating certain measures that were not valid or reliable. One of the major factors leading to success at Wooster College was that the Assessment Committee thoroughly reviewed all assessment reports and provided timely feedback on each component so that, if necessary, program faculty could make enhancements to their assessment process in the future. In addition, the senior administration of the college increased the resources dedicated to support of assessment initiatives.

A similar process for formal review of assessment reports is conducted at California State University, Dominguez Hills, according to Shirley Lal and Mary Cruise (see Resource A, p. 281). The University Student Learning Outcomes Assessment Committee consists of key faculty members who formally evaluate assessment processes to document student learning and program quality across the campus. This ongoing process requires program faculty to submit a three-year progress report and a six-year self-study that includes a description of the learning outcomes assessment process and evidence of program quality.

A formal review of assessment reports across the campus completed by a group of faculty members can provide crucial insights regarding how different groups of instructors in various disciplines are using their assessment results to make targeted changes in their programs. Illustrations of key changes can be shared widely so that other faculty may learn how assessment can be meaningful in shaping their own curricula.

Ensuring Use of Assessment Results

Using the results from assessment should not be a burden, especially for faculty members who typically adapt and regularly modify their courses with the intention of improving student learning. Some individuals may be inclined to make decisions based on intuition, but the critical value of assessment is that faculty have real data or concrete information that can be utilized to make informed, strategic changes. As Suskie (2004, p. 300) notes, "assessment results should never dictate decisions to us; we should always use our professional judgment to interpret assessment and make appropriate decisions."

Faculty frequently use results from their assessments to reform their undergraduate programs. In the Department of Engineering Education at Virginia Tech (John Muffo, see Resource A, p. 288), undergraduates are regularly assessed with a variety of measures, including pre- and post-tests, attitudinal and learning styles inventories, electronic portfolios, course exit surveys, and focus groups. Through these assessments, faculty discovered that students did not fully understand their ethical values and how these affect their thinking about ethical dilemmas in engineering. Based on these assessment results, the faculty intentionally devotes more attention to helping their majors understand that engineering is not ethically neutral and that it sometimes involves difficult ethical decisions. They also added more videos and skits to their courses to emphasize the relevance of ethics.

At the University of North Dakota, faculty discovered through a formal analysis of students' transcripts that undergraduates received significantly less exposure to diversity than to other stated goals within their general education experience (Kelsch and Hawthorne, see Resource A, p. 294). They also found that although some students graduate with a high level of understanding and appreciation of diversity, other students graduate with a serious weakness in their understanding of diversity. The provost initiated a reform process in 2005 in which a task force was charged with reviewing all assessment information. Through this formal review, faculty were able to identify needed changes and implement them in their general education goals. The university senate approved a new "Essential Studies" program that places a greater focus on diversity through the development of a new "social-cultural diversity" goal. Now students are required to take courses that are intentionally designed to focus on diversity. In addition, the faculty utilize assessments that actually gauge student learning in reference to this crucial goal.

Assessment results may also provide faculty and administrators with vital information to inform key decisions about the allocation of resources. At Ohio University (OU), a comprehensive study of the First Year Experience was conducted for two years by using the National Survey of Student Engagement, Policy Center surveys on improving the First Year Experience, and a comprehensive Current Practices Inventory (Joni Y. Wadley and Michael Williford, see Resource A, p. 288). The task force at OU derived evidence from these assessments to create thirty-three recommendations for change. Some of the key recommendations that were acted on by senior academic leaders included providing new resources to appoint a director of retention and an office that addresses first-year student success. Additional resources were also provided to expand the learning communities program and attrition intervention programs as well as the common reading program. This OU example illustrates that as faculty interpret assessment information, they may more clearly see the necessity for creating new services or expanding interventions that address students' needs more effectively. Academic leaders who seriously value assessment provide the required resources and identify new funding to support the implementation of these changes based on the assessment results. As Dolinsky, Matthews, Greenfield, Curtis-Tweed, and Evenbeck (2007, p. 11) note, university communities that prefer evidence-based statements and actions typically utilize assessment results as a key source of information for making decisions to allocate new revenue streams or reallocate existing ones. When financial support is provided to make informed, targeted changes based on assessment results, it becomes evident that an institutional culture is embracing assessment and making enhancements that serve students.

Evaluating the Assessment Process

The assessment process itself can be evaluated by faculty and staff as they seek to improve how information is gathered (Banta & Associates, 2002; Jones, Voorhees, & Paulson, 2002). Faculty in the industrial design department at Savannah College of Art and Design regularly assess both undergraduate and graduate-level learning (Laura Ng, see Resource A, p. 291). An assessment panel selects random samples of student work. Faculty members who serve on this panel then judge the student work according to rubrics that the instructors have designed to determine the levels of student performance. As instructors applied these rubrics to student work, they discovered that better rubrics were needed for specific drawing courses. Therefore, the faculty created and utilized more nuanced rubrics that were increasingly more reliable.

California State University Sacramento's Student Affairs Division staff also reconsidered certain assessment measures (Castillon and Varlotta, see p. 201) based on their assessment results. For the Women's Resource Center, the staff modified certain test items that they had used but found were vague to students. Staff in the Student Health Center redesigned instruments to ensure that they incorporated more relevant direct measures of student learning. Finally, other units are changing their assessment designs by preparing to use multiple measures to collect longitudinal data from students.

These two examples reveal that assessment is a continuous process that is constantly open to change and reform as evidence is examined by faculty and staff. In some cases, such evidence can suggest the need for modifying the actual assessment measures so that faculty and staff can gather more precise and relevant information about student learning and development. In other cases, the assessment results suggest the need for a different assessment design so that more meaningful information can be gathered about students.

The State Higher Education Executive Officers (SHEEO, 2005, p. 15) note that providing better evidence of accountability requires substantial improvements in the quality and utilization of data. Faculty and staff are making substantive changes in their courses, academic programs, and overall curriculum with the intention of advancing student learning (Jones, 2002). Frequently they develop their own systematic assessments that yield meaningful results and identify the types of targeted changes that should be made to strengthen student learning experiences. Results derived from these comprehensive assessments can be useful for both internal and external stakeholders. Faculty and staff are implementing transparent learning assessments that should enhance student learning, institutional practice, and public confidence in their graduates' capabilities (SHEEO, 2005). When faculty and staff are able to glean useful insights about their students' performance and make relevant changes with sufficient resources, there is greater likelihood that these assessments will be sustained over time.

PART TWO

PROFILES OF GOOD PRACTICES IN OUTCOMES ASSESSMENT

In Part Two we continue to pursue the major themes of planning, implementing, and improving and sustaining assessment that were introduced in Part One. There we presented principles of effective practice in connection with each of these themes. Here we draw on 49 profiles selected for inclusion in their entirety from the 146 profiles sent to us by assessment practitioners in response to our call for contributions to this book. We illustrate the principles associated with these themes through relevant profiles.

Chapters 4 and 14, focused respectively on planning assessment initiatives and improving and sustaining assessment, contain no subdivisions. Because implementing assessment contains so many variations, we have divided that topic into two subsections—campuswide examples in Chapters 5–9 and assessment in specific contexts in Chapters 10–13. Each section contains an overview of the relevant profiles followed by the profiles themselves.

Chapters 5–9 include the following campuswide examples:

- General education profiles
- Undergraduate academic majors profiles
- Faculty and staff development profiles
- Use of technology profiles
- Program review profiles

Chapters 10–13 contain examples in the following specific contexts:

- First-year experiences, civic engagement opportunities, international learning experiences profiles
- Student affairs profiles
- Community colleges profiles
- Graduate programs profiles

CHAPTER FOUR

GOOD PRACTICE IN IMPLEMENTING ASSESSMENT PLANNING

As indicated in Chapter 1, effective assessment requires a plan that (a) engages stakeholders, (b) connects with goals and processes such as mission-related planning that are valued within a particular college or university, and (c) describes a sequence of data-gathering activities that will take place over a period of several years. The campus profiles selected for this section embody these basic planning principles and illustrate additional concepts that provide guidance for implementing and sustaining division- and institution-wide assessment.

At Brigham Young University (BYU), staff in institutional research and assessment developed a campuswide Wiki site using consistent definitions and a common template and invited stakeholders to contribute expected student learning outcomes for each degree program. Students were actively involved in the process, issuing invitations to other students to participate. Faculty were encouraged to contribute to the Wiki site in invitations from the university president, vice presidents, deans, department chairs, and other faculty. According to Gerrit Gong and Danny R. Olsen, the BYU plan for assessment, which includes the invitation process combined with use of the Wiki site, is now producing evidence that assessment of learning related to the stated outcomes does yield findings that guide improvements.

Staff in the Division of Student Affairs at the University of Alabama recently adopted a new mission statement linked to student learning outcomes in the areas of personal development, community, participation, and skill development. Through curriculum mapping, Katie Busby and other division staff ensured that the programs and activities they offer enable students to attain the mission-related outcomes. Engagement of appropriate staff and connection to the valued process of strategic planning have led those in the division to be more intentional in assessing the learning outcomes associated with their programs and activities.

Ten broad, multidisciplinary learning outcomes span all programs on the eight campuses of Miami Dade College. Five tasks with accompanying rubrics have been designed by faculty to assess nine of the ten outcomes, and a commercial computer skills test is employed in assessing the tenth. Joanne Bashford, S. Sean Madison, and Lenore Rodicio describe how assessment results have been used to inform both curricular and cocurricular learning experiences. Connection of the assessment plan to Miami Dade's strategic planning, and widespread involvement of faculty and top administrators, ensures that continuous improvement of the assessment process itself will be a priority for the foreseeable future.

The mission of the U.S. Military Academy is expressed in its academic program through an overarching academic goal and ten specific goals for learners. Each goal has stated learner outcomes, standards for each outcome, and faculty-developed rubrics for assessing student work. Thomas P. Judd and Bruce Keith tell us how an interdisciplinary faculty team uses curriculum-embedded direct measures of learning, as well as indirect measures, to gauge student achievement of each goal. Commitment of senior leadership, broad engagement of faculty, and a strong connection with the institutional mission have made the plan for assessment of the intellectual domain the model for assessing West Point's five other developmental domains—physical, military, social, moral-ethical, and the human spirit.

Kennesaw State University is a recipient of the 2008 Award for Institutional Progress in Student Learning Outcomes given by the Council on Higher Education Accreditation. According to Thomas P. Pusateri, Kennesaw's plan for assessing generic skills and discipline-specific learning outcomes in each academic degree program is integrated with other valued institutional processes such as strategic planning, program review, and faculty development. The Faculty Senate has endorsed a set of Principles of Assurance of Learning as well as an Assurance of Learning Council with representatives from each of seven colleges that reviews annual assessment reports from each degree program and provides commentary. Assessment findings helped to convince Kennesaw's leadership to adopt "Global Learning for Engaged Citizenship" as a five-year strategic initiative, and outcomes assessment will continue as the means of gauging progress in promoting global learning.

Institutions

Doctoral and Research
    Private
        Brigham Young University; Provo, Utah (34,000 students)
    Public
        University of Alabama; Tuscaloosa, Alabama (25,000 students)

Master's
    Public
        Kennesaw State University; Kennesaw, Georgia (21,000 students)

Baccalaureate
    Public
        United States Military Academy; West Point, New York (4,000 students)

Associate
    Public
        Miami Dade College; Miami, Florida (58,000 students)

Putting Students at the Center of Student Expected Learning Outcomes

Gerrit W. Gong, Danny Olsen, Brigham Young University

◆ ◆ ◆

Look for a campuswide Wiki site that uses consistent definitions and a common template for recording expected student learning outcomes for each degree program. Invitations from the Brigham Young University president and from faculty to faculty and students to students have encouraged widespread participation in outcome development, assessment, and use of assessment findings.

Background and Purpose(s) of Assessment

Using a common template (outcomes, evidences, assessment), faculty at Brigham Young University (BYU) identified and published student expected learning outcomes for each of its 267 major degree programs on a campuswide, open and transparent Wiki site—LearningOutcomes.BYU.edu.

Putting students at the center of expected learning outcomes has helped BYU create a shared student-faculty framework to improve learning and teaching while addressing on-campus priorities and accreditation requirements in cost-effective ways. Articulated learning outcomes also contribute to other ongoing priorities, such as focused mapping of direct and indirect evidence and curriculum alignment.

Assessment Method(s) and Year(s) of Implementation

Over the past 10 to 12 years, BYU faculty have sought to establish expected student learning outcomes but at different levels (courses, programs, majors); different degrees of skill, commitment, and success; different definitions and measures across different colleges and units, such as engineering and humanities—in some cases because of different (or nonexistent) specialized accreditation requirements.

Over the past three years, BYU has introduced a more consistent and effective approach to expected student learning outcomes by developing a campuswide Wiki site that uses consistent definitions and a common template, teaming a university advisory task committee with established campus governance bodies, and especially by involving students.

Student peer-to-peer invitations and invitations from university leaders (university president, vice presidents, deans, department chairs, individual faculty) encouraged every student and faculty member to review the learning outcomes in their degree program(s). University-level surveys monitored student awareness of learning outcomes and the extent to which students felt that degree programs fulfilled stated outcomes.

Required Resources

Wiki applications are efficient and cost-effective. Campus Wiki specialists demonstrated a prototype campuswide Wiki site within 7 days and credentialed Wiki editing rights. Learning outcomes began to be published on the Wiki within 30 days. Existing IT budgets covered technical support and server needs.

Faculty Center and Center for Teaching and Learning staff trained with consistency through college, department, and individual faculty consultations;

online Frequently Asked Questions were developed; and assessment literature, strategies, templates, and guidelines for writing good learning outcomes were disseminated.

College and department faculty hosted retreats, lunches, work sessions to develop and post outcomes, evidences, and assessment on the Wiki for their degree programs. Degree program faculty invited and involved students at each stage of identifying, publishing, implementing, revising, and adapting their Wiki material.

Findings

1. *Large-scale involvement of students and faculty* in a systematic process to identify, publish, use, and refine expected student learning outcomes for each BYU degree program.
2. *Identification and publication of expected learning outcomes for each BYU degree program at LearningOutcomes.BYU.edu campus Wiki.* The Wiki site provides for the first time a single location including a common framework of (a) stated outcomes, (b) evidence, and (c) assessment for program improvement and improvement of learning and teaching.
3. *Widespread student and faculty use of the Wiki site as evidenced by use to date*: 290,479 Wiki page views and 60,607 unique visitors (as of March 31, 2008).
4. Side-by-side teaming of *University Advisory Task Committee, Deans Council, University Curriculum Council, and Graduate Council* to develop campuswide approaches for stating all aspects of learning outcomes, documenting evidence for them, and using them in systematic assessment and improvement. The University Advisory Task Committee included Student Advisory Council (SAC) leaders, freshmen, and graduate student representatives—who then worked peer-to-peer with college and department student groups to invite each student to visit the Wiki and review their degree program's expected learning outcomes.
5. *Deepening of culture of assessment* across campus where (a) faculty and students have an emerging common vocabulary and conceptual framework to improve learning and teaching and fine-tune curriculum within the university's mission; (b) faculty, program and department chairs, and college administrators are systematically gathering evidence to document that students who graduate have achieved degree program stated outcomes; and, (c) faculty, program and department chairs, and college administrators are establishing and using evidence consistently across programs showing that results of assessment activities lead to improved teaching and learning.

Use of Findings

BYU seeks to move to the next level by using findings to

1. develop, refine, implement, and improve use of expected student outcomes by continuing to invite every student and faculty member to review degree-program stated outcomes as part of the open and transparent processes of campuswide student and faculty review
2. incorporate student and faculty review suggestions into degree-program outcomes and align stated outcomes at the course, program, and institutional levels
3. publish and post degree-stated program outcomes in campus departments and advisement centers for student and faculty access and use
4. continue training and support by Center for Teaching and Learning through faculty assessment consultations and online Frequently Asked Questions

Impact of Using the Findings

Besides engaging students, involving campus entities with line responsibility for program improvement, curriculum, and assessment (for example, Deans Council, University Curriculum Council, University Graduate Council) inculcates and deepens use of expected learning outcomes.

These groups also continue work to assess and benchmark how to envision, identify and publish, implement, document, and improve using ongoing data-based review. For example, the University Curriculum Council now requires documented learning outcomes as part of the process to establish a new course or program.

Students involved in peer-to-peer sharing of learning outcomes created a short DVD to document their efforts. The DVD is now used in student orientation and has been shared with the U.S. Department of Education as evidence of how to sustain assessment by putting students at the center of student learning outcomes. (The student DVD project helped fulfill an expected learning outcome for a film major.)

Continuing impact in other areas includes ongoing work to

a. invite, train, popularize, and monitor widespread, regular use of the university-wide Wiki site
b. discuss, implement, and iterate a common, consistent approach (including formatting, writing, and so on) to expected learning outcomes in each degree

program through regular progress updates within established university structures (such as the Dean's Council, University Curriculum Council, college councils, department staff meetings)

c. train and consult with colleges, departments, degree programs, individual faculty through the Faculty Center, the Center for Instructional Design, and the University Curriculum Council

d. provide ongoing input and perspective from analysis of best practices, surveys of relevant academic literature, and student and peer responses to learning outcomes

e. disseminate learning outcomes information and decisions across campus, including through Wiki feedback and college- or department-level focus groups with students

Success Factors

- *Wiki site—LearningOutcomes.BYU.edu*—is an easily updated, transparent, cost-effective place where students and faculty can see and compare expected learning outcomes for each degree.

- *Personal invitations* by the University president, deans, department chairs, and individual faculty to invite each BYU faculty member and BYU student to become familiar with the expected learning outcomes for their degree program(s)—and to discuss how an understanding of degree-program expected outcomes can facilitate deep learning and effective teaching.

- *Linking* expected learning outcomes Web site to other sites where students, faculty, and the public find information about BYU's degree programs—for example, MyMap, where students plan their course of studies.

- *Inviting* each student and faculty member to provide feedback energizes a *dynamic process* of clarifying and refining program outcomes. This process also deepens student and faculty understanding and commitment to stated program outcomes. The process of definition and dissemination heightens campus consciousness and focus regarding what each program is seeking to accomplish within the overall university mission.

Relevant Institutional Web Sites Pertaining to This Assessment Practice

Campuswide Wiki and Student DVD—Student Expected Learning Outcomes:

http://learningoutcomes.byu.edu

This example of one college's assessment summary Web site provides a working repository for college program learning outcomes, measures, and assessment activities:

http://humassessment.byu.edu

Planning Assessment in Student Affairs

A. Katherine Busby, University of Alabama

◆ ◆ ◆

Look for a comprehensive assessment planning process in an office of campus activities. Through curriculum mapping, staff have ensured that their programs and activities enhance students' personal and skill development and decision-making skills.

Background and Purpose(s) of Assessment

The Division of Student Affairs at the University of Alabama (UA) is evolving to serve a growing student population. As part of that evolution the division adopted a revised mission statement in 2007 to reflect its commitment to student learning and development on a dynamic campus and to support the university's efforts in teaching, research, and service. The mission of the division is to maximize each UA student's learning experience. The division comprises campus activities, career center, counseling center, office of the dean of students, housing and residential life, and university recreation. Each unit is uniquely suited to execute the division mission through a variety of programs and services. Upon the adoption of the division mission statement, staff in several units continued to utilize best practices in planning and revised their own mission statements and learning outcomes to ensure consistency within their area, with the division, and with the university.

Assessment Method(s) and Year(s) of Implementation

The Office of Campus Activities staff fully embraced a comprehensive assessment planning process after the new division mission was adopted. The Office of Campus Activities, which includes the community service center, university programs, student involvement (including leadership-related activities), and the

Ferguson Center (student union), revised its mission statement and established unit-wide learning outcomes. Whereas each office has a unique purpose, all offices operate under the campus activities mission of maximizing every UA student's learning experience through exploration, enjoyment, and service. The Office of Campus Activities staff have operated with current unit-wide learning and development outcomes since summer 2007.

Required Resources

The assessment planning process required time from the Campus Activities staff. This group met on four separate occasions with meetings as short as one hour to longer planning sessions of approximately four hours. These meetings were held over a three-month period.

Findings

Through a series of facilitated discussions, the Campus Activities staff articulated the role of their office on campus and developed several learning outcomes to which all contributed. The outcomes that were established are related to personal development, community participation, and skill development and include analyzing issues related to the campus, state, nation, and world as well as exhibiting decision-making skills.

Use of Findings

The process of reviewing and revising the unit mission statement and establishing learning and development outcomes was itself a beneficial activity for staff. However, simply developing outcomes is not enough. The outcomes should be used to guide further planning efforts within the unit. To that end, the Campus Activities staff used the newly established learning outcomes and conducted a curriculum mapping exercise to ensure that programs and activities were consistent with the outcomes and to minimize duplication of efforts and close any gaps. The staff will use a similar process to inform their selection of assessment measures.

Impact of Using the Findings

As a result of participating in the planning process and establishing learning outcomes, the staff within Campus Activities is more intentional when planning programs, services, and events. The unit-wide outcomes also allow for common assessment measures to be used by multiple offices within Campus Activities, thus allowing for improved utilization of existing data. The establishment of common learning outcomes across the unit and the subsequent curriculum mapping exercise allowed the Campus Activities staff to consider how their efforts influence student learning and development; to examine the assessment measures they were using; and to utilize measurement tools more effectively and efficiently.

Success Factors

Staff members in the Office of Campus Activities were particularly engaged in the process. The planning process was broken down into manageable steps that allowed staff the opportunity to contribute, reflect, and finalize decisions in a progressive manner that was neither prolonged nor rushed. The staff were particularly attentive to the contributions of their respective offices as well as a broader perspective that was common among all offices. They focused on the unit mission and carefully examined their own practices and how those practices contributed to students' growth and development through active participation on campus.

Relevant Institutional Web Sites Pertaining to This Assessment Practice

www.sa.ua.edu/assessment/

E Pluribus Unum: Facilitating a Multicampus, Multidisciplinary General Education Assessment Process

Joanne Bashford, S. Sean Madison, Lenore Rodicio, Miami Dade College, Miami, Florida

◆ ◆ ◆

Look for a detailed description of general education assessment plans and implementation processes in a multicampus system. Faculty employ locally developed scoring rubrics to performance-based tasks designed to assess student development of specified learning outcomes.

Background and Purpose(s) of Assessment

Since opening its doors in 1960, Miami Dade College (MDC) has grown to become one of the largest colleges in the nation, delivering a wide range of higher education programs responsive to the educational and career needs of the diverse South Florida community. Today the college has eight campuses and enrolls nearly 160,000 students, including more Hispanic and African American undergraduates than any other college in the United States. MDC offers associate's degrees and certificates in more than 200 areas of study and continuing education geared toward professional skills enhancement and the myriad interests of the lifelong learner. The college also offers bachelor's degrees in education, public safety management, and nursing.

How does a multicampus, geographically dispersed institution facilitate and implement general education initiatives without compromising the collective identity of the institution? How do geographically dispersed, multidisciplinary faculty members collaborate to meet the demands and opportunities of general education reform initiatives?

MDC has met this challenge by revising its original set of 25 general education goals; and by doing so, the college adopted a new set comprising ten learning outcomes that are broad, multidisciplinary, and span all programs. These outcomes now provide the foundation for learning at the college and reflect expectations for future graduates that are consistent with new and emerging workforce, global, and technological demands.

This assessment work also is a key goal of one of the five pillars of the 2004–2010 MDC Strategic Plan: Student Achievement and Success.

Assessment Method(s) and Year(s) of Implementation

With ten new learning outcomes, MDC faculty and administrators recognized the importance of sustaining assessment practice in the college's complex, multicampus system. They also recognized, however, that implementing this practice might evoke resistance, especially among those closest to the teaching and learning event—the faculty. As a strategy to facilitate faculty engagement across eight campuses, administrators established an assessment infrastructure that included two key features: an assessment philosophy that rested on seven tenets about assessment at the college and an intercampus assessment design strategy that positioned faculty as the "drivers" behind this initiative.

In August 2006, the provost for academic and student affairs invited faculty members from around the college and from various disciplines to participate as members of the Miami Dade College (MDC) Learning Outcomes Assessment Team (formerly known as General Education Assessment Team). This move represented the next phase in MDC's general education program development initiatives and provided an opportunity to gather evidence about students' attainment of MDC's learning outcomes.

After the 2006–07 team was approved by the Academic Leadership Council and appointed by the provost, the associate provosts for academic affairs and for institutional effectiveness (IE), with the support of college training and development (CTD), coordinated a general education outcomes assessment retreat on September 29–30, 2006. At the retreat, nationally known experts facilitated the team's work in developing assessment tools, including scoring rubrics and performance-based assessment tasks.

From November 2006 to May 2007, the team, with continued support from the district offices of IE and Academic Affairs, participated in a variety of institution-level assessment activities such as (1) identifying students and classes to include in the assessment sample, (2) surveying faculty proctors and students, (3) developing anchor papers, (4) scoring assessments, (5) analyzing evidence of validity, and (6) sharing assessment results with colleagues at Conference Day 2007, a professional development convening of faculty and staff from all eight campuses on one of the larger campuses.

Five tasks with accompanying rubrics were developed to cover nine of the ten MDC learning outcomes. Most of the tasks covered more than one of the outcomes and all required students to integrate and apply knowledge and abilities to complete the tasks. The tenth outcome was assessed using a commercially developed computer skills test. The tasks were field tested in October, revised, and administered in selected classrooms at the end of fall term 2006.

Required Resources

The district president of Miami Dade College has demonstrated a strong commitment to assessment by not only inspiring interest in the process but also allocating resources to support this institutional work. The college employed a district director of learning outcomes assessment to coordinate activities across this eight-campus institution. The director's role and responsibilities are under the auspices of the Office of Institutional Effectiveness that includes a director of institutional research, a director of test administration and program evaluation, senior researchers, and several research associates. The director of learning outcomes assessment facilitates the work of a faculty-driven assessment team comprising 25 full-time faculty members from various academic and workforce disciplines, five student affairs professionals, and eight resource members who have collective expertise in outcomes assessment. All eight campuses are represented on the team, which is cochaired by an MDC faculty member and the director of learning outcomes assessment.

In addition, college administrators have convened a Learning Outcomes Coordinating Council (LOCC) to oversee all initiatives related to learning outcomes and assessment. This council is appointed by the provost for academic and student affairs and is composed primarily of faculty with representation by academic and student affairs administrators.

Resources for the Learning Outcomes Coordinating Council and the Learning Outcomes Assessment Team include the Office of College Training and Development (CTD), which supports faculty professional development endeavors by coordinating workshops and consultants.

Findings

The first round of assessments was administered to students who were eligible to graduate upon completion of the term. Assessment results were reported in aggregate and established benchmark data to inform the college dialogue about curricular and cocurricular learning experiences related to the ten outcomes and student attainment of those outcomes. These data revealed the need for particular emphasis on a number of outcomes including critical thinking, quantitative analysis, and appreciation for aesthetics and creative expression. Students were least likely to perform up to faculty expectations in these areas. The assessments also revealed that students demonstrated their highest proficiencies in scientific and environmental literacy, social responsibility, ethical thinking, and computer competence outcomes.

In terms of the assessment process, most faculty demonstrated a willingness to support these initiatives, as indicated by their participation in pilots, motivation of students, and administration of assessment tasks within their classrooms. Faculty also provided observation notes regarding the assessment process that were supportive, yet provided important suggestions to improve the process. This faculty feedback included comments on student efforts, administrative support, and test format.

Use of Findings

The results from this first administration of the General Education Assessment Tasks were shared during the college's annual Conference Day 2007. At Conference Day, personnel in each discipline, school, and the student services division reviewed and discussed the results and how courses and cocurricular experiences contributed to the attainment of learning outcomes. Through these discussions specific actions were identified to enhance students' attainment of the outcomes prior to graduation, including greater intentionality in addressing the outcomes, introduction to performance-based assessments in courses, and formative student-centered assessment strategies for the classroom and beyond.

The Learning Outcomes Assessment Team reviewed results and observations made by faculty who administered the assessments, and the team implemented numerous suggestions for strengthening the administration process. Examples of these enhancements include revisions to task prompts, instructions, and graphics, more opportunities for disciplinary groups to review tasks, earlier notification of class selection, information sessions for participating faculty, and computer-based administration of tasks.

The Office of Institutional Effectiveness staff reviewed the sampling process and suggested alternatives as appropriate to maximize faculty and student participation in subsequent assessment administrations. They also used regression analyses to relate results to other indicators of learning and thus identified potential threats and sources of bias.

Additional evidence of graduates' attainment of the learning outcomes, such as common discipline and course-level assessments, Gordon Rule course writing assessments, Graduating Student Survey results, Community College Survey of Student Engagement (CCSSE) results, and transfer student performance by discipline were also considered when reviewing learning outcomes assessment results. When combined with this additional evidence, the learning outcomes assessment results provide valuable and actionable information for the college to use to increase student learning.

Impact of Using the Findings

As the college considers subsequent implementation phases of this assessment process, the college also must recognize and address, as appropriate, lessons learned that will strengthen future iterations of the assessment process:

Lesson Learned 1. Consistent and open communication about the assessment process is imperative for faculty buy-in and administrative support. In fact, faculty and college community engagement is of such concern that a number of initiatives have been developed to increase awareness of not only outcomes-based assessment but also of learning outcomes curriculum initiatives. These initiatives include an all-day, multicampus faculty retreat titled "General Education and Assessment: An Academic Dialogue." At the retreat, faculty led other faculty in discussion about the college's learning outcomes and assessment practice within the classroom. The college also hosted a public covenant signing ceremony to acknowledge faculty, student, and college commitment to attainment of the ten learning outcomes through intentional learning experiences and sound assessment practice.

Lesson Learned 2. Students must have multiple opportunities to become familiar with performance-based assessment design, format, and evaluation throughout the college curriculum. In addition, more emphasis and intentionality are needed to provide faculty with opportunities to gauge students' attainment of the college's learning outcomes through formative assessment techniques. In fact, faculty are engaging in a curriculum mapping process to analyze course competences to determine where and at what levels learning outcomes are addressed. At the conclusion of this process, faculty will be able to identify not only gaps in the curriculum but also opportunities for potential collaboration and innovation.

Lesson Learned 3. MDC leaders recognize the challenges in performance-based assessment and must continue to validate strategies through disciplinary and external expert review. Steps have been taken to continue training and development of the Learning Outcomes Assessment Team in designing rubrics and determining interrater reliability. Strategies to maximize student motivation are also being explored and implemented.

Lesson Learned 4. MDC leaders must continue to explore ways to use emerging technology in outcomes assessment to streamline the process, making it both user-friendly and cost-effective. For example, the college is experimenting with Web technology to administer the performance-based assessments in a manner that conserves paper and maintains test security.

Success Factors

At MDC a multilevel culture of assessment across disciplines, programs, and cocurricular experiences is emerging. All related activities must continue to advance the established assessment philosophy and a faculty-driven process that is centered on continuous improvement. Implementation of the aforementioned lessons is paramount. Although nominal incentives have been provided for faculty participants, one of the greatest success factors for this process has been the involvement of faculty, even at the earliest stages of the process. This inclusiveness has fostered motivation among the faculty to improve the teaching-learning process using the results of the collegewide assessments.

Relevant Institutional Web Sites Pertaining to This Assessment Practice

www.mdc.edu/learningoutcomes

Triangulation of Data Sources in Assessing Academic Outcomes

Thomas P. Judd, Bruce Keith, United States Military Academy

◆ ◆ ◆

Look for a well-organized plan for assessing ten academic goals using direct evidence of student performance embedded in course work and surveys of students, graduates, and employers of graduates.

Background and Purpose(s) of Assessment

Assessment has become an integral part of the academic system at the United States Military Academy (USMA) since the inception of the process in 1996. Originally conceived as a goal-based system that is responsive to decision makers and informs faculty about the need for curricular change, the development of the process has been largely the work of faculty. The mission-based process includes assessment of the major components of curriculum: the learning model, program design, program implementation, and goal achievement. The mission of USMA—*to educate, train, and inspire the Corps of Cadets so that each graduate is a commissioned leader of character committed to the values of Duty, Honor, Country; and prepared for a career of professional excellence and service to the Nation as an officer in the United States Army*—is expressed in the academic program through the overarching academic goal: *Graduates anticipate and respond effectively to the uncertainties of a changing technological, social, political, and economic world.* Faculty groups have defined this overarching academic goal as ten more specific goals, ensuring that graduates are able to (1) think and act creatively; (2) recognize moral issues and apply ethical considerations in decision making; (3) understand human behavior; (4) be aware of culture; (5) be cognizant of history; (6) listen, read, speak, and write effectively; and (7) be self-directed learners who are proficient in the fundamentals of (8) engineering, (9) mathematics and science, and (10) information technology. Each of the goals has a set of stated student outcomes, standards for each outcome, and rubrics for assessing students' work. These ten goals provide the framework for the 30 courses of the core curriculum taken by all USMA students.

To ensure that the system is effective and efficient, assessment projects make maximum use of existing evidence. A high level of confidence in the data is critical when inferences result in curricular decisions. In order to reduce measurement error and to increase confidence in the data, four sources and types of evidence are used at multiple points in time to assess all ten goals: direct evidence of student performance embedded in ongoing student work, surveys of students, surveys of graduates, and surveys and interviews of graduates' supervisors.

Assessment Method(s) and Year(s) of Implementation

Each of the ten academic goals is assessed by a goal team composed of faculty from diverse disciplines. The goal team leaders together form the Assessment Steering Committee, which oversees the outcomes assessment process. In the years prior to full operation, the goal teams developed the outcome statements, goal standards, and assessment rubrics for each goal. Finally, the teams identified places in the core curriculum where student work could be used to demonstrate achievement of the goal standards. These embedded indicators include projects, papers, tests, and final exams, either in whole or in part. It was critical that the teams identify a variety of embedded indicators that give direct evidence of achievement of each component of the outcome standards. These embedded indicators are the first of the sources of evidence in the triangulation of assessment data and represent the most direct evidence collected by the goal teams.

The second source of evidence comes from survey data. Students are surveyed at three points in time: at the end of their freshman year, at the end of their senior year, and three years after graduation. All three surveys have been in use in their present form since 1999, and were developed with clear linkages to the ten academic goals. Students and graduates alike are asked to indicate their level of confidence in performing and/or applying skills associated with various dimensions of the ten academic goals.

The third source of evidence comes from surveys and focus-group interviews of our graduates' employers. The surveys are administered to supervisors of graduates in conjunction with the administration of the graduate survey. As in the graduate survey, supervisors are asked to indicate a level of confidence in our graduates' abilities to accomplish tasks directly related to the ten academic goals. Although the supervisors may not actually have seen graduates perform skills in areas associated with every goal, they can nonetheless speak to how confident they are that the graduate could perform such tasks if the opportunity presented itself. The focus-group interviews are held annually with former supervisors and are conducted by members of the goal teams and the Assessment Steering Committee.

When used in conjunction with the freshman, senior, and graduate surveys and the direct evidence of student performance collected by the goal teams, the employer survey data complete a comprehensive picture of academic program outcomes. The goal teams use all of these sources in their annual reports summarizing the current status of assessing outcomes of the academic goals.

Required Resources

This approach requires substantial effort from faculty. Staffing the goal teams is an annual event, but the continual rotation of the membership ensures new viewpoints, widespread awareness and familiarity, and a workload shared by many. The survey data collection process requires an appropriately staffed and skilled institutional research office, equipped to develop and administer surveys tailored to the outcome statements. Ensuring the institutionalization of the process requires a committed team leader who understands and values assessment and is willing to rely on assessment results to make decisions and implement the requisite changes.

Findings

Assessment must be a viable process. The assessment rubrics used with the embedded indicators provide consistent data that inform outcome goal achievement. This information, supplemented by the survey data, gives a picture of students' performance while undergraduates, their changing levels of confidence in the outcome skills, and their supervisors' perceptions of their performance. The close alignment of embedded indicators and survey questions with outcome goal statements facilitates the analysis of outcomes data. However, the triangulation of data and outcomes is not always as clear as it might be. For example, evidence for all of the defined outcomes for the moral awareness and continued intellectual development goals is not yet completely aligned.

As in most complete assessment processes, the act of defining and specifying outcome goals has refined our understanding of what we intend to accomplish with students in our core curriculum. The analysis of data that informs faculty of the results of the education of our students has validated both the process and the goals.

Use of Findings

Faculty in disciplines aligned directly with the outcome goals immediately saw the effectiveness of their contributions to students' achievement of the goals, and often were motivated to make small curriculum adjustments as the findings highlighted areas in need of strengthening (such as history, English, engineering, information technology). In the 2006–07 academic year the Assessment Steering Committee and goal teams used assessment findings to conduct a review of the core curriculum, resulting in several recommendations to the dean for curriculum changes.

Impact of Using the Findings

The broad success of the assessment of the academic goals has been recognized across the institution and is in the process of being replicated in other developmental domains. The USMA mission requires development not just in the academic area, but in six domains: intellectual, physical, military, social, moral-ethical, and the human spirit. The intellectual domain is dominated by the academic program, and was the first to develop a comprehensive assessment process. As the institution proceeds to develop comparable processes for the other domains, the assessment of the academic program has become the model process for the other five, and the lessons learned are helping smooth the path. Teams of faculty in each of the domains are developing outcome statements, standards, and a learning model.

Success Factors

Several key factors have contributed to the success of the academic assessment process. First, senior-level administrators committed to supporting academic assessment established the process. Their commitment to use the process for curriculum decisions and recognition of faculty effort was essential in maintaining faculty support. Second, a faculty willing to engage in designing and implementing the process was critical for success. Third, rotating membership of the goal teams of faculty close to the disciplines contributed to widespread acceptance among faculty and recognition of the utility of assessment. Fourth, engaging faculty from programs accredited by the external agencies (for example, ABET in engineering) made use of faculty with experience and facility with assessment who were able to develop faculty members new to outcomes assessment.

Relevant Institutional Web Sites Pertaining to This Assessment Practice

A rationale and description of the ten academic goals, the goal standards, the learning model, and the assessment model are available at:

www.dean.usma.edu/support/aad/EFAOCW.pdf

Assurance of Learning Initiative for Academic Degree Programs

Thomas P. Pusateri, Kennesaw State University

◆ ◆ ◆

Look for an award-winning Assurance of Learning initiative that focuses assessment of student achievement in general education on capstone experiences and integrates assessment of learning outcomes with faculty development, program review, and other strategic initiatives such as global learning.

Background and Purpose(s) of Assessment

In 2003, Kennesaw State University (KSU) established its Assurance of Learning (AOL) initiative for continuous program improvement via assessment of general education and discipline-specific student learning outcomes within each academic degree program. The AOL initiative is strategically integrated with comprehensive program review, faculty development, and other university-wide strategic initiatives.

Assessment Method(s) and Year(s) of Implementation

Annually from 1994 through 2003, KSU's Office of Institutional Planning collected and archived assessment reports from all academic departments. Beginning in 2003, KSU developed a more comprehensive and systematic reporting system for (a) assessing student learning outcomes in general education and all academic degree programs, (b) using assessment results for quality enhancement, and (c) integrating assessment processes with university-wide strategic initiatives.

To facilitate this assessment system, KSU administrators and faculty established the Assurance of Learning (AOL) Council, whose membership is comprised of faculty representatives from each of KSU's seven colleges. The AOL Council provides campuswide coordination, consultation, and workshops to assist program faculty in articulating student learning outcomes, collecting and reporting evidence of student achievement of these outcomes, and using these findings to improve program quality.

In November 2004, KSU's Faculty Senate endorsed a set of Principles of Assurance of Learning drafted by AOL Council members with broad faculty input. Faculty members from each academic degree program and KSU's general education program prepared reports comprising seven key sections, the first five of which were submitted in 2005, and the remaining two in 2006. The AOL Council reviewed and provided feedback at each stage of report completion. The seven sections of the comprehensive AOL reports are:

1. *Articulating student learning outcomes* that focus on end-of-program outcomes rather than outcomes linked to any specific course or instructor.
2. *Connecting outcomes to program requirements* via a curriculum matrix mapping each outcome to courses or other experiences in the program's degree requirements.
3. *Connecting outcomes to measures* (for example, assignments) that the program's faculty collect to assess student achievement of the outcomes.
4. *Articulating expected and hypothesized findings* based on criterion-referenced, norm-referenced, best-practice, value-added, or longitudinal standards.
5. *Articulating the plan and timetable for collecting evidence of AOL* for the next three years.
6. *Collecting, analyzing, and interpreting evidence of AOL* and submitting annual reports.
7. *Using findings of AOL for quality enhancement* such as modifications in curricula, improvements to the assessment system, and faculty development.

In 2006–07, the AOL Council sought input from each program concerning the AOL process and used this input to develop a streamlined reporting structure for annual follow-up reports, which were collected for review in December 2007.

Required Resources

Each college appoints a representative to serve on the Assurance of Learning Council, which reviews AOL reports and conducts assessment-related workshops. Department chairs appoint faculty to oversee the AOL process for each program and to submit the annual report. Some colleges have subscribed to assessment management systems such as Chalk & Wire or Digital Measures to facilitate data gathering, analysis, and report writing.

Findings

KSU academic leaders identified 14 competences for graduating seniors and expect each degree program faculty to articulate and assess discipline-specific student learning outcomes related to these competences within their degree requirements. This approach puts the focus of summative assessment of general education competences within each discipline's capstone experiences toward the end of a student's undergraduate career rather than in the first year or two, as is done at many institutions.

KSU's University College faculty submitted an AOL report, "Competences for Graduating Seniors," that includes a detailed matrix linking (a) the general education competences to relevant competences within each undergraduate degree program, (b) the courses in which those competences are measured, and (c) the measures used by each degree program to assess those competences. Although not all 14 competences have been measured by all academic units, there is substantial articulation and assessment of them within each degree program, and KSU faculty are able to demonstrate that most graduates have attained most competences.

Of the 34 undergraduate degree programs that provided data on student learning outcomes in their AOL reports, 33 (97 percent) included data assessing the competence of *thinking critically and analytically;* 25 (74 percent) assessed the competence *analyzing quantitative problems;* 24 (71 percent) assessed *using computing and information technology;* 22 (65 percent) assessed *writing clearly and effectively;* 21 (62 percent) assessed *working effectively with others;* and 18 (53 percent) assessed *speaking clearly and effectively.* The data indicate that the majority of students in the 34 disciplines meet or exceed expectations on these competences based on a variety of assessment methods (for example, senior theses, presentations, or simulations in capstone experiences; student portfolios; and other course-embedded assignments).

Use of Findings

Data from KSU's AOL initiatives and other sources were particularly useful recently when KSU leaders developed a five-year strategic initiative, "Global Learning for Engaged Citizenship." Typically, three-fourths of KSU seniors who complete the National Survey on Student Engagement report that KSU experiences contributed to their development of many of KSU's 14 competences for graduating seniors. However, only half of the seniors who responded to NSSE recently (53 percent in 2005, 50 percent in 2004) reported that KSU contributed to understanding people of other racial and ethnic backgrounds. In addition, fewer KSU seniors (8 percent in 2005) than their national peers (13 percent at Master's I and II institutions) reported having completed a study abroad program, and fewer KSU seniors (35 percent) had taken foreign language course work than their national peers (41 percent).

The AOL report submitted by KSU's University College provided additional evidence that many KSU students may not be developing sufficient competence related to understanding people of other races and ethnic backgrounds. Although faculty in 21 (62 percent) of 34 undergraduate degree programs indicated that they assess this competence, most of those programs focus on cognitive learning outcomes and assessment methods that involve little to no multicultural or cross-cultural behavioral and attitudinal experiences.

Impact of Using the Findings

Data from the NSSE and AOL reports were useful in helping university administrators, faculty, staff, and students commit to KSU's five-year strategic initiative, "Global Learning for Engaged Citizenship." University administrators have made a strong commitment to provide resources to identify, track, and enhance global learning opportunities, outcomes, and achievements on campus. A "Get Global" Web site contains resources for students and faculty. An appointed faculty member in each college serves as a global learning coordinator, whose responsibility it is to advocate for enhanced opportunities for students to develop global learning competences. AOL Council members are contributing to this initiative by consulting with faculty members in degree programs to articulate discipline-appropriate student learning outcomes and assessment methods related to global learning. The AOL Council also will track the development and assessment of student learning outcomes related to global learning over the next five years.

Success Factors

In July 2006, the leadership for AOL initiatives was transferred from the assistant vice president for academic affairs to a new associate director for the scholarship of teaching and learning in the Center for Excellence in Teaching and Learning (CETL). Recently, the CETL associate director also assumed leadership for KSU's comprehensive program review (CPR) process, which had been directed previously by KSU's director for institutional effectiveness. This transfer of responsibilities reflects KSU's commitment to two key principles concerning the assessment of student learning outcomes and program quality. First, the primary purpose of AOL and CPR should not be to serve accountability, even though that is an important function. Instead, the primary purpose should be to enhance the quality of teaching and learning within degree programs. Second, assessments of student learning outcomes should be sufficiently strong and sophisticated to be leveraged into peer-reviewed presentations and publications on the scholarship of teaching and learning. The CETL associate director coordinates an annual faculty development competition for Scholarship of Teaching and Learning

(STLT) Funding Awards. These awards have provided a venue for faculty from several colleges and departments to form interdisciplinary research teams that support and learn from each other as they conduct research on the scholarship of teaching and learning and develop conference presentations and publications from their research.

For integrating assessment of student learning outcomes with program review, faculty development, and university-wide strategic initiatives, KSU's Assurance of Learning initiative was awarded the Council on Higher Education Accreditation's 2008 CHEA Award for Institutional Progress in Student Learning Outcomes.

Relevant Institutional Web Sites Pertaining to This Assessment Practice

Assurance of Learning:

www.kennesaw.edu/cetl/aol

Comprehensive Program Review:

www.kennesaw.edu/cetl/cpr

Faculty Development via the Scholarship of Teaching and Learning Team Funding Awards:

www.kennesaw.edu/cetl/faculty_funds/teaching_learning.html

"Get Global" Initiative:

www.kennesaw.edu/getglobal/

CHAPTER FIVE

GENERAL EDUCATION PROFILES

Assessment of student achievement in general education begins with the identification by faculty of basic skills that all students should develop, such as writing, thinking, and information literacy. This section opens with three profiles that focus on assessment of one or two of these generic skills. Three subsequent profiles describe assessment methods that have been applied more broadly.

At North Carolina State University, Patti H. Clayton, Sarah Ash, and Jessica Katz Jameson have worked with colleagues to develop a detailed model for assessing demonstration of critical thinking in student reflection products. The reflection model, called DEAL for the three steps of **D**escription, **E**xamination, and **A**rticulation of **L**earning, incorporates guiding prompts specific to the learning goals of academic enhancement, civic learning, and personal growth. Linking the prompts to learning objectives grounded in Bloom's Taxonomy (1956) enables faculty to use the objectives as a rubric, scoring students' reflections at levels ranging from identification to evaluation. A second holistic rubric based on Paul and Elder's Standards of Critical Thinking (2001)—accuracy, clarity, precision, relevance, depth, breadth, significance, logic, and fairness—provides students additional detail about the quality of their learning. Faculty on other campuses, including Indiana University–Purdue University Indianapolis (see Enrica Ardemagni, Lisa McGuire, and Patricia Wittberg, Resource A, p. 285), have adapted the DEAL model to the assessment of critical thinking in a wide range of courses and disciplines.

Teresa Flateby and colleagues at the University of South Florida have created a different approach to assessing writing and thinking that also has been applied on other campuses. The Cognitive Level and Quality of Writing Assessment (CLAQWA) rubric incorporates five major categories, each with multiple traits, and five operationally defined performance levels. A separate scale assesses the cognitive levels reached in student papers and helps faculty construct assignments that develop progressively more complex levels of learning. An online version of CLAQWA gives faculty an opportunity to provide students more comprehensive and useful feedback about their work than is typically possible. In addition, the online system enables faculty to aggregate and store data about students' writing and thinking strengths and weaknesses.

At William Paterson University, faculty embarked on an initiative to assess four learning literacies: information seeking and understanding (information literacy), technology competence, critical thinking, and numerical literacy. As Sharmila Pixy Ferris and Anne Ciliberti report, several years of work convinced them that although the four skills should be integrated across the curriculum, assessment of each skill should be the focus of effort in a separate semester. To assess information literacy, faculty developed an instrument based on the information literacy competence standards advanced by the Association of College and Research Libraries. The instrument has been applied to student work in freshman general education courses and senior capstone courses. Experience in assessing information literacy is providing guidance for assessing the three remaining literacies—critical thinking, technology literacy, and numerical literacy—in subsequent semesters.

Since 2003, faculty at Northeastern Illinois University have been developing a plan for assessing six goals for general education. Angeles L. Eames describes the methods employed in assessing student achievement of three of the abilities identified in the goals: communication (writing and speaking), integrating information (critical thinking), and use of quantitative methods. Course-embedded assessment using locally developed rubrics, standardized testing using the Academic Profile, and items from two national surveys as well as a locally developed alumni survey provide direct and indirect evidence of student learning. Faculty have based several new courses and programs on assessment findings, including a First Year Experience course, Writing in the Disciplines, and several new math courses. In addition, a coordinator has been appointed for English composition courses and new pedagogical enhancement activities are under way in the campus Center for Teaching and Learning.

According to Pam Bowers, faculty at Oklahoma State University formed the General Education Assessment Task Force in 2000. This group developed assessable learning outcomes for general education and a series of student portfolios for use in assessing written communication skills, math problem-solving skills, science problem-solving skills, critical thinking, and appreciation of diversity. Each skill is the subject of its own portfolio and students populate the portfolios with course assignments collected throughout the undergraduate curriculum. Faculty members, who are paid summer stipends for their work, use standardized rubrics to evaluate the work in each portfolio. Data aggregated across student portfolios in a skill area provide evidence of the effectiveness of the general education curriculum in strengthening student achievement in that area.

With leadership from Uche Ohia and colleagues, faculty at Florida Agricultural and Mechanical University employ a variety of direct and indirect measures in assessing student attainment of eight core learning outcomes. Direct measures include the standardized test, Measure of Academic Proficiency and Progress, and portfolios containing artifacts from general education courses scored using rubrics developed by faculty groups. Indirect measures include the National Survey of Student Engagement and student focus groups. Information obtained from the portfolio, the standardized test, and the focus groups raised concern about students' critical thinking skills and led to the adoption of an institution-wide plan for enhancing these skills.

Institutions

Doctoral and Research
> Public
>> Florida Agricultural and Mechanical University; Tallahassee, Florida (12,000 students)
>> North Carolina State University at Raleigh; Raleigh, North Carolina (31,000 students)
>> Oklahoma State University–Main Campus; Stillwater, Oklahoma (23,000 students)
>> University of South Florida; Tampa, Florida (45,000 students)

Master's
> Public
>> Northeastern Illinois University; Chicago, Illinois (12,000 students)
>> William Paterson University of New Jersey; Wayne, New Jersey (11,000 students)

Assessing Critical Thinking and Higher-Order Reasoning in Service-Learning Enhanced Courses and Course Sequences

Patti H. Clayton, Sarah Ash, Jessica Katz Jameson, North Carolina State University

◆ ◆ ◆

Look for a model for integrating critical reflection and assessment in service-learning courses as well as in a sequence of courses that lead to a minor in nonprofit studies.

Background and Purpose(s) of Assessment

We have been conducting a project focused on formative and summative course-based assessment of student learning outcomes within and across service-learning enhanced courses at North Carolina State University (NCSU). In particular, we are interested in building both faculty and student capacity to deepen and document learning in the three categories of service-learning's outcomes: academic enhancement, civic learning, and personal growth. We knew—from our own experience and from the literature—the challenges of achieving significant rather than superficial and problematic outcomes via service-learning, and we were aware of the need to assess learning outcomes through the demonstration of actual student learning, not just through self-report of satisfaction, as a way to legitimate the use of this nontraditional educational strategy.

Assessment Method(s) and Year(s) of Implementation

Over several years (formalized in 2003, but dating back to 2001 informally) and several service-learning courses, a group of NCSU faculty, staff, and students reviewed student reflection products for evidence of learning and concluded that a much stronger design of, and greater support for, critical reflection was needed. As a result, we developed a core reflection model called DEAL, for the three steps of **D**escription, **E**xamination, and **A**rticulation of **L**earning, with sets of guiding prompts specific to each of the general learning goals (academic enhancement, civic learning, and personal growth). The prompts, in turn, were linked to a set of learning objectives, grounded in Bloom's Taxonomy (1956). Because of the hierarchical nature of the taxonomy, we were able to use these objectives as a rubric, scoring the students' reflection products based on their ability to meet each level in the hierarchy, from identification to evaluation.

Our continued examination of student writing led us to the realization that students could meet each level, but do so badly. Therefore we also incorporated Paul and Elder's Standards of Critical Thinking (2001)—accuracy, clarity, precision, relevance, depth, breadth, significance, logic, and fairness—into the model to further guide the students toward higher-quality learning. A four-level holistic rubric was created to assess demonstration of critical thinking in student reflection products.

These two rubrics have been used ever since for research purposes and by instructors for both formative feedback and final grading. Success in achieving the desired learning outcomes can be assessed across categories of learning goals or across time within each category, from early to late in the semester, and from first to final drafts.

Required Resources

The primary resources are the student and faculty time needed to learn how to use the critical reflection model and associated assessment tools, along with faculty and staff time for training. Students and faculty alike, of course, need access to materials on the DEAL model and associated rubrics. Additional time for coding, de-identifying, and recording is necessary if the student work is being collected for research purposes.

Findings

In a research project in which a group of trained faculty, staff, and students scored student reflection products from two different courses, we found that use of the DEAL model for critical reflection and its associated rubrics did in fact improve students' higher-order reasoning abilities and critical thinking skills relative to our learning goal categories of academic enhancement, civic learning, and personal growth. This happened across drafts of an essay as well as across multiple assignments over the course of the semester. However, given the "counter-normative" (Howard, 1998; Clayton & Ash, 2004) nature of learning through critical reflection, we found that students needed a lot of support and feedback in order to be successful in articulating their own learning. In addition, we found that students had the greatest difficulty in the academic learning category.

Use of Findings

The assessment results led to the refinement of both reflection prompts and rubrics and faculty development processes and materials. In addition, because of the need to build greater capacity for students to learn how to learn through critical reflection, we created a tutorial, which introduces students to service-learning, critical reflection, and critical thinking in general and to the DEAL model and its associated rubrics in particular; it guides them step-by-step through the application of the model to their own service-learning experiences.

As a result of the overall success in using the Bloom-based objectives to guide and assess reflective thinking in individual service-learning courses, we created a modified version of this integrated reflection and assessment process for use across a series of NCSU courses that make up a service-learning enhanced nonprofit studies minor. Here the learning goals are expressed in terms of five leadership challenges facing the nonprofit sector, each understood to be at the intersection of academic content and civic learning: aligning mission, methods, and resources; balancing individual interests and the common good; earning and maintaining the public trust; moving beyond charity to systemic change; and capitalizing on opportunities associated with diversity. Again, learning objectives in each of these arenas are expressed hierarchically from identification to evaluation; and the course sequence is designed to support students in gradually moving up the taxonomy (for example, the introductory course targets student learning up to the level of application in each of the five arenas, an intermediate course has as its goal the level of evaluation, and a capstone course aims to have the students evaluating in an integrative manner across the multiple service-learning experiences that they have had throughout the minor). We are gathering student products from introductory, intermediate, and capstone courses and scoring them using Bloom-based rubrics, to examine the extent to which the sequential design of service-learning across the minor is in fact helping the students to achieve the desired learning outcomes, and to determine whether there are differences in the students' abilities to think at the desired level of reasoning across the five leadership challenges.

Impact of Using Findings

Faculty who have participated in this assessment process have improved their teaching by using service-learning and, more generally, by paying closer attention to the connection between stated learning objectives and actual student learning. We have become better critical thinkers and more skilled at designing and facilitating reflection, at giving students effective feedback, and at grading reflection products.

For the minor in nonprofit studies, this assessment process contributed to the refinement of cross-course learning objectives and related course design. It also revealed limitations in our current methods of teaching toward and measuring learning outcomes across multiple courses, which come from a variety of disciplines and are taught by faculty who have varying levels of familiarity with service-learning in general and the DEAL model in particular. Therefore, we realize the need to work with faculty teaching in the minor to build their capacity to incorporate the leadership challenges into their courses by using the prompts and rubrics. However, despite these challenges, we will be able to bring an evidence-based argument regarding learning outcomes to NCSU leadership as part of seeking increased support for the minor.

Faculty on other campuses have become interested in the DEAL model and its associated rubrics as they have learned of our research findings, and this has led to the development of interinstitutional collaboration focused on further adaptation through ongoing research with student products from a wider range of courses and disciplines. In addition, we hope to be able to use the evidence from the assessment of student learning to promote the use of reflective learning across our own campus more generally, to encourage more faculty and departments to adopt service-learning in their courses, and to invite more faculty and students to join us in ongoing scholarship of teaching and learning projects grounded in learning through critical reflection.

Success Factors

In our experience, it is important to integrate teaching and learning strategies (in this case, service-learning, with its emphasis on critical reflection) closely with assessment strategies through well-articulated learning objectives. Grounding the approach to assessment in educational theory (such as Bloom's Taxonomy or Paul and Elder's Standards of Critical Thinking) enabled us to fulfill our goal of assessing student learning as demonstrated versus as self-reported. Also important were taking the time to read student products carefully and to iteratively refine the reflection process and associated rubrics as well as our use of them.

One innovation that helped us use our time effectively was a faculty-student learning community within which to build capacity, experiment, mentor, and collaboratively score products. Students have given us some of our core insights, posed significant questions, and brought useful perspectives to this assessment project; and faculty have used the space and support provided by a learning community structure to take risks and to generate substantial scholarship.

Indeed, a focus on scholarship and capacity building has also been crucial in this work as it has led us to a very disciplined and thoughtful engagement with our students' thinking and has reinforced for us continuously the importance of making the teaching and learning process explicit and visible to students, to ourselves, and to our colleagues.

Relevant Institutional Web Sites Pertaining to This Assessment Practice

www.ncsu.edu/curricular_engagement

Improvement in Students' Writing and Thinking through Assessment Discoveries

Teresa Flateby, University of South Florida

◆ ◆ ◆

Look for a model for teaching and assessing students' writing and thinking skills that uses an online system and peer review by students. Faculty report an increased understanding of assessment as an integral part of students' learning processes and of improving instruction.

Background and Purpose(s) of Assessment

The assessment of writing and thinking at the University of South Florida (USF) was begun in 1999 primarily in response to regional accreditation demands. More recently, assessment is becoming more formative and embedded in our undergraduate curriculum.

Prior to 1999 I led the assessment of writing and thinking, which was a focus of the university's Learning Community, a two-year team-taught general education program. In 1999, coordination of general education assessment for our ten-year Southern Association of Colleges and School's reaffirmation was added to my responsibilities as the director of evaluation and testing. Understanding the value of assessment conducted by a team of stakeholders and embedded within courses (the approach used in the Learning Community program), I hoped to continue with a similar orientation.

Several factors affected the assessment approaches selected. USF's general education program was not centrally coordinated and was a distributed model, allowing students to choose from a wide array of courses. This model reflected seat time rather than learning outcomes. In addition, factors such as a very small budget, modest support from the upper administration, my other full-time responsibilities, and the newness of assessment to the university affected the approach selected. I had gathered, however, a small number of key advocates, referred to as "fixers" in the political science literature, who help advance assessment (Hill, 2005). These "fixers" helped by either becoming members of an *ad hoc* assessment committee or by recommending faculty who had a basic understanding of assessment and who valued general education.

Although we had constraints, the committee agreed that writing was central to our institution's general education goals and that we must focus on assessing the quality of our students' writing, as well as the thinking associated with effective writing.

Assessment Method(s) and Year(s) of Implementation

The initial assessment of writing and thinking began in the Learning Community and resembled a standardized test, with students writing on a specific standard topic under timed conditions at particular points in the curriculum. Raters external to USF, who also evaluated essays for the state's rising junior exam, scored our students' essays. Employing a holistic rubric, they assigned scores of 1–6, ranging in proficiency levels from "below" to "exceeds" expectations. Our assessment practices were basically acceptable, but slightly outdated according to writing assessment practices advocated by composition professionals. Although our results confirmed our anecdotal evidence that some students were more than acceptable writers, many more were not. We also discovered that this approach did not produce meaningful results; it provided little formative information to identify specific student writing weaknesses. Just as important, we involved very few faculty members in this process.

Additional Learning Community assessment results revealed needs to assist faculty with the assessment of student writing and thinking. We discovered inconsistencies in grading students' essays and in the emphasis given to higher-order thinking skills in the program. In response, Elizabeth Metzger, program coordinator and former director of USF's composition program, and I began developing a rubric to provide a consistent method to evaluate writing and thinking skills for faculty from diverse disciplines. Based on commonly used writing handbooks, such as *St. Martin's Handbook* (Lunsford & Connors, 1992), *Harbrace College Handbook* (Hodges et al., 1998), and *Scott Foresman Handbook for Writers* (Hairston, Ruskiewicz, & Friend, 1999), the writing rubric that we developed has a comprehensive writing focus (Flateby & Metzger, 1999, 2001). The resulting Cognitive Level and Quality of Writing Assessment (CLAQWA) rubric is analytic; it has five major categories with multiple traits within each category and five performance levels operationally defined. It is jargon-free, flexible, and useful in its entirety or with a smaller number of traits, depending on the demands of the assignment or discipline and the achievement levels of students. Recently, based on the American Philosophical Association's Delphi Report (1990) and Bloom's Taxonomy of Educational Objectives-Cognitive Domain (1956), we have added critical thinking traits to complement the original "reasoning" traits on the writing portion of the CLAQWA rubric.

The separate cognitive scale, representing a holistic view of thinking revealed in a text, is based on Bloom's Taxonomy. This scale was developed to assess the cognitive levels reached in students' papers, as well as to help faculty construct assignments to reflect cognitive levels accurately and to encourage them to think about the developmental nature of assignments.

The CLAQWA analytic rubric was created for use in the Learning Community program, but the ad hoc USF faculty assessment committee formed to guide general education assessment also recommended using CLAQWA. Although the assessment was more consistent with instruction (students wrote their essays out of class), results confirmed those obtained from the previously collected holistically evaluated writing: that typically students' performance levels were lower than desired. The analytic scale provided more actionable findings; the traits related to thinking were the most problematic.

Required Resources

The type and extent of needed resources to assess writing and thinking depend on the approach selected. If the assessment is focused at the program or institutional level, resources for faculty development and stipends are needed. If the assessment is embedded, faculty development to effectively use the rubric or online assessment system is essential. Implicit in these plans is the need to organize the process, communicate and offer the development activities, and manage the data, including how data are used.

Findings

Over a seven-year period of collecting writing and thinking data, results consistently revealed lower-than-desired performance. More specifically, students' weakest skills were related to reasoning, supplying evidence to support their ideas, and cohesively presenting their ideas. In response to these findings, the General Education Council added "process" writing courses in which feedback and revision are essential, and also began requiring a focus on critical thinking in all general education courses. Due to the weaknesses revealed, we surveyed faculty to determine their perceptions of student writing and their writing and thinking evaluation processes. Faculty described problems with students' writing and suggested obstacles that prevented them from addressing these problems. Some reported needing guidance to evaluate students' writing, some wanted more assistance to help students with writing instruction, and others mentioned that large classes prohibited the inclusion of writing.

Use of Findings

During the assessment process, several USF instructors who were involved with the general education assessment adapted the CLAQWA rubric for peer review in composition classes. Although they were already applying peer review, they found that their students' writing and thinking skills improved more with the new CLAQWA adaptation. Shortly after, faculty from other disciplines, including fine arts and engineering, began using this peer-review process. Finding the results to be beneficial, they have continued to use the process and have encouraged their colleagues to apply peer review.

In addition to using the results to revise the general education curriculum, we created assessment and instructional tools to address weaknesses and faculty concerns. Realizing the importance and potential of technology, we began developing an electronic platform for the CLAQWA rubric nearly three years ago. Our goals were to provide faculty with a flexible rubric, one that can be adapted to most written work, and to give students fuller explanations about faculty expectations and more instructional feedback. Thus we included examples to improve students' writing and thinking about the course content. This system, which evolved from the rubric, has multiple benefits. Students are able to apply the system for peer review, thus providing meaningful writing and thinking feedback to their fellow students. The CLAQWA Online system can be used for faculty wishing to offer feedback either with the CLAQWA rubric or with instructor-generated comments. In addition, the general education assessment team uses the system to evaluate students' texts, giving more comprehensive and useful feedback to students than is typical for program assessment. Results are stored and aggregated to identify students' writing and thinking strengths and weaknesses quickly.

Impact of Using the Findings

Using peer review and the online system have produced several benefits. Both reveal that student writing and thinking skills improve in the courses in which these resources are implemented. Faculty often report greater collaboration among students after engaging the peer-review process. In addition, faculty have a better understanding of how assessment is an integral part of instructional improvement and of the student learning process, as opposed to an administrative or external mandate.

Success Factors

Especially in settings where assessment is not yet part of an institution's fabric, identifying early adopters is critical. Because meaningful assessment and a culture shift require adequate support, both tangible resources (funding and time) as well as leadership support are needed. Without these supports, individual faculty will engage in the assessment process and learning will improve to a limited degree, but not achieve the potential associated with a change in culture.

Relevant Institutional Web Sites Pertaining to This Assessment Practice

CLAQWA information and Web site may be found at:

http://usfweb2.usf.edu/assessment/index.shtml

Assessing Learning Literacies

Sharmila Pixy Ferris, Anne Ciliberti, William Paterson University

◆ ◆ ◆

Look for faculty-developed rubrics for assessing four learning literacies: information seeking and understanding, technology competence, critical thinking, and numerical literacy. Initial use of the rubrics indicates that seniors in capstone courses have developed more competence in information literacy than have freshmen in general education courses.

Background and Purpose(s) of Assessment

Our assessment addresses issues of lifelong learning relevant to general education, basic skills, the Technology across the Curriculum and Writing across the Curriculum initiatives, and the goals of the Center for Teaching Excellence at William Paterson University.

Our initial impetus was a requirement by our regional accreditor, the Middle States Commission for Higher Education, that we demonstrate that information literacy skills are successfully integrated into the curriculum. However, we found in 2004 through data from local assessments and anecdotal reports from faculty and staff that with respect to the need for improved information literacy skills, our students were similar to their counterparts across the nation in urgently needing assistance in understanding basic math concepts, effectively using technology tools, and evaluating the credibility of information resources.

To this end, our purpose was the assessment of four "learning literacies," the umbrella term used at William Paterson University to denote four dimensions of learning: information seeking and understanding, technology competence, critical thinking, and numerical literacy (see Exhibit 5.1 for a detailed definition). Two years of preliminary work led our learning literacies team to conclude that these four competences should be studied together. Our immediate goal was to assess mastery of the four competences in our curriculum, whereas our long-term goal is to assist in integrating these skills across the curriculum.

EXHIBIT 5.1. LEARNING LITERACIES

At William Paterson University the term "learning literacies" is used as an umbrella phrase to denote four dimensions of learning: information seeking and understanding, technology, critical thinking, and numerical literacy. Two years of preliminary work led our Learning Literacies Strategy Team to conclude that four lifelong learning skills are closely connected—information and technology skills, critical thinking and numerical literacy—so that the four competences should be studied together.

Information Literacy

- Recognize and articulate an information need
- Develop effective research strategies
- Analyze and critically evaluate information
- Organize and synthesize information
- Understand legal and ethical issues related to information and apply this understanding to technology literacy

Technology literacy

- Engage in global and collaborative outreach through electronic communication
- Engage in face-to-face communication through technology-enhanced presentations
- Use emerging technologies to collect and manage data and information
- Use technology to analyze data more effectively
- Demonstrate familiarity with major legal, ethical, privacy, and security issues in information technology

Critical Thinking

- Identify and examine assumptions and premises
- Distinguish belief, opinion, and empirical truth
- Think open-mindedly; think critically about personal beliefs

- Present and assess the quality of supporting data and empirical evidence within a context
- Draw conclusions based on evidence, prior knowledge, and context
- Create or generate ideas, processes, experiences, or artifacts

    Numerical Literacy

- Identify and examine assumptions and premises
- Distinguish belief, opinion, and empirical truth
- Think open-mindedly; think critically about personal beliefs
- Present and assess the quality of supporting data and empirical evidence within a context
- Draw conclusions based on evidence, prior knowledge, and context
- Create or generate ideas, processes, experiences, or artifacts

Assessment Method(s) and Year(s) of Implementation

In 2004, a learning literacy team was formed under the leadership of the director of the library. We began with extensive time devoted to the creation of assessment rubrics. We then moved into a multilevel and multiphase plan for engaging faculty and assessing the four literacies (see Figure 5.1).

Faculty engagement was promoted through two campuswide forums in 2005 and 2006 and ongoing meetings with deans, department chairs, and Faculty Senate members. Once this was under way, we decided to assess one learning literacy

FIGURE 5.1. MULTILEVEL AND MULTIPHASE PLAN FOR ENGAGING FACULTY AND ASSESSING THE FOUR LITERACIES.

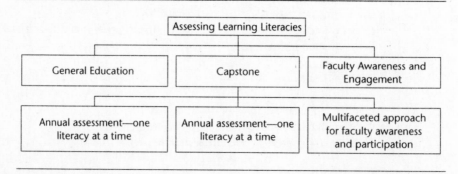

per semester, to support data collection of one literacy skill set concurrent with data analysis, and to allow for concomitant "closing the assessment loop" through action on results. Our schedule for data collection began with assessment of information literacy, to be followed on a semester-by-semester basis with assessment of critical thinking, technology literacy, and numerical literacy.

To assess information literacy, we developed an instrument based on the definition outlined by the Association of College and Research Libraries (ACRL) Information Literacy Competence Standards for Higher Education (ACRL, 2000), which have become the nationally accepted standard. Our assessment was piloted in spring 2007, with a questionnaire on information literacy posted on an external web site, Zoomerang.com (to ensure anonymity, at the union's request). A stratified random sample of 20 percent of faculty in general education (GE) and capstone courses was selected to participate in the pilot project. The pilot helped us refine the instrument, and we rolled out a complete assessment of all GE and capstone courses in fall 2007.

We assessed students in courses from the general education and capstone programs for carefully considered reasons. Implicit in assessing the four competences is the recognition that learning skills evolve and develop as students progress through undergraduate study and that advanced learning literacy skills are requisite for academic success, future careers, and/or graduate work. The general education program is a natural place in the curriculum to investigate student mastery of learning literacies because so many of William Paterson University's 12 GE goals and objectives correspond to the learning literacies of this project. Key among these are: to practice and refine fundamental learning skills; to foster effective written and oral communication; to foster critical and creative thinking. There is also strong correspondence between the university's student learning outcomes and objectives and the information literacy learning competences. Capstone courses are important as they help determine the degree to which students achieve mastery of the advanced learning skills.

In our assessment, faculty who teach these selected courses were asked to assess the skill levels of three students randomly identified by the last few digits of their student identification numbers. Student data remain anonymous and confidential. Participating faculty were asked to select any one significant class assignment, project, or examination as a basis for judging student performance on a subset of the literacy measures as set out in a rubric (see Exhibit 5.2) developed for this purpose. Space was also provided for qualitative and open-ended feedback on the assessment and method. For the complete assessment, GE and capstone faculty were personally invited by e-mail from the provost to participate, with follow-up reminders from the chair of GE and the director of the Center for Teaching Excellence.

EXHIBIT 5.2. SAMPLE ASSESSMENT RUBRIC

5 Inquiry

Beginning: Student demonstrates only a basic or rudimentary ability to state an information need; the chosen topic demonstrates minimal understanding of the field or course content.

Competent: Student clearly states the question or problem to be addressed; the topic demonstrates adequate knowledge of the field of study or course content.

Advanced: Student states the question or problem clearly, poses the question in a particularly thoughtful, unique, or creative manner and reflects a deep understanding of the field of study.

The student demonstrates the ability to recognize and articulate an appropriate topic at the following level of proficiency:

Beginning	Competent	Advanced	Not Applicable
(1)	(2)	(3)	(4)

6 Appropriateness of Research

Beginning: Based on the citations provided and the presentation or description of the materials, few of the resources used by the student are relevant. There is little evidence of care in the selection of resources. Inaccurate or incomplete citations make it difficult to determine appropriateness.

Competent: Based on the citations provided and the presentation or description of the materials, some of the resources used are relevant. The use of popular versus scholarly materials or media and other forms of evidence is somewhat appropriate and balanced.

Advanced: Based on the citations provided and the presentation or description of the materials, the selection of resources is thoughtful, appropriate, and balanced. The student identifies highly relevant resources or studies in the field.

The student demonstrates the ability to identify and document appropriate resources:

Beginning	Competent	Advanced	Not Applicable
(1)	(2)	(3)	(4)

7 Evaluation: Analyze and Critically Evaluate Information

Beginning: Student selects some appropriate sources; however, most sources don't fit the essential criteria required by the assignment or fail to consider alternative views. The evidence provided poorly supports the arguments presented or the requirements of the project.

Competent: Essential criteria were considered in the selection and evaluation of sources. Sources are relevant and alternative views are considered where appropriate. Most of the evidence supports the arguments or the requirements of the project. Analysis of the sources is adequate.

Advanced: Sources selected clearly relate to the information need and address the essential criteria required by the assignment. Alternative views are analyzed and considered in the development of an argument. The evidence presented strongly supports the arguments or requirements of the project. Analysis of sources is thoughtful and insightful.

The student demonstrates the ability to analyze and critically evaluate the information sources used for this project:

Beginning	Competent	Advanced	Not Applicable
1	2	3	4

8 Synthesis

Beginning: Sources used are not well-integrated into the project. The organization and presentation of the information is weak or occasionally contradictory.

Competent: Information, conclusions, or inferences are presented clearly and in a logical, coherent manner. The student demonstrates a general understanding of the materials and the ability to integrate much of the information gathered for the project. The student addresses the purposes of the project in an acceptable manner.

Advanced: Information, conclusions, or inferences are clear, logical, and coherent and relate strongly to the project requirements. New information is well-integrated with course material. The presentation is well-structured and provides evidence of insight, original work, and an enhanced understanding of the topic.

The student demonstrates the ability to use the information to accomplish a specific purpose for an identified audience:

Beginning	Competent	Advanced	Not Applicable
(1)	(2)	(3)	(4)

Data were analyzed by learning literacy (LL) team members with assistance from the Office of Institutional Research and Assessment and the Center for Teaching Excellence. The LL team disseminates the data. We have also completed an assessment rubric for critical thinking, which is currently being piloted. We propose to assess technology literacy in fall 2008, and numerical literacy in spring 2009. This will ensure that we can concurrently analyze data on one learning literacy while working on closing the loop by acting on data already collected.

Required Resources

The essential resource for this assessment has been a strongly committed assessment team that is comprehensive in representing a wide range of constituents: the library, general education, basic skills, First Year Seminar, Technology across the Curriculum, Writing across the Curriculum, and the Center for Teaching Excellence. Support from the Office of Institutional Research and Assessment has proved crucial in identifying faculty who teach GE and capstone courses, and the Office of Instructional Research and Technology plays an important role in posting and maintaining the survey on Zoomerang.

Findings

Response (35 percent returning questionnaires) for the full-faculty assessment of information literacy was gratifying. Results were interesting in that they support the curricular progression of information literacy skills through students' courses of study at the university. We found differences in information literacy (IL) skills between seniors in capstone courses and freshmen in GE courses. Information literacy scores indicate that seniors in capstones receive higher ratings than do freshmen in GE courses. Specifically, fewer seniors than freshmen were rated at "beginning" competence, and more seniors than freshmen were rated at "competent" or "advanced" levels. Significance was confirmed through a chi-square test with a value of 14.433, p < .001.

This finding was heartening as it suggests that the university is successful in teaching information literacy skills as students progress through their undergraduate studies, and that advanced learning literacy skills do evolve and develop as students progress through their majors. The dimension with the largest difference between seniors and freshmen was "appropriateness of research materials," and the one with the smallest difference was "synthesis of information."

These findings notwithstanding, not all significant findings had positive implications. One very telling finding was the degree to which faculty rated each of the information literacy skills as not applicable in their selected assignments. For example, the information skill most often regarded by faculty (39 percent) as "not applicable" in their assignments relates to Integrity (the ability to adhere to research protocols and guidelines, including documentation requirements). "Appropriateness of research" was the second skill most frequently cited as "not applicable" (29 percent).

Given faculty concerns about the amount of plagiarism evident in student work, both at William Paterson and nationally, the finding that integrity issues are not relevant in many assignments suggests pedagogy needs examination at all levels of the curriculum.

Taken as a whole, the data gained from this assessment raise questions about information literacy and student outcomes throughout the undergraduate curriculum, and provide support for further study of the four competences targeted for assessment.

Use of Findings

Our initial assessment of the first learning literacy is useful on several levels. It provides us with valuable data on students' information literacy skills at entry and exit levels. It also guides us in our upcoming assessments—of critical thinking in spring

TABLE 5.1. INFORMATION LITERACY SCORES.

Not Applicable	Capstone	%	GE	%	Combined	%
Inquiry	1	11.1	3	2	4	2.6
Appropriateness	2	22.2	43	29.4	45	29
Evaluation	0	0	17	11.6	17	10.9
Synthesis	3	33.3	26	17.8	29	18.7
Integrity	3	33.3	57	39	60	38.7
TOTAL	9	100	146	100	155	100

2008, technology literacy in fall 2008, and numerical literacy in spring 2009. As we analyze data on one learning literacy, we are beginning to work concurrently on closing the loop with data already collected. As we complete assessment of all four learning literacies, we can establish benchmarks to determine whether the student mastery of these skills needs work. If this research indicates that students' learning literacy competences fall below the university's expectations, further work will need to be done to integrate the competences in our courses.

Impact of Using the Findings

Although we have just begun our full-scale assessment, results already have had an immediate impact. First, as the university is in the process of general education curriculum review, our data will be valuable in helping to guide the process of overhauling the GE curriculum. Second, our data have already had an impact on the preparations for our decennial accreditation review in 2011. The data provide "direct measures" of quality in the teaching and learning of "information literacy" — identified by Middle States as a *specific* skill set that must be successfully integrated across the curriculum. This assessment is doubly valuable in that it is based on the examination of information literacy, and the other learning literacies, as specific outcomes distinct from other classroom assessments, not related to any particular course, major, or discipline.

Success Factors

The data from the initial assessment have proved useful in a number of ways, as outlined above. But perhaps the largest success factor has been engaging faculty and administration in a discussion about student performance on the four learning literacies. Our assessment has brought to the forefront an awareness of student needs in today's information- and technology-rich society where these four competences are highly interconnected. Our assessment has initiated a consideration of how the university's mission of educating students for lifelong learning should be addressed at various stages throughout the curriculum.

Relevant Institutional Web Sites Pertaining to This Assessment Practice

Learning Literacies Web Site:

www.wpunj.edu/academics/cte/literacy.htm

General Education Web Site:

www.wpunj.edu/academics/gened/

William Paterson University Home Page:

www.wpunj.edu/default.htm

Using Direct and Indirect Evidence in General Education Assessment

Angeles L. Eames, Northeastern Illinois University

◆ ◆ ◆

Look for the use of multiple measures, including locally developed rubrics and a standardized test as well as national and local surveys, to assess student achievement in writing and speaking, critical thinking, and using quantitative methods. Faculty have used assessment findings to strengthen the writing and mathematics curricula and to add a new First Year Experience.

Background and Purpose(s) of Assessment

Northeastern Illinois University serves many first-generation students and students for whom English is their second language. Graduates of the university tend to pursue careers in teaching, business, and public service. The general education curriculum has remained basically unchanged for the last twenty years and includes six goals (see the Web site for more information). We address three of these in this profile:

General education assists students in developing
1. the ability to communicate both in writing and orally
2. the skills required to gather, analyze, document, and integrate information
3. the ability to use quantitative methods in the natural, social, and behavioral sciences

Within recent years, the faculty began to wonder if the changing population and marketplace might necessitate reform in the general education curriculum. A new provost thought that an effective assessment program would help to clarify the purposes and goals of the general education program and point to needed improvements. He charged the Faculty Senate's Committee on General Education with developing and implementing a new plan for general education assessment. His decision was fortuitous; the regional accrediting body was due to pay a visit within three years.

The committee worked diligently to develop the assessment plan during the 2003–04 academic year. The final plan was approved and endorsed by several faculty governance groups. The full plan can be accessed at: www.neiu.edu/~neassess/pdf/GenEd_Assessment_Plan_FINAL_APPROVED.pdf

The big question to be answered by general education assessment is "What impact does our current general education program have on our students' learning?" One way to address this is to see how well our students meet the expected learning goals and outcomes for general education. The assessment plan provides the framework for answering this question and involves faculty and students, each playing a different role.

Assessment Method(s) and Year(s) of Implementation

Since spring 2005, the methods we have used include: embedded assessment; locally developed instruments (rubrics) to examine student writing and critical thinking abilities; standardized testing, including the Academic Profile (now Measure of Academic Proficiency and Progress, or MAPP); locally developed instruments to assess oral communications skills; and an item analysis of NSSE, CIRP, and alumni surveys to discover trends in responses related to general education. In the coming year, we will pilot an instrument we are designing to assess the development of literary and aesthetic sensitivities and another developed by math and psychology faculty that will examine students' use of quantitative skills in greater depth. Not all of these methods are used every year, but standardized testing and item analysis from existing surveys occur on an annual basis. Locally developed tests require pilot testing and academic review before they can be implemented on a larger scale; one such instrument is chosen for administration each year.

Required Resources

University leadership from the administration as well as the Faculty Senate and the faculty in general are vital for the success of this effort. Faculty and staff are needed to administer the process, analyze and communicate the findings, and make recommendations for improvements. Without someone to administer the process and coordinate efforts, this plan would not work. Between $5,000 and $10,000 is needed annually to purchase testing materials, for professional development activities for the committee, for faculty stipends if faculty panels are used, and for analysis and communication of results. The coordination function for this effort is performed by the executive director of Assessment and Institutional Studies.

Findings

During the spring 2005 term we examined student responses at three points:

1. At entry—new first-time freshmen
2. At completion or near completion of general education requirements
3. One year out from graduation

In assessing the first goal, "to develop students' abilities and skills in written communication," a faculty panel used a rubric with a 4-point scale that examined the following dimensions in student writing: thesis clarity, support/reasoning, writing style, and writing conventions. Two samples of student writing were assessed. The first sample was drawn from the writing placement tests taken by incoming freshmen; the second from assignments made to students in upper-level classes, typically juniors and seniors. In comparing the mean scores of the two groups, we found that students' writing had improved. Across the board, the strongest area for students was thesis clarity. Their area of greatest difficulty was in providing support for their assertions and in putting together coherent reasoning to support their assertions. Use of the Academic Profile indicated that there were no significant differences between the performance of Northeastern Illinois University students and those at peer institutions with regard to writing.

To assess the next goal, "to develop students' abilities and skills in critical thinking," we used a locally developed rubric as well as the Academic Profile test. Following a similar approach to that used above for obtaining samples of student work, a faculty panel read 150 student papers obtained from upper-level courses. The panel determined that work collected from entering freshmen was not of sufficient length to be able to judge critical thinking skills. The rubric criteria used included the student's ability and skill to: identify issues, recognize context, evaluate evidence, and evaluate implications and conclusions. The results showed that students could identify main issues and summarize. Students showed some understanding of various contexts, and could identify data and information that count as evidence. Students were weaker in demonstrating their ability to evaluate evidence for its credibility or legitimacy. And though they could suggest consequences, they tended to do so without clear reference to context, assumptions, data, and evidence. The results from the Academic Profile again indicated that there were no significant differences between the performance of our students and that of students at peer institutions.

The assessment of quantitative skills relied solely on the Academic Profile for the first year. This proved to be an area that needed improvement for our students. That year was seen as a way to begin to develop a baseline for reviewing our performance. Over 500 students participated in either the testing program or the embedded assessment process that year. Almost 100 faculty were actively involved at different points in the process.

Similar results were obtained a year later. That year we also examined the trends for the indirect measures. Paradoxically, we found that although students' writing needed improvement, their confidence as entering freshmen in the area of writing had soared. Most felt they were in the top group. Now knowing that students had a false sense of confidence despite needing help in developing their writing abilities, the staff at the Writing Center made stronger outreach efforts. They set up tables in the library, in the student center, and in the classroom buildings for "drop-in service," in addition to their main location. The Center director reports that the approach was very successful in reaching students who might not otherwise have come to the Center.

The university continues to assess general education. Each year we ask additional questions and as we learn the answers to these, changes are made to improve student learning.

Use of Findings

We share results through presentations and discussion in college academic affairs committees, in Faculty Council for Academic Affairs, in faculty assemblies for each college, at the department level, and at the senior administrative level. The results are shared with retention committees, student support services, advising staff, and enrollment management professionals.

Impact of Using the Findings

The findings and ensuing discussions, along with other studies, provided strong support for the establishment of several new programs at the university. These include a First Year Experience program and the Writing in the Disciplines program. In addition, a coordinator for English composition courses has been appointed to align the composition and writing courses in terms of learning outcomes, pedagogies, and assessment to increase the impact of these courses on student learning. New mathematics courses aim to increase the quantitative literacy of our students. The Center for Teaching and Learning is working with faculty to enhance pedagogies to improve student performance in identified areas of weakness.

At the beginning of the assessment process, the faculty thought that we might want to change our approach to general education, but didn't know what needed changing or fixing. The assessment results point to some of those directions. In the coming year, we anticipate a deeper dialogue aimed at restructuring the general education curriculum to support student success more effectively.

Success Factors

Precipitating factors for assessment include a new provost, upcoming regional accreditation, and faculty unease about the goals of general education. Later, a new president fueled the momentum. Our efforts are sustained by the commitment of the faculty and administration working together. As results became known, these served as catalysts for more discussion, and consequently more investment on the part of the faculty. Through it all, people committed to the idea of improvement of student success through general education need to keep the momentum going. Finally, a well-thought-out plan endorsed by the faculty provides direction.

Relevant Institutional Web Sites Pertaining to This Assessment Practice

The university Web site is undergoing redesign and consequently, the general education Web site is currently being revised. However, the assessment plan can be found at:

www.neiu.edu/~neassess/pdf/GenEd_Assessment_Plan_FINAL
_APPROVED.pdf

Institutional Portfolio Assessment in General Education

Pam Bowers, Oklahoma State University

◆ ◆ ◆

Look for cross-disciplinary teams of faculty paid to apply locally developed rubrics in assessing portfolios of student course assignments for each of five general education outcomes. Preliminary findings have encouraged faculty to institute a writing requirement for all courses approved for the general education curriculum.

Background and Purpose(s) of Assessment

This summary is based on historical documents in the Office of University Assessment compiled prior to the author's employment there.

The Oklahoma State University (OSU) Assessment Council and Office of University Assessment formed a faculty General Education Assessment Task Force in May 2000 for the purpose of developing and implementing a new plan to assess the effectiveness of OSU's general education program. Although general education and "midlevel" assessment methods such as standardized tests and surveys had been conducted intermittently at OSU since 1993, no sustainable approach to evaluating the general education curriculum had been established. The task force formed in 2000 was the first group of faculty members paid to work on such a university-wide assessment project and this development marked a renewed commitment to general education assessment at OSU.

Following the assessment standard of articulating desired student outcomes first, and in collaboration with the General Education Advisory Council (general education policy-making body), task force members revised OSU's *Criteria and Goals for General Education Courses* document and identified "assessable" outcomes for the general education program. The task group developed the following guidelines for effective and sustainable general education assessment:

- The process must not be aimed at individual faculty members or departments.
- The process should be led by faculty members and faculty participation should be voluntary.
- The process should use student work already produced in courses.
- The process should assess all undergraduates, including transfer students, because general education outcomes describe qualities expected of all OSU graduates.

In 2001, task group members agreed to initiate an institutional portfolio assessment method that was consistent with these guidelines to assess student achievement of the expected learning outcomes for the general education program. In 2003, the name of the task force was changed to the General Education Assessment Committee. This committee is charged with continuing to develop and implement general education assessment and reports to the Assessment Council and General Education Advisory Council; membership on these committees is intentionally overlapping. Committee members serve rotating 3-year terms, are extensively involved in undergraduate teaching at OSU, represent a range of disciplines, and are paid summer stipends for their work on general education assessment.

Assessment Method(s) and Year(s) of Implementation

Institutional Portfolios. Committee members have developed institutional portfolios to assess students' written communication skills (data collection in 2001, 2002, 2003, 2004, 2005, and 2006), math problem-solving skills (data collection in 2002, 2003, and 2005), science problem-solving skills (data collection in

2003, 2004, 2005, and 2007), and critical thinking (data collection in 2005, 2006, and 2007). The committee began developing a rubric for assessment of students' knowledge, skills, and attitudes regarding diversity in 2006, pilot tested the rubric with a small number of samples of student work in summer 2006, and conducted the first assessment using the rubric in 2007.

Separate portfolios are developed to evaluate each general education learner goal, and each portfolio includes students' work from course assignments collected throughout the undergraduate curriculum. Faculty members, including GE Assessment Committee members and additional faculty involved in undergraduate teaching, work in groups to evaluate the work in each portfolio using standardized scoring rubrics to assess student achievement relative to a given learner goal. The results provide a measure of the extent to which students are achieving OSU's general education learning goals. The committee plans to continue to develop institutional portfolios to assess the learner goals for general education as described in the *Criteria and Goals for General Education Courses*.

Required Resources

Each of the six faculty members of the General Education Assessment Committee is paid one month's salary and benefits during the summer for work performed throughout the year. Additional faculty members are paid a stipend of $1,000 each to serve as reviewers. Administrative support for this assessment work is provided by the Office of University Assessment and Testing. The assessment office is funded by a per-credit-hour fee, which also supports the general education and other assessment activities.

Findings

It has taken us two to three years to collect and evaluate enough samples of student work in each portfolio to attain the number needed to achieve the desired statistical power. As the portfolio to assess students' achievement of the learning goal of "effective written communication skills" was the first developed, this was the first for which assessment results led to specific action for program improvement. Faculty determined that results of the writing portfolio assessment indicated a need for improvement in students' writing performance. Supporting information was provided by data from the National Survey of Student Engagement, which indicated that students' perceived engagement in writing was lower at this institution than at comparison institutions.

Use of Findings

As a result, the faculty implemented a policy change for courses with the general education designation to increase significantly the amount of writing required in these courses, and to ensure that students had the benefit of receiving feedback on their writing from the instructor.

Effective August 2004, all new requests for general education designations had to meet the new writing requirement. However, courses with approved general education designations that met all criteria and goals except the writing requirements were allowed to retain the general education designation, with the expectation that the new writing standards would be implemented prior to the next course review. The General Education Advisory Council reviews each course every three years, or when course modifications are submitted. Each course must satisfy all criteria and goals, now including the writing requirements, to retain the general education designation.

Impact of Using the Findings

The requirement for increased writing has been phased in gradually, as general education designated courses come up for review every three years. There has been some resistance to the increased writing requirement from faculty who teach large classes. The policy change has led to the development of faculty workshops to help faculty use the assessment rubric to clarify expectations for their students and to provide feedback to students about the strengths and weaknesses demonstrated in their writing for class assignments. Faculty members who need assistance due to the increased grading workload are also encouraged to work through their departments and colleges to request financial support for assistance. The writing assessment was not conducted in the most recent cycle (not all portfolios are assessed every year), but we expect that improvement in students' writing performance will be demonstrated in future assessment cycles.

Success Factors

Faculty believe the portfolio process is useful, and its eight-year history has proved that it is sustainable over time. Portfolios for five general education learning outcomes have been created, and three are assessed each summer. The writing portfolio was the first one developed, and faculty have taken action, based on assessment results, to improve students' achievement of that learning outcome. Given that it takes two to three cycles to amass the sample size needed for an institution our size and we have developed five portfolios since the project's inception, we are just reaching the critical stage of using results for improvement regarding two additional learning goals—critical thinking and science problem solving.

In addition to the information provided by the results of the assessment, we consider the process to be a success factor, as it has led to program and teaching improvements. Our process provides the opportunity for faculty across disciplines to determine jointly their expectations for student learning regarding each of the general education learning goals, and to describe in specific terms the criteria and characteristics of students' work that constitute achievement of the goal. Faculty members who serve as reviewers for the assessment have the experience of reviewing class assignments—both the instructions given to students and students' performance of the assignments—from across the university. This provides them with an opportunity to consider how class assignments in their own programs compare with those in other disciplines.

This experience has also led to faculty discussions about the content of class assignments. Each year General Education Assessment Committee members conduct faculty workshops to discuss the assessment process and results, and to engage faculty in discussions about their own class assignments and how they might be modified to engage students more effectively in practicing and demonstrating knowledge and skills in critical thinking, for example. This activity helps provide samples of student work for the assessments but, more important, helps align activity in individual classrooms with the institutional general education learning goals.

These cross-disciplinary workshops have been well received by faculty and have helped generate support for the general education assessment process. In addition, the portfolio method has been adopted by many academic programs, both undergraduate and graduate, and two colleges are conducting collegewide assessments using this method.

Relevant Institutional Web Sites Pertaining to This Assessment Practice

http://uat.okstate.edu/assessment/index.html

Faculty Ownership: Making a Difference in Systematic General Education Assessment

Uche O. Ohia, Florida Agricultural and Mechanical University (FAMU)

◆ ◆ ◆

Look for a plan for general education assessment that encompasses graded writing samples collected in a portfolio, a standardized test of generic skills, a national measure of student engagement, and focus-group interviews. Concerns about students' critical thinking skills have led to the development of a Quality Enhancement Plan to increase student achievement in this area.

Background and Purpose(s) of Assessment

Institutional systematic assessment activities began at Florida Agricultural and Mechanical University (FAMU) in 2004. Assessment at FAMU serves three major purposes: program and service improvement, accountability to external constituents, and progress toward institutional effectiveness to meet public and accrediting agency requirements.

Our general education assessment initiative was undertaken largely in response to a Southern Association of Colleges and Schools (SACS) standard on assessment and the Academic Learning Compact mandated by the Florida Board of Governors (FBOG). Faculty ownership of this initiative has made a big difference and has produced a systematic general education assessment program.

Following its establishment in summer 2004 as an oversight committee, the General Education Assessment Committee (GEAC) developed the first-ever general education assessment plan that identified and recommended focusing assessment on eight institutional core student learning outcomes: communication skills, critical thinking skills, technology literacy, collaboration skills, ethical values, lifelong learning, cultural diversity, and quantitative reasoning.

Assessment Method(s) and Year(s) of Implementation

The GEAC plan identified a variety of methods for use in assessing the five outcomes that became the focus of the first two years of the process. A direct method, the General Education Institutional Portfolio, made it possible to collect artifacts, such as projects, papers, test questions, assignments, and lab reports. The GEAC piloted this portfolio in spring 2006 with writing samples from 30 percent of students taking an English writing course, ENC 1102.

In fall 2006, writing samples were collected and evaluated for 192 students enrolled in various general education courses. These samples were scored using rubrics developed by faculty groups to ensure consistent evaluation of each learning outcome.

Another direct method employed was the Measure of Academic Proficiency and Progress (MAPP), a standardized instrument developed by the Educational Testing Service (ETS). This test of general education outcomes was administered to opportunity samples, first to over 950 students during the 2005 ETS pilot test of MAPP and subsequently to 124 students in fall 2006 as a pre-post measure to incoming freshmen and other students who had earned 60 credit hours.

Two indirect measures, the National Survey of Student Engagement (NSSE) and focus-group interviews, were used. The interviews have been conducted once per semester since fall 2006 in three groups of 7–10 students each. Groups include students from diverse disciplines and, when possible, from diverse races, ages, and genders. GEAC efforts have resulted in the completion of two assessment cycles and assessment planning forms documenting the results and recommendations for improving the outcomes and the process.

Required Resources

The committee's work was facilitated by the Office of University Assessment, which has four full-time employees. In addition, administrative support has always been assured, including release time for the committee members and a stipend paid to the faculty member coordinating the portfolio effort by collecting and distributing artifacts to the Faculty Assessment Scoring Team (FAST). Other budgeted items include travel and MAPP. Another key resource in the process are the students who participate in the surveys, focus groups, and testing, or who complete other instruments used to assess the general education learning outcomes and students' satisfaction with their preparation.

Findings

The results of the fall 2006–07 General Education Institutional Portfolio assessment showed that 68 percent (80 of 118 student writing samples) received a passing score in communication skills; 70 percent (96 of 138 writing samples) received a passing score in critical thinking skills; 51 percent (63 of 125 samples) were given a passing rating in ethical values; whereas 56 percent (69 out of 124 mathematics artifacts) received a passing score in quantitative reasoning.

The MAPP results indicate some slight improvement in many of the tested subscales of MAPP over the two years of administration. In particular, from the fall 2006 testing, respectively 71, 78 and 64 percent of students were at the proficient and marginal levels of Level 1 Reading, Writing, and Mathematics. For Level 2 of the three skills, 25, 33 and 35 percent, respectively, of students were reported to be proficient. Overall, fewer students were found to be proficient at Level 3, particularly in Critical Thinking, with about 96 percent of freshmen reported as not proficient in critical thinking. However, entering freshmen's MAPP mean scores have continued to improve, though they remain below the national average.

The National Survey of Student Engagement (NSSE) was administered for the first time at FAMU in spring 2005 to about 950 students for the purpose of measuring perceptions of such desired educational outcomes as critical thinking, problem solving, effective communication, and responsible citizenship. The results were analyzed, and areas of strength and weakness of our programs were identified and communicated as appropriate. The findings suggest the following: When compared with selected peers and its Carnegie group, FAMU's freshmen and seniors showed **no significant differences** in their mean responses to the Level of Academic Challenge and reported **higher** levels of engagement in Active and Collaborative Learning, **higher** levels of engagement in Student-Faculty Interaction, **lower** levels of engagement in Supportive Campus Environment, and **no significant differences** in engagement in Enriching Educational Experiences. On items related to critical thinking skills, FAMU students had more favorable self-assessments than students at peer institutions.

The consensus of students participating in focus-group interviews indicated satisfaction with the opportunities they have at FAMU to enhance their communication and critical thinking skills, prepare for cultural diversity, and understand the concept of "ethical value." Students gave mixed responses to questions about critical thinking. In one group students said that English courses had made them think critically because they "had to elaborate on topics."

Use of Findings

The GEAC carefully reviewed all the results, discussed the findings as a team, and recommended that more effort be put into increasing the proficiency levels of students across the general education curriculum. In particular, based on the MAPP results, GEAC suggested enhancing instructional skills of the faculty to enable them to teach all the skills. They also suggested enhancing the general education curriculum coverage of identified areas of deficiency.

The GEAC used "assessment roundtables" as a forum to share progress on the plan and to disseminate findings from the assessments. Committee members' reflections on the assessment results prompted them to recommend that the university continue to focus on improving student learning outcomes by requiring faculty to provide curricular activities that cover the expected learning outcomes in greater depth. They also recommended special emphasis on ways to teach each skill to ensure outcomes improvement. Finally, they asked that conscious effort be made to distribute and ensure broader coverage of the general education outcomes in the majors or disciplines. The committee has discussed and identified strategies to motivate students to take the MAPP posttest.

Based on the NSSE results, GEAC members produced an action plan for addressing the areas of concern raised by students' responses. The committee will continue to use the same methods and study the impact of the implemented interventions over time.

Impact of Using the Findings

In general, student performance on the Critical Thinking (CT) skill dimension of the MAPP has become a concern for the university. For this reason, and mindful of the fact that this is one of the FBOG mandated learning outcomes, members of the university community have selected the topic "enhancing performance in critical thinking skills" as its Quality Enhancement Plan (QEP), which is a SACS accreditation requirement. Based on a GEAC recommendation, faculty are developing an assessment policy that will state the consequences of students' nonparticipation in posttesting with MAPP, the NSSE, or any other instrument.

Overall, this collaborative approach involving students, faculty, and administrators in the university's assessment process has noticeably raised the level of awareness of the necessity to achieve the institution's mission of educational excellence through ongoing conversations aimed at improving students' learning in the core curriculum.

Success Factors

Administrative support contributed greatly to the success of this initiative. So did the timely identification and selection of two committed individuals to cochair the GEAC. As leaders, these faculty members not only had the vision and respect but also the ability to motivate and keep the group focused on the time lines, results, and their responsibilities as change agents to help students succeed.

Other success factors include the delivery of a series of workshops and coaching, hosting regular communication forums using assessment roundtables, making funds available to sponsor faculty travel to outside conferences, and establishing an assessment Web site as a resource.

Relevant Institutional Web Sites Pertaining to This Assessment Practice

Office of University Assessment:

www.famu.edu/assessment

General Assessment Plan:

www.famu.edu/Assessment/UserFiles/File/ge.pdf

CHAPTER SIX

UNDERGRADUATE ACADEMIC MAJORS PROFILES

Undergraduate program faculty members within certain disciplines or professional fields work together to define important learning outcomes for their students. They reflect on their individual courses and determine how the course-level outcomes reinforce program-level learning outcomes. Once these decisions are made, they identify the best methods to assess student learning. The profiles in this chapter focus on undergraduate programs and suggest the variety of methods being used to assess student learning. Portfolios enable students to submit examples of their work over time, along with reflections on how well they have achieved learning outcomes. Rubrics can be developed by faculty to gain meaningful information about students' performance. Where assessment is valued, academic leaders closely review assessment reports to identify patterns or trends in how faculty are assessing undergraduate student learning and using the results to make enhancements. Such information can provide faculty and other academic leaders with crucial evidence about assessment successes and challenges that present opportunities for assessment to be strengthened.

Physics faculty at Miami University collaborated with other science department chairs and the assessment office to identify overarching learning outcomes for science majors. According to Jennifer Blue et al., the faculty identified seven traits associated with a high-quality experimental research project. They developed a rubric that described four levels of performance on each of these traits.

Faculty members applied the rubric to assess the research paper required in the research capstone course. Instructors found that for most of the criteria, students had successfully achieved the important research skills that would effectively prepare them for graduate work. However, the most problematic areas were students' abilities to reflect on their own work and to suggest steps for further inquiry. The faculty discussed these assessment results and incorporated changes in several physics courses to address these areas.

The next two profiles illustrate the implementation of portfolios in two different undergraduate programs. At the University of Akron, Steven C. Myers, Michael A. Nelson, and Richard W. Stratton report that the economics faculty articulate crucial learning outcomes for their majors. Students demonstrate their competences by selecting examples of their work from numerous courses. They write reflections regarding how each assignment demonstrates the specific learning outcome, what they have learned from the assignment, and how their work might be improved. Students also present a poster session in which they demonstrate their completed work to the department, the broader university community, and area employers. In addition, faculty provide incentives for students to validate their work by presenting at "professional conferences, undergraduate paper competitions, and similar venues."

At Alverno College, teacher candidates are required to develop a portfolio to demonstrate their achievement of the college's curriculum-wide abilities. According to Lake et al., faculty members provide feedback to students on their performance using explicit criteria designed to judge students' individual work. Instructors "intentionally assist students to develop their capacity to independently" be responsible for their own learning. They guide students so that undergraduates learn how to assess themselves. The most significant resource commitment is the amount of time faculty invest in their reviews of each student's portfolio to determine if she is ready for student teaching.

At Moravian College, the College Assessment Committee (CAC) regularly provides feedback to faculty on their departmental assessment plans. Robert T. Brill reports that as the CAC evaluates plans, members look for linkages between assessment strategies and specific learning outcomes. They review the types of assessment methods used and expect some authentic measures. They also expect to see a clear, detailed assessment process in which information is discussed among the faculty members. Finally, they examine the feasibility of the assessment plan given current levels of resources. Ultimately, CAC members identify patterns across the assessment plans of key strengths and areas that need attention or improvement in the future.

In each of these profiles, faculty developed their own authentic assessment measures and gathered meaningful information about student learning. The assessment results provided key insights regarding how well students were mastering the program-level learning outcomes.

Institutions

Doctoral and Research
> Public
>> University of Akron; Akron, Ohio (25,000 students)
>> Miami University; Oxford, Ohio (14,000 students)

Master's
> Private
>> Alverno College; Milwaukee, Wisconsin (2,600 students)

Baccalaureate
> Private
>> Moravian College and Theological Seminary; Bethlehem, Pennsylvania (1,500 students)

Assessing Scientific Research Skills of Physics Majors

Jennifer Blue, Beverley A. P. Taylor, Jan M. Yarrison-Rice, Herbert Jaeger, Miami University

◆ ◆ ◆

Look for a faculty approach to developing explicit, clear learning outcomes for undergraduate physics majors and to assessing student learning using a common rubric.

Background and Purpose(s) of Assessment

In the spring of 2004, the physics department chair agreed to participate with other science department chairs and Assessment Office staff in a project to identify overarching student learning outcomes for science majors and to assess those outcomes. The science chairs met regularly for two semesters to determine expected outcomes and assessment methods.

Assessment Method(s) and Year(s) of Implementation

One of the most important skills identified for science majors was the ability to carry out an experimental research project. This ability was broken down into seven skills or traits, and a rubric was developed that described four levels of performance on each of these traits. The traits were:

- Identifies and summarizes the problem or question to be investigated
- Identifies existing, relevant knowledge and views
- Uses appropriate equipment and experiments to collect data
- Analyzes data in an appropriate manner
- Draws sound inferences and conclusions from data
- Reflects on own work to assure that conclusions are justified
- Suggests appropriate steps for further inquiry

The physics department offers a research capstone course at least once per year. Students plan and carry out a research project and write a final paper describing their project and its results. All the participating students and their faculty mentors meet biweekly to discuss progress and problems. For three consecutive offerings of the capstone (spring 2005, spring 2006, and summer 2006), faculty mentors used the rubric to assess the final papers. Each faculty member rated each paper. The scale on the rubric went from 1 (inadequate) to 4 (substantially developed). The rubric is available at the Web site given below. A score of 4 sets a high standard for an undergraduate and is in fact what one might expect of a typical master's level graduate student. In early fall 2006, the results were compiled and analyzed.

Required Resources

No monetary resources were required. Increased faculty time was devoted to examining the papers of the capstone students, as previously each faculty member had only graded the papers of his or her own students.

Findings

Table 6.1 shows the means on the seven criteria as well as the percentage of papers that were rated either "moderately developed" (rating of 3) or "substantially developed" (rating of 4).

The faculty felt that these results were quite good and indicated that on the whole our majors were prepared for the research work they would carry out in

TABLE 6.1. RESULTS FROM THE ASSESSMENT

Criteria	Mean Rating	Ratings of 3 or 4 (%)
Problem statement	3.3	88
Existing knowledge	3.1	84
Equipment and experiments	3.6	98
Data analysis	3.4	95
Inferences and conclusions	3.4	97
Reflects on own work	3.1	77
Further inquiry	3.1	76

graduate school. However, there were some individual scores that were much lower than desired. The most problematic areas were reflecting on one's work and suggesting steps for further inquiry.

Use of Findings

The department faculty identified PHY 293, Contemporary Physics Lab, a course required of all physics majors, as the appropriate place to begin trying to help students develop these skills in a more organized way. During spring 2006, the two faculty members who usually teach this course planned revisions to specifically address the experimental inquiry skills. New pre-lab questions on existing knowledge were used for all experiments and three experiments were modified to include post-lab extended discussion sessions that focused on data analysis and drawing conclusions from data, as well as reflections on the experiments. The revised course was taught for the first time during fall 2006. The assessment rubric for experimental science was utilized to score student lab reports from the earliest lab and then compared to a lab write-up from the end of the semester. At the outset, students generally scored from "inadequate" to "minimally developed" on the seven criteria; later in the course they scored from "inadequate" through "minimally to moderately developed."

As with the seniors, the areas of most concern in the assessment of students enrolled in PHY 293 were the last two rubric items about reflecting on their work and considering further steps. Students simply did not provide this information. In the fall of 2007, we changed the requirements for the lab report to include more questions that lead students to consider their work more critically, and we provided more class time for discussion and reflection. This time we assessed a total of four experiments throughout the semester rather than just two. In this second round of revision, the rubric was changed to reflect the level of work required in the class in one of the areas ("uses appropriate instruments and experimental procedure"). Because this course provides the instruments and the procedure, we changed that rubric element to "Student conveys understanding of how instruments work and in what form data are provided by the experiment."

Physics students begin to learn experimental skills in PHY 183, Physics Laboratory, so modifications were also made to the rubric to adapt it for this course and an assessment was carried out. The rubric was modified to reflect the tasks and level of understanding expected of students in this course. The traits were rearranged and grouped under the same headings found in the formal laboratory reports: Introduction, Apparatus and Procedure, and Results and Discussion. Some of the traits that would not be expected of student reports at the first-year level were eliminated from the rubric.

Students in PHY 183 write three formal lab reports; the second and third reports from fall 2006 were analyzed with the modified rubric. Students often have trouble with the first report, which in many cases is the first lab report they have ever written. Even after the extensive modifications to the rubric to make it appropriate to the expectations of this course, students performed poorly, often scoring at the lowest level on the last three traits ("draws sound inferences and conclusions," "reflects on own work," and "suggests further inquiry"). Further, students did not notably improve their scores on the rubric between the second and third reports.

Impact of Using the Findings

The first students to take the revised PHY 293 course have not yet taken their research capstone, so we do not yet have data to show the impact of the changes. However, input we have received via exit surveys of the PHY 293 students suggests that we should reduce the number of experiments the students conduct, while increasing the discussions about data analysis and drawing conclusions. In fall 2008, the course will be radically modified to make this possible with three focus areas of experiments, discussions with each experiment, and fewer lab reports so that students may use their time for more in-depth analysis of each of the three required reports.

In PHY 183 the instructions the students receive about how to write the lab report have been changed to reflect the student learning outcomes that are embodied in the rubric. We have improved the training of the teaching assistants who deliver the course. The teaching assistants now better understand the importance of encouraging students to find answers for themselves as they are doing the activities; rather than always answering students' direct questions, teaching assistants now have the skills to lead the students to the answers by asking questions of their own. In addition, we realized that the PHY 183 lab manual itself needed to be changed in order to give students the chance to do more critical thinking. As the course stood in the fall of 2006, students had few opportunities to make choices and were not asked enough questions to prompt deep reflection. Some improvements have already been made, and more are coming. The plan is to have each lab activity require a bit more from the students than the one before.

Success Factors

The physics department at Miami is strongly committed to students and their scientific education. As a result, faculty members were willing to participate in the assessment process despite the fact that it required an additional time commitment on their part. Also, members of the department were eager to act on the results of the assessment in order to improve student learning. The project would probably not have taken place without the initial invitation from the Assessment Office.

Relevant Institutional Web Sites Pertaining to This Assessment Practice

Scientific Inquiry Rubric:

> www.units.muohio.edu/led/Assessment/Assessment_Basics/Sample_
> Rubrics/Scientific_Inquiry.pdf

Department of Physics:

> www.cas.muohio.edu/physicsweb

E-Portfolios and Student Research in the Assessment of a Proficiency-Based Major

Steven C. Myers, Michael A. Nelson, Richard W. Stratton, The University of Akron

◆ ◆ ◆

Look for economics faculty assessing student learning using portfolios and rubrics to determine student achievement of key program-level learning outcomes.

Background and Purpose(s) of Assessment

The development of an assessment plan for an academic program is challenging when there is no discipline-specific licensing or accreditation process to guide the formulation of the plan. Economics department faculty at the University of Akron confronted this challenge as part of an overhaul of their undergraduate major. The revised curriculum is proficiency based and culminates with an independent student research project. Student achievements are documented and assessed using an electronic portfolio.

Assessment Method(s) and Year(s) of Implementation

After a year of wide-ranging and sometimes contentious discussion, department faculty chose to base student learning outcomes on the Hansen Proficiencies (Hansen, 1986, 2001), one of several competing notions of what economics programs are supposed to accomplish. These proficiencies are roughly parallel to the six categories in Bloom's taxonomy (1956) in the cognitive domain. Beginning with the simplest activity and increasing in difficulty to the most complex (creation of new knowledge), these proficiencies provide the framework to measure what students should achieve, setting goals of what students should know and be able to do. Yet they do not dictate content or specific delivery technologies, as competence can be demonstrated in multiple ways.

Students are provided with opportunities to demonstrate competence in one or more of the proficiencies in each of the courses they take for the major. These "artifacts" may take many forms, including but not limited to homework assignments, exams, and other written assignments. For all but the highest proficiency level (senior paper) students are afforded several opportunities to demonstrate competence in each learning outcome (proficiency) as they proceed through the major.

Students select one or more artifacts from their course work to demonstrate their skill in each proficiency and then post them in an electronic portfolio. They also write a "reflective statement" that describes how each artifact demonstrates the proficiency, what they have learned from the exercise, and how their work might be improved. Each student's portfolio is individually tailored to meet her or his own needs and interests, subject to some broad parameters. The scaffolding skills necessary to accomplish this are developed as part of the Computer Skills for Economic Analysis course that students take early in the major.

Portfolios are reviewed periodically by the department's undergraduate advisor. With the exception of the senior project, each artifact is evaluated using the grade earned in the course. The senior project is independently evaluated by two faculty members using a faculty-approved standardized grading rubric. All projects are publicly presented to department faculty and students. Most are also presented at a poster session sponsored by the department and open to the broader university community and area employers. External validation of this work is accomplished by creating incentives for students to make presentations at professional conferences, undergraduate paper competitions, and similar venues.

Required Resources

Faculty time is necessary to identify, modify, and create artifacts for their courses that reflect the proficiencies. Additional time is needed to create the rubrics for the artifacts and the portfolio. The department's undergraduate advisor must periodically review all portfolios and provide feedback on reflective statements written by students. This person is also given the responsibility to ensure that each graduating student's portfolio is complete and to report assessment data and summary statistics to the department chair and undergraduate curriculum committee for further analysis.

Student time and effort is required to create, populate, and maintain the portfolio. Two core classes in the undergraduate curriculum are devoted in part or entirely to activities surrounding the portfolio. These include the aforementioned computer skills course, in which, among other things, students develop their portfolio templates, and the senior project course. Class time is also needed periodically to educate students on how the portfolios can be useful to them.

Allowing students to construct their own portfolios saved the expense of using standardized portfolio software, the cost of which varies widely, as does the amount of university support required to maintain the system. Computer resources are still needed, however, to maintain the portfolios of current students and to archive those of program graduates. Travel dollars are also needed when students present their research to external audiences.

Findings

All program graduates to date have produced portfolios that are judged to be "satisfactory" or "excellent" in each proficiency area. Most interesting are students' accomplishments regarding the "create new knowledge" proficiency—the highest level of Bloom's cognitive domain (1956). Students produced research that successfully competed in external research competitions for undergraduates. One student won a competition that featured undergraduates from some of the most prestigious universities internationally. Perhaps more noteworthy has been that students with modest academic abilities have produced some exceptional research projects. In fact, anecdotal evidence suggests that some of the largest value-added gains (the confidence and analytical skills of students entering the program compared to where they finished) occurred among this group. Not all such students were successful, however, as a small number of students each year did not complete the project and hence did not graduate.

An incentive system is needed to ensure that students update their portfolios as they proceed through the curriculum. Without such incentives, many students would wait until their final semester to make any changes to the template they developed much earlier in the major.

Department faculty also observed a change in culture among undergraduate majors. With each succeeding cohort, students seemed more ready to accept the challenge of finding a senior project research topic and conducting the analysis. Greater numbers were also willing to present their findings to external audiences.

Use of Findings

Using a standardized template, the undergraduate advisor reviews and assesses completed portfolios, and the results are reported to the department chair and undergraduate curriculum committee for further discussion and analysis. The results are also reported to university central administration in various ways, including the department annual report, and to a university student assessment committee. The success of the senior project has been used in marketing materials designed to attract majors, especially students from the Honors College.

As the electronic portfolio system has only been in place for three years, many of the findings to date have centered on ways to make the process work more smoothly. Faculty members have given more attention to ensuring that their courses will provide students with suitable portfolio artifacts. Incentives have been put in place to ensure that students will update their portfolios as they proceed through the major.

Some faculty members have modified their course requirements to provide better scaffolding for students to conduct the senior project. For example, one instructor now requires an annotated bibliography rather than a term paper as a strategy to prepare students to develop a proposal for their senior project.

Impact of Using the Findings

The assessment process has raised the visibility of the department within the university. Central administrators have asked department faculty to present the plan as a "case study" of programmatic assessment at a statewide learning outcomes assessment process in Columbus, Ohio. Anecdotal evidence also suggests that the marketing materials have attracted more majors, especially students with strong academic credentials. However, sufficient time has not yet elapsed to evaluate the process and course content changes made based on assessment results.

Success Factors

A change in the composition of the faculty by specialty field, a declining number of majors, and an undergraduate program that had not been updated in more than ten years were the catalysts for changing the curriculum. At the same time there was increased pressure from central administration for more accountability at the program level. Together these factors created the opportunity and provided the incentive to address program assessment at the same time the curriculum was updated.

A small but dedicated core faculty took up the challenge with the support of the department chair. This does not mean that a successful outcome to the process is more problematic in a department with a large faculty. However, for skeptical or nonengaged faculty outside the core it is important that the assessment plan respects academic freedom, as this will help to mitigate active opposition to the process.

The University of Akron was selected by the Carnegie Academy for the Scholarship of Teaching and Learning to participate in a leadership program with a theme focused on undergraduate research. This initiative has resulted in the university administration encouraging and supporting undergraduate research. Among other things, administrators have offered matching funds to help students fund travel to present their work at external venues.

Finally, the findings of the assessment process to date have generated information valued by the faculty because it aligns directly with the learning outcomes that faculty members agree are essential for a student graduating with a major in economics.

Relevant Institutional Web Sites Pertaining to This Assessment Practice

For more information and related papers, visit the Assessment link on the University of Akron Department of Economics Web site:

http://www.uakron.edu/colleges/artsci/depts/econ/

Integrating Student and Program Assessment with a Teacher Candidate Portfolio

Kathy Lake, Judith Reisetter Hart, William H. Rickards, Glen Rogers, Alverno College

◆ ◆ ◆

Look for portfolio assessment for teacher candidates and how this information is shared with relevant internal and external stakeholders, including accreditors.

Background and Purpose(s) of Assessment

Assessment of student learning outcomes at Alverno College is an integral part of developing and documenting each student's learning. Grounded in this shared commitment to learning, assessment also provides faculty with performance data that they use to improve their teaching and the broader curriculum for which they take collective responsibility. As appropriate, faculty and educational researchers develop summaries and provide examples of student performance from these curriculum-embedded assessments for the purposes of accountability and broader dialogue with external publics.

The specific teacher candidate portfolio assessment we describe here is a milestone assessment in the teacher education program. It is used to support each teacher candidate's integrative learning, to validate prior determinations of readiness for progression into student teaching, to improve the teacher education program, and to support the program's external accountability. The distinctive contribution of this portfolio to these multiple purposes needs to be understood in the context of the college's overall curriculum, of which it is a part and with which it shares many educational principles.

All students at Alverno are required to demonstrate achievement of the college's curriculum-wide abilities, which are integral to the degree. These complex, multidimensional abilities are infused with the disciplinary and interdisciplinary content that is articulated and assessed within each course and program. Faculty continually review how these abilities are articulated, how students perform on assessments of them, and the overall coherence of the assessment system. Their goal is to ensure that each student experiences the curriculum as gradually guiding her toward an increasingly sophisticated performance within a course and within her chosen field. Thus, the explicit criteria for effective performance at the level of the course, program, and college are cumulatively and developmentally specified.

Alverno faculty, in their role as teachers, give each student feedback on her performance in relation to explicit criteria that are specifically articulated within individual assessments. In doing so, faculty intentionally assist students to develop their capacity to independently take hold of their learning. A critical component is coaching students in how to self-assess their performance qualitatively in relation to the criteria for the assessment and the associated curriculum-wide abilities. To this purpose, the feedback a faculty member gives to a student reinforces or redirects her analysis of her performance.

Assessment Method(s) and Year(s) of Implementation

As a general process for assessing individual teacher candidates, the ED 420 portfolio assessment has been in place for over fifteen years. The contents of the portfolio are selected, developed, and organized by the teacher candidate as a cumulative and qualitative picture of her performance across courses and field placements. She develops the portfolio in support of her progression to her more extended 18-week student teaching placement. Faculty members give candidates extensive written and oral guidance on what to include in the portfolio. The bulk of the portfolio consists of artifacts, including lesson plans and assignments, samples of K–12 student work with feedback she gave, self-assessments of lessons she carried out in the field, video excerpts of her teaching in two field placements, an analysis of these teaching episodes, and all field evaluations she has received from supervisors and cooperating teachers. The candidate provides a brief rationale for her selection of each artifact in relation to the program's conceptual model and state standards for teaching. Then, as overarching, binding elements, each candidate develops a reflective essay on her development as a pre-service teacher and sets goals for her student teaching experience.

An integral part of the portfolio assessment is an interview with a K–12 teacher or administrator and an Alverno faculty member. During this interview the candidate highlights aspects of the portfolio, including the videotape of her teaching. Her assessors, who have familiarized themselves with the portfolio, probe the candidate's evidence of readiness and give oral and written feedback. Assessors are supported by sample interview questions.

In 2005, ongoing faculty discussions of candidates' performance on the portfolio were further enhanced by a formal qualitative analysis of 19 portfolios. This independent analysis was conducted by three researchers from Alverno College's Department of Educational Research and Evaluation (ERE), who articulated a developmental scoring system in relation to the state standards for teachers. The formal scoring scheme was derived from the Alverno Education Department Program Level Benchmarks for Teacher Licensure and Development, which developmentally specified at what levels each of the state's ten standards for teachers must be met at points in the program in order for candidates to progress. These progression milestones are admission to the program, admission to student teaching, and recommendation for licensure.

Required Resources

The most significant resource required is the time that faculty invest in reviewing each candidate's portfolio to determine whether or not she has met criteria for progressing to student teaching. Each faculty member assesses two to three portfolios each semester. The assessment consists of the review of the portfolio by faculty and community assessors and an interview. Candidates prepare an "evidence record" that guides the assessors in their review. Often, community assessors are graduates of the program and have experienced the portfolio assessment themselves. Others, although not graduates, are experienced assessors who come back semester after semester to participate in the assessment experience.

The ongoing faculty conversations on how candidates are generally performing on the portfolio assessment and department deliberation on implications for curricular improvement are integral to each faculty member's work as an educator. A week after the assessment interview, a faculty meeting is held for the purpose of sharing insights and findings, and discussing each candidate's readiness for student teaching. At this time, written feedback from the coassessors related to the portfolio assessment is shared across the faculty.

Findings

The findings of the study conducted by ERE contribute to faculty discussions about the portfolio assessment. Findings in relation to some of these summary dimensions included:

- Candidate rationales ranged from clear internalization of the state standards and program conceptual model to less analytical descriptions.
- Candidates consistently had strong lesson plans with articulated outcomes, often including subject matter standards.
- Candidates effectively constructed their subject matter knowledge in pedagogical terms, but only infrequently included artifacts from their content area courses.
- Candidates demonstrated strong attention to monitoring student performance through assessments, and many developed creative ways of assessing students

that fostered further learning. At the same time, candidates infrequently paid close attention to articulating explicit criteria for use in assessing students. Candidates generally did not address standardized testing and measurement.

Use of Findings

Results of the portfolio assessment are integral to the determination of progression to student teaching. Each teacher candidate receives written feedback about her portfolio and interview.

Department faculty selected a range of portfolios for the 2005 external review of the program by the Wisconsin Department of Public Instruction (DPI) and the National Council for Accreditation of Teacher Education (NCATE), including all of those from the previous semester. The 30-page written report on the qualitative analyses was provided as evidence of student learning outcomes. This report was reviewed by members of the department, who also met with Alverno's educational researchers in a department meeting devoted to discussing recommendations from the report.

Impact of Using the Findings

Ongoing faculty observations from the portfolios have led to modifications of the portfolio requirements and curricular program elements.

Based on the report findings, the department expanded a one-credit field course into a two-credit course with a focus on assessment. In addition, the department has revised the portfolio assessment. For example, portfolio instructions now recommend that elementary education candidates include papers and presentations that demonstrate their subject matter knowledge and that secondary education candidates include artifacts from their content area courses. In lieu of the teaching philosophy statement, candidates are given a different integrative task. Candidates are asked to write a letter to a student just entering the program about how the candidate now understands the department's conceptual model and the state standards. Likewise, the purpose of the rationale for each artifact is further clarified as "a key place for you to demonstrate your ability to analyze and deeply reflect on your teaching and learning." Criteria for the portfolio have been augmented to include more explicit instruction on the kind of educational theory that candidates should demonstrate they have mastered. Candidates are provided with a list of major theorists whom they have studied over the course of their program, and faculty model how these theorists are integral to the program of study and the conceptual framework.

Success Factors

The shared commitment to making assessment foremost about individual student learning has produced the kind of assessment evidence that department faculty can readily use to improve the teacher education program. This is possible because a culture of shared responsibility for developing curriculum supports ongoing faculty review and discussion of teacher candidate performance across the portfolios, as well as other performance-based assessments of curriculum-defined abilities.

The resulting student's investment in creating a cumulative and integrative portfolio of her learning has provided a distinctively broad and detailed view of the curriculum.

Through documentation of rigorous analyses, specific written recommendations, and dialogue with faculty, educational researchers enabled both internal and external stakeholders to use independent qualitative findings effectively.

Relevant Institutional Web Sites Pertaining to This Assessment Practice

Related publications on "Assessment at Alverno College: Student, Program, Institutional," "Student Assessment-as-Learning at Alverno College," and "Self Assessment at Alverno College" are available at:

www.alverno.edu/for_educators/publications.html

A Review and Feedback Process for Developing and Improving Departmental Assessment Plans

Robert T. Brill, Moravian College

◆ ◆ ◆

Look for a review process conducted by faculty to critique department-level assessment programs across the college and to provide constructive feedback for improvement.

Background and Purpose(s) of Assessment

After extensive workshops and other initiatives to educate and motivate faculty about the assessment of student learning outcomes, the College Assessment Committee (CAC) of Moravian College directed academic departments to initiate two manageable assessment projects. The idea was to have departments start small, but also to experience success in applying assessment principles learned in the workshops. In this manner, the CAC would help guide and nurture faculty toward a full successful assessment project, building their confidence before developing a more comprehensive assessment plan. Assessment coordinators from each department were given guidelines for completing a departmental assessment plan. They were required to collaborate with departmental colleagues to identify two student learning outcomes and develop a specific plan to collect, analyze, and reflect on implications of the assessment data for both outcomes. The committee received plans that spanned a wide range of quality and scope. The CAC was in need of a review process that would extend its educational goals and provide an "assessment of the assessment plans" in order to promote greater likelihood of a formative, successful completion of the assessment projects initiated by academic departments.

Assessment Method(s) and Year(s) of Implementation

The CAC was divided into three subgroups based on college divisions (humanities, social sciences, and natural sciences). Each departmental proposal was reviewed by a four-person subgroup of the CAC. Two faculty members from that division, an administrator, and the CAC chair served on all three subgroups. During fall semester 2005, members did an individual review and then discussed their perceptions collectively. The review was based on five dimensions:

1. *Linkage:* Is the link between the assessment strategies and the learning outcomes clear?
2. *Authenticity:* Are assessment measures exclusively self-reported? Are more authentic measures possible?
3. *Adequacy:* Are assessment measures adequate? Are other assessments outside the course structure necessary or possible?
4. *Utility:* Is there a clear and detailed (for example, with a time line) process in which assessment information is discussed by the department (or representative body) in order to discern possible program improvements or refinement of the outcome assessment plan?
5. *Feasibility:* Does the assessment plan seem overly ambitious or in need of extensive resources? Is the assessment project "do-able," given the resources and support available?

Feedback for each departmental proposal was summarized in a written report and sent to the faculty author of the proposal with the invitation to discuss the feedback with the subcommittee or the CAC chair. In the month following feedback distribution, subcommittees held an open meeting for assessment representatives within divisions to come together and discuss common concerns and individual challenges, and share resources and experiences related to the assessment project.

Required Resources

A relatively large, representative committee of dedicated members knowledgeable about assessment is needed. Member skepticism of assessment should not necessarily be avoided, but should be constructively channeled. A document of clear guidelines for departmental assessment plans that includes the evaluative criteria should be provided early in the process, and, if at all possible, integrated as part of a faculty development experience in the area of outcomes assessment. We wished we had developed the feedback process prior to our initiative request. The guidelines would have been strengthened by a more explicit reference to these dimensions, and this also would have bolstered acceptance of the subsequent feedback. As it happened, we only learned the review would be needed after initial plans were submitted.

Findings

Suitable assessment plans were submitted by 16 of 18 departments (89 percent) submitted. All were reviewed and a feedback report was generated for each plan. The review process identified several trends to be addressed. First, a leading concern for the majority of departments (56 percent) was that the submitted plan did not include a formalized time line. Relatedly, more than a third of the plans (38 percent) failed to identify a deliberate process of departmental reflection or discussion of the implications and improvement-oriented change suggestions that might flow from the assessment results (utility criterion). Second, it was a common judgment that the departments (50 percent) were taking on too much data collection and needed to find a more manageable scope and focus in their assessment efforts (*feasibility* criterion). This led to a dialogue that suggested departments were generally overreacting to the assessment requests and attempting to design plans that were ambitious beyond feasibility. A third constructive trend was the identification that some departments' measurement efforts were possibly drifting from, or out of sync with, the targeted outcomes (*linkage* criterion). Finally, two departments seemed to be relying exclusively on self-report sources of assessment, where more authentic sources were feasible and, in some cases, already available via existing assignments embedded in courses (*authenticity* criterion).

Suffice it to say that the review process prevented a series of massive data collection efforts that would have lacked proper focus and prohibited closing the feedback loop toward curriculum improvement, a frustrating trend that faculty veterans recalled from department self-studies in the 1980s. In addition, the feedback attempted to be reinforcing as well, by providing strong praise and encouragement for well-developed aspects of the assessment plans.

Regarding faculty development and education, seven departments (44 percent) requested post-feedback follow-up meetings and thirteen of the participating departments (81 percent) were represented at the divisional open meetings. Dialogue in both contexts was highly constructive in clarifying assessment issues, sharing ideas, and exchanging available resources or models (from CAC and with other departments), as well as in communicating needs so that CAC could advocate for or provide necessary resources.

Use of Findings

By the end of the fall 2006 semester, all sixteen of the participating departments submitted a progress report on how their efforts had evolved, particularly in terms of data collection, analysis, and use of the results. Three progress reports made direct, positive reference to the CAC's feedback. It was evident that all departments discussed in the previous section made substantive revisions to their assessment plans. All indications suggest that these revisions were improvements by either making full follow-through on the plan (for example, completing the loop by initiating improvements) feasible, or refining the measures and data collection efforts to be more manageable or aligned with the targeted outcomes. Specific benefits are outlined below.

Impact of Using the Findings

As documented in the progress reports, 13 departments reported multiple substantive assessment-driven changes. Collectively, there were 12 curriculum modifications (for example, portfolio requirements implemented, learning outcomes shifted to more appropriate courses, increase in a field experience requirement, and initial planning underway for a new senior seminar); 9 teaching improvements (such as adjustments in time lines for assignments, refined strategies and focus for early draft feedback, greater emphasis on information literacy skills that did not seem to transfer from a first-year course, and use of assessments for placement into groups for projects); as well as 16 refinements to the assessment process itself (recognizing the need for a standardized tool, development of a May departmental retreat to handle these issues, breaking a targeted outcome into three more specific learning outcomes, and the development of rubrics for assessing writing samples). These highlights were gathered into a report and shared with the faculty.

Success Factors

Given the challenge of developing assessment plans for most faculty members and departments without prior experience, and given the moderate dose of faculty development workshops we were able to provide, the review process was a necessary and critical supplemental resource to assist departmental assessment efforts.

Key success factors included knowledgeable and dedicated members of the CAC. Also, providing very specific written feedback in what were clearly critical criterion dimensions armed departmental representatives with credible documentation of possible improvements. This allowed them to discuss comments knowledgeably and to collaborate with departmental colleagues on constructive revisions to the plan. Where praise was appropriate, the wording of the feedback was very complimentary and encouraging, thus bolstering motivation in what was typically a new, challenging, and often frustrating endeavor for the department. The opportunity for follow-up discussion in either a voluntary one-on-one format or in divisional open meetings was lauded by representatives and seen as a clear indication of (a) the importance of the assessment tasks at hand, (b) institutional support for the efforts, and (c) the value of providing departments with constructive clarification of issues raised by the feedback. Finally, the anticipation of a required formal progress report was a critical and effective incentive and source of accountability for departmental assessment representatives.

Relevant Institutional Web Sites Pertaining to This Assessment Practice

To see examples of the feedback reports provided to departments by the CAC, the request and guidelines for the initial department assessment plan, or the progress report guidelines, go to:

http://home.moravian.edu/users/psych/mertb01/

CHAPTER SEVEN

FACULTY AND STAFF DEVELOPMENT PROFILES

On some campuses faculty and administrators provide sustained, in-depth learning opportunities for colleagues over time. Often instructors with substantial experience in assessment offer workshops to help their peers consider new ideas. Lopez (2004, p. 43) notes that "institutions that have been successful in educating their faculty about assessment have high rates of faculty involvement in the assessment program at both the institutional and departmental levels."

The University of Northern Iowa provides an interesting example of a well-conceived and implemented professional development plan that supported faculty members for assessment and subsequently to take "coordinated action steps for change," according to Barry J. Wilson. Initially the professional development seminars focused on curriculum mapping to demonstrate how all courses addressed and assessed key learning outcomes. A second series of workshops addressed course-level assessment of student outcomes. A professional development day followed where faculty members examined program data and evidence from the curriculum mapping process to design an action plan indicating key improvements that should be made at the individual, department, or program level.

Faculty learning communities (FLCs) furnish another example of a sustained professional development initiative aimed at helping faculty improve their assessments. According to Catherine M. Wehlburg and Edward McNertney, FLCs were created at Texas Christian University for each of the six major areas associated with the core curriculum: religious traditions, historical traditions, literary traditions, global awareness, cultural awareness, and citizenship and social values. Each FLC was designed to create and maintain key assessment strategies as well as to share results of the assessment process with other faculty members. Participating faculty moved from a focus on what they are teaching to what they want students to learn in taking their courses.

Reorienting the campus environment to emphasize learner-centeredness is an important goal for many professional development activities. At Ferris State University, Roxanne Cullen and Michael Harris developed a rubric for assessing learning-centered qualities. Faculty and administrators used this rubric as they evaluated their syllabi to determine the degree of learner-centeredness present within individual courses and their current teaching practices. This rubric consisted of major categories focused on "fostering group work and team projects as well as providing other opportunities to learn from one another, as opposed to viewing the professor as the single source of knowledge." Another major category focused on empowering undergraduates so that they would develop intrinsic motivation to learn. The third category focused on types of assessments given within courses and the extent to which students were afforded the opportunity to revise their work. This formal review of course syllabi has produced insights regarding the specific types of faculty development initiatives that are needed in the future.

Another strategy for identifying the types of professional development activities that should be offered is to conduct a faculty needs-assessment survey. According to Brigitte Valesey at Widener University, the Task Force for Student Learning surveyed faculty members to gather feedback about faculty development needs, assessment resources, and the status of assessment implementation within all academic programs. Task force members used the results to provide direction for faculty development workshops. They also identified effective assessment practices within the university as well as priorities for planning and sustaining continuous assessment. Based on the survey results, one of the first steps undertaken was to define common assessment terminology. This information was communicated by task force members using multiple venues. Administrative support was vital to help assessment become a long-term institutional commitment and the necessary resources were provided to help sustain assessment over time.

Institutions

Doctoral and Research
   Private
      Texas Christian University; Fort Worth, Texas (8,900 students)
      Widener University; Chester, Pennsylvania (6,700 students)

Master's
> Public
>> Ferris State University; Big Rapids, Michigan (13,000 students)
>> University of Northern Iowa; Cedar Falls, Iowa (14,000 students)

From Assessment to Action: Back-Mapping to the Future

Barry J. Wilson, University of Northern Iowa

◆ ◆ ◆

Look for ways to design and sustain a professional development plan for faculty over time. This incremental plan helps instructors demonstrate linkages between learning outcomes within individual courses and program-level outcomes, as well as to identify areas needing improvement based on assessment results.

Background and Purpose(s) of Assessment

The institutional mission at the University of Northern Iowa includes the preparation of teachers in all six colleges, two schools, and thirty-two academic departments. Our assessment system for the program has been in place for four years and provides rich data from multiple sources on program outcomes for teaching majors. These data include evidence from student teacher evaluations, teacher work samples, and survey data from student teachers, alumni, and employers. We wanted to provide professional development activities to support faculty in moving from assessment to positive, coordinated action steps for change. The first phase of our work was curriculum mapping; the second phase was course-level assessment workshops; and the third, a professional development day devoted to study and interpretation of data and the development of action plans for change.

Assessment Method(s) and Year(s) of Implementation

During the 2006–07 and 2007–08 academic years, university faculty participated in a series of curriculum mapping workshops titled "From Assessment to Action: Back-Mapping to the Future." The workshops focused primarily on learning outcomes for teaching candidates in the areas that a recent accreditation visit identified as needing improvement: diversity, assessment of learning, and classroom management. Our purpose was to identify gaps and redundancies in the program and improve the articulation of program outcomes across all segments. Half-day workshops on curriculum mapping were conducted in the fall of 2006, and the summer and fall of 2007. Eighty-eight faculty from all program areas participated. The end product, taken from individual course maps, was a visual display in Excel of how all courses across the entire program addressed and assessed professional standards. Separate displays were created for elementary and secondary programs.

This activity led to offering workshops on course-level assessment of student outcomes, an area in which faculty discovered they needed additional knowledge and skills. They had thought that they "covered" content that addressed important learning outcomes. They were not satisfied that they were assessing those outcomes so that they could say with some confidence that learning outcomes for the course had been met. During the initial workshop, faculty were given support material and assessment assignments to complete during the spring 2008 semester. Faculty also will be meeting at the end of the semester to discuss changes made and to exchange ideas on any issues and problems encountered.

Communication and collaboration across all elements of the program were facilitated by a professional development day. The agenda included a keynote speaker who addressed the challenges of preparing teachers for the twenty-first century. In the morning sessions, participating faculty examined program data and evidence from the curriculum mapping process. Given the size of the group (120 faculty and 20 administrators), we used laptop computers at each table to record group discussions and consensus on key topics, including questions about the program outcomes data collected as well as the compiled curriculum map of the elementary and secondary teaching programs. Small groups represented a cross-section of the program at each of 13 tables. At the end of the day, faculty returned to their departments and program areas to develop a draft action plan to address improvement at the individual, department or area, and program level. This initial draft will be refined and resubmitted by each department. Our teacher education council and council of academic department heads are assigned responsibility for follow-up.

Required Resources

Half-day workshops were held to introduce faculty to the curriculum-mapping process. Faculty were paid a small stipend for participation. Several follow-up meetings were held to discuss any issues or problems encountered and to assess findings.

Our provost also authorized the cancellation of classes for a day to give the 120 faculty and 20 administrators time to review data summaries. These included direct and indirect evidence of student outcomes as well as curriculum mapping data.

We used WebCT courseware and laptop computers for faculty teams to record responses to questions regarding their interpretations of the data and recommendations for change. Our IT team provided necessary support for online access and setup.

Findings

Faculty involved at various levels of the program identified how their individual course(s) addressed professional standards through the curriculum mapping workshops. Faculty members uploaded their course maps, and individual maps were combined in an Excel spreadsheet. We were particularly interested in how foundational courses, methods courses, and clinical experiences addressed standards and how components meshed (or not). We also wanted to provide faculty with opportunities to discuss issues and collaborate across program areas. The process helped us identify gaps where preparation appeared to be lacking as well as areas of possible redundancy. Many faculty also discovered that although they indicated "covered" content, course-level assessments needed to reflect professional standards and end-of-program outcomes more effectively.

Workshops devoted to assisting faculty in developing course-level assessments to support program outcomes were held in January 2008 for 33 faculty. Support material was provided on our WebCT courseware site to provide opportunity for continued online support and communication among participants. At the end of the semester, changes in assessment practices will be reviewed to determine the degree to which change in assessment practices was accomplished.

Finally, in the spring of 2008, classes were cancelled for a day of professional development devoted to study of data (including compiled curriculum maps), recommendations for change, and the development of action plans for change. Outcomes from the day were recorded at each table using laptop computers and WebCT courseware. Resulting data are being used for systematic follow-up and documentation of our program improvement activities.

Use of Findings

Work to date has resulted in action plans for coordinated change at the individual, department, and program levels. The application of technology to support change in a complex environment has been helpful as we continue to refine the improvement part of the assessment cycle.

Impact of Using the Findings

Engaging faculty in using data for program improvement is challenging in our large, complex university. We are modifying our assessment plan to incorporate the mapping and professional development day every three to four years. This timing would allow us to detect the impact of our action plans on student outcomes data as well as to provide a basis for continued conversation, collaboration, and action between accreditation cycles.

Success Factors

We were assisted by a small grant from the Iowa Teacher Quality Enhancement initiative to support faculty stipends and some printing costs. The most critical factors were the involvement of key faculty and administrators in the planning and implementation of the project. We were also aided by our instructional technology staff to make maximum use of technology to support our goals.

Relevant Institutional Web Sites Pertaining to This Assessment Practice

Curriculum Mapping Workshop Materials and Outcomes:

www.uni.edu/coe/epf/Assessment

Assessment Data Web Site:

www.uni.edu/coe/epf/Assess

University Assessment Web Site:

www.uni.edu/assessment/

Faculty Learning Communities as an Assessment Technique for Measuring General Education Outcomes

Catherine M. Wehlburg, Edward McNertney, Texas Christian University

◆ ◆ ◆

Look for ways in which faculty learning communities (FLCs) provided a context for essential dialogues and support to make important assessment decisions for the core curriculum. These FLCs fostered greater agreement among faculty within each core area regarding specific common course-embedded assessments that were implemented across courses.

Background and Purpose(s) of Assessment

At Texas Christian University (TCU), a core curriculum was designed and implemented by the faculty. As part of the development of this program, student learning outcomes were built into the program and were approved by the faculty at the same time that the entire core curriculum was approved.

In order to develop appropriate and meaningful assessments for each of the categories within the curriculum, the Office of the TCU Core Curriculum, the Center for Teaching Excellence, and the Office for Assessment created and funded a faculty learning community (FLC) for each of six of the categories within the TCU core curriculum. All faculty who are teaching a course within a particular category are members of that particular FLC. Each FLC has two faculty facilitators that call the FLC meetings. The discussions that occur within each FLC are designed to do three things:

- Create and maintain appropriate assessment strategies for the category
- Share the results of the assessment process with faculty who teach in that category (in other words, share with the FLC members)
- Enhance the discussions on teaching within that particular TCU core category

Assessment Method(s) and Year(s) of Implementation

The assessment methods created by members of each of the six FLCs vary widely based on the actual outcome that is measured and the methods that are developed by the FLC members. The six categories include: religious traditions, historical traditions, literary traditions, global awareness, cultural awareness, and citizenship and social values. Because the outcomes for each of the core curriculum categories were approved by the faculty at the time of the implementation of the new core, each FLC was charged with creating a method for measuring student learning of their specific outcomes within the category. FLCs were given a due date for their assessment plans and strategies and support to create their own plans. Faculty in the Historical Traditions FLC chose to do pre- and posttests of student descriptions that focus on their outcome. This has been in place since 2007. Religious Traditions FLC members tried two different types of posttest exam items. During their first attempt in 2007, all faculty used the same set of items as part of the final exam. However, faculty encountered difficulties because of the contextual and content differences within the courses that were vetted and approved for the Religious Traditions FLC. Therefore, the 2008 assessment is based on a set of approved, but different, items that are included on final exams. A rubric was developed to look across courses and items and determine how well students had met the outcome. The members of the Cultural Awareness FLC first began with a survey for faculty about their course and a survey for students about their experiences in this category of courses. After much discussion, however, the faculty embedded a common set of items in their final exams in fall 2007.

Required Resources

Each FLC facilitator was paid an annual stipend of $200. Because there are two facilitators for each of the six categories, our annual stipend budget is $2,400. In addition, FLC facilitators shared their practices during three paid lunches a year (a total of $1,000). Additional funds were provided to the faculty learning communities for refreshments when they met (approximately $1,000). The most important resource, however, was the time that faculty committed to this process.

Findings

Each FLC developed specific measures for their core curriculum outcome. Therefore, findings are different for each area. The Religious Traditions FLC surveyed students to find out their initial responses to questions regarding "What is the study of the past?" and "How do we understand the events of the past?" Based on student responses, the faculty rated each statement. A list of student statements was then developed that ranged from demonstrating little understanding of the purpose of studying history ("a study of all events of the past") to a greater understanding of why history is important ("understanding how events of the past have shaped the future"). During the fall 2007 semester, students were sent an e-mailed pretest (N = 531) consisting of two forced choice items. On the first, asking "What is the study of the past?" students provided the following responses:

- "events that shaped the present" (42 percent)
- "a study of all events of the past" (17 percent)
- "understanding of what causes change over time" (16 percent)
- "a record of human history" (12 percent)
- "search for truth and supposed facts of the past" (12 percent)

For the fall 2007 (N = 415) posttest, the responses of students had changed, with 64 percent responding that the study of the past is focused on "events that shaped the present."

Use of Findings

Members of the Historical Traditions FLC used these findings to shape discussions during their meetings. Even the creation of the items caused faculty to reevaluate and articulate more effectively how their course met the outcomes stated for this core category. Some course modifications focused on additional student assignments and the sequencing of material. The Religious Traditions FLC findings have prompted faculty within that FLC to reexamine how their different courses have a common theme that makes the courses appropriate for this core curriculum category. The theme is articulated within the agreed-on outcomes and faculty created their end-of-semester assessment tool that meets the needs of the individual courses while still measuring the common outcome.

Impact of Using the Findings

Faculty within the FLCs used the agreed-on outcomes as one assessment of their course. Many of the courses within the core curriculum also meet other aspects of student requirements. Some might be within the student's major; others satisfy a writing emphasis requirement or could even meet an additional core requirement. Therefore, the findings for one area of the core could affect a course and then have an indirect impact on other areas. As a result of the core curriculum assessment, courses have been modified, in-class assessment methods have been added, and students are being asked to learn how a specific course is actually a part of the larger core curriculum.

Success Factors

The support of three areas (the Core Curriculum Office, the Office for Assessment and Quality Enhancement, and the Center for Teaching Excellence) greatly contributed to the ongoing growth and success of this assessment process. With one of the initial tasks focused on creating assessment methods for a specific core category, members of the FLCs modified their initial approaches to teaching a course within the core. Their focus is now more on what students are learning rather than on what they are teaching. However, as part of their discussion of findings, the circle is completed as they must use their findings to influence students at the course level. Having colleagues within the FLCs has meant that these discussions take place over time and feedback from others is provided.

TCU Core Curriculum and Assessment:

www.core.tcu.edu/

Assessing Course Syllabi to Determine Degree of Learner-Centeredness

Roxanne Cullen, Michael Harris, Ferris State University

◆ ◆ ◆

Look for development of a learner-centeredness rubric that is applied to course syllabi. Results are used to identify professional development experiences necessary in certain areas.

Background and Purpose(s) of Assessment

Professional development is a key element in pushing forward the learner-centered agenda. Academic leaders should foster professional development for everyone and support benchmarks as well as continuous improvement efforts. Professional development in the learner-centered paradigm should reflect the values of fostering individuality while developing community and focus on common, core values. Toward that goal, we recommend a model for developing an agenda for professional development that is based on assessment and conducted collaboratively, with faculty and administration working in concert toward a common goal.

Assessment is crucial to shift effectively toward complete learner-centeredness. We developed a rubric for assessing learning-centered qualities through a review of course syllabi (see Table 7.1). Faculty and administrators within academic units or departments use this rubric to review course syllabi and determine the degree of learning-centeredness present in current teaching practices. Subsequently they reassess periodically to determine if progress is being made toward achieving an increased level of learning centeredness. A formal review of course syllabi is offered as a single measure for beginning to assess this strategic and complex transition.

TABLE 7.1. RUBRIC FOR DETERMINING DEGREE OF LEARNING-CENTEREDNESS IN COURSE SYLLABI.

Community	1	2	3	4
Accessibility of Teacher	Available for prescribed number of office hours only; discourages interaction except in class or for emergency.	Available for prescribed number of office hours; provides phone and e-mail but discourages contact.	Available for more than prescribed number of office hours; offers phone, e-mail, fax, home phone; encourages interaction.	Available for multiple office hours, multiple means of access including phone(s), e-mail, fax; holds open hours in locations other than office (such as library or union); encourages interaction.
Learning Rationale	No rationale provided for assignments or activities.	Explanation of assignments and activities but not tied directly to learning outcomes.	Rationale provided for assignments and activities; tied to learning outcomes.	Rationale provided for assignments, activities, methods, policies, and procedures; tied to learning outcomes.
Collaboration	Collaboration prohibited.	Collaboration discouraged.	Collaboration incorporated; use of groups for work and study.	Collaboration required; use of groups for class work, team projects; encourages students to learn from one another.

(continued)

TABLE 7.1. *(continued)*

Power and control	1	2	3	4
Teacher Role	No shared power. Authoritarian, rules are written as directives; numerous penalties; no flexibility in interpretation; not accommodating of differences.	No shared power. Though teacher is ultimate authority, some flexibility is included for policies and procedures; some accommodation for differences among students.	Limited shared power. Students may be offered some choice in types of assignments or weight of assignments or due dates.	Shared power. Teacher encourages students to participate in developing policies and procedures for class as well as input on due dates and assignments.
Student Role	Student is told what he or she is responsible for learning.	Student is told what he or she is responsible for learning but encouraged to go beyond minimum to gain reward.	Student is given responsibility for presenting material to class. Some projects rely on student generated knowledge.	Students take responsibility for bringing additional knowledge to class via class discussion or presentation.
Outside Resources	No outside resources other than required textbook. Teacher is primary source of knowledge.	Reference to outside resources provided but not required.	Outside resources included with explanation that students are responsible for learning outside the classroom and independent investigation.	Outside resources included with explanation that students are responsible for learning outside the classroom and independent investigation. Students expected to provide outside resource information for class.

TABLE 7.1. *(continued)*

Power and control	1	2	3	4
Syllabus Focus	Focus is on policies and procedures. No discussion of learning or outcomes	Weighted toward policy and procedures with some reference to content covered.	Includes course objectives. Balance between policies and procedures and focus on learning.	Syllabus weighted toward student learning outcomes and means of assessment; policies are minimal or left to class negotiation.

Evaluation-Assessment	1	2	3	4
Grades	Focus is on losing points; grades used to penalize.	Emphasizes the accumulation of points disassociated from learning performance.	Grades are tied directly to learning outcomes; students have some options for achieving points.	Grades are tied to learning outcomes; option for achieving points; not all work is graded.
Feedback Mechanisms	Midterm and final test grades only. Students not allowed to see or retain copies of tests.	Midterm and final test grades with minimal other graded work. Tests not cumulative. Students may see but not retain copies of tests.	Grades and other feedback in the form of nongraded assignments, activities, opportunities to confer with teacher.	Periodic feedback mechanisms employed for the purpose of monitoring learning (lecture response slips, ungraded quizzes, graded quizzes, tests, papers, SGID or other feedback on learning).

(continued)

TABLE 7.1. *(continued)*

Evaluation-Assessment	1	2	3	4
Evaluation	Tests (not comprehensive).	Tests, quizzes, and other summative evaluation.	Summative and formative evaluation, written work required.	Summative and formative evaluations including written and oral presentations, group work, self-evaluation and peer evaluation.
Learning Outcomes	No outcomes stated.	Goals for course stated but not in the form of learning outcomes.	Learning outcomes clearly stated.	Learning outcomes stated and tied to specific assessments.
Revision or Redoing	No rewriting or redoing of assignments allowed.	Some rewriting or redoing of assignments is allowed, but penalized.	Rewriting and redoing of assignments is allowed.	Rewriting and redoing of assignments is encouraged.

The rubric is divided into three major categories that reflect the learner-centered approach. The first dimension is community, which is defined as fostering group work and team projects as well as providing other opportunities to learn from one another, as opposed to viewing the professor as the single source of knowledge. Another facet of community involves developing relevance. Does the professor attempt to create a sense of relevance to the learning environment by providing a rationale for learning and learning activities, thus establishing a sense of purpose, trust, and, subsequently, community? The accessibility of the professor is another indication of community as it represents the academic community's investment in the students.

The second dimension is creating power and control within the students. Undergraduates should develop an intrinsic motivation for learning that fosters a sense of control over one's learning. Ascertaining students' sense of intrinsic motivation cannot be easily determined by a review of syllabi; however, a syllabus can reveal attempts to create an environment where control is shared. The manner in which policies and procedures are presented is one indicator. Another indicator is the amount of choice provided to students as well as the responsibilities expected of the student. Is the student a partner in the learning experience?

The third dimension is assessment and evaluation. We made a distinction between evaluation and assessment for both are key to a learning-centered approach. We use assessment as ongoing, formative feedback from professor to student, so that an undergraduate can gauge his or her own progress, as well as feedback from student to professor in order for the instructor to determine if learning is taking place. We use evaluation to mean the summative determination of whether students have met specific learning outcomes. A review of course syllabi using these criteria is intended as a formative measure to guide future faculty development initiatives.

Assessment Method(s) and Year(s) of Implementation

The course syllabus is routinely used to assist reviewers of classroom teaching in gaining insight into the standards and practices of an individual teacher's course, as well as into the current practices within a unit or department. A thoughtful review of a course syllabus can reveal important information about teaching philosophy, attitude toward students, course goals, and additional areas.

Each academic department collects course syllabi from faculty each semester. Using the rubric we developed, the department head can review these syllabi in order to gain a sense of the climate of learning within the department or unit. The review provides a picture of the attempts faculty are making toward establishing community, sharing power and control, and building assessment and evaluation. The department head can then use the results as a starting point for discussion with department faculty regarding faculty development goals and opportunities. This review is intended to provide data to inform and guide professional development.

Required Resources

Required resources include course syllabi and the rubric.

Findings

We piloted this assessment practice with two academic units. The syllabi from the first unit revealed a consistency of approach: the greatest degree of learner-centeredness was related to the creation of community. However, it was clear that in most cases, no tie was made between learning outcomes and learning rationale, or between learning outcomes and evaluation. We anticipated that once the concept of learning outcomes was clearly understood, the professors who were already providing explanation of assignments and activities would consider tying those explanations to learning outcomes. Also, none of the syllabi revealed evidence of sharing power and control with students. Because the unit had only begun discussions about adopting more learner-centered practices, we determined that a further discussion of learning outcomes and learning rationale would be the best starting point in working with this particular unit. The idea of sharing power and control is generally a more difficult concept to accept and practice.

The review of the second unit had very different results. Faculty in this unit had worked for two years to revise the curriculum to reflect learner-centered practices. They were accustomed to discussing pedagogy and learner-centered goals together as a unit. The review of their syllabi revealed evidence that evaluation and assessment were built into every facet of all courses, and assessments were tied to learning outcomes. The area that emerged as a point of interest for discussion was the relationship between learning outcomes and the learning rationale. Syllabi were heavily focused on rules and procedures, which was understandable considering that the academic unit prepares health care professionals and many procedures are dictated by state health codes. As faculty in this unit were more advanced in their understanding and acceptance of learner-centered principles, we determined that they could benefit from a discussion regarding loosening some of the rigidity present in the presentation of the rules and procedures. By tying the necessity of the rules to workplace habits and employer expectations, they could develop a rationale connected to lifelong learning that would subsequently reduce the sense of arbitrary or authoritarian control on the part of the professor.

Use of Findings

We found the discussions with faculty in these two units to be rewarding and productive based on the results of reviewing course syllabi. Both units had been working with our Faculty Center on issues related to learner-centered pedagogy, so the discussions, in these cases, fed into an already established larger unit goal. The faculty knew that we would be reviewing the syllabi and that the purpose was purely formative in nature. We conducted the assessment prior to the beginning of the academic year so that the faculty could use the results as they met to plan their professional development initiatives in the fall semester.

Success Factors

A review of this nature, conducted by the academic administrator, *should not* be the initial step used to foster a discussion of learner-centered pedagogy in a unit or department, as the likelihood that its formative nature could be misperceived is high. It is best used as a gauge after faculty have begun experimenting with learner-centered teaching strategies and other discussions regarding this shift have taken place. If this rubric is used as a benchmark in an ongoing process and is owned and directed by the faculty, the likelihood of success will be greater.

Implementing Annual Cycles for Ongoing Assessment of Student Learning

Brigitte Valesey, Widener University

◆ ◆ ◆

Look for a faculty needs-assessment survey utilized to identify the types of professional development that would be useful and meaningful for instructors.

Background and Purpose(s) of Assessment

The merger of new strategic directions and reaccreditation processes beginning in 2004 prioritized student learning assessment at Widener University. The Task Force for Assessment of Student Learning was charged to create an institutional foundation and formal framework for collecting, reporting, and reviewing assessment of learning data. Regional accreditation expectations for formal assessment activities and cycles compelled the task force to determine faculty perceptions, prevailing practices and exemplars, and assessment gaps. In addition, the task force members recognized the need to build on existing assessment reporting structures and identify the persons responsible for assessment. For the task force, the challenge was to formalize anecdotal information and to fold current assessment practices into an ongoing institutional process that would regularly inform teaching and learning.

Assessment Method(s) and Year(s) of Implementation

The task force conducted a questionnaire in fall 2005 to gather input for faculty development needs and assessment resources, as well as the status of implementation of student learning assessment in all academic programs. This questionnaire was administered again in spring 2006 to reassess faculty needs and perceptions concerning assessment. Each inventory focused on key questions concerning student learning expectations, assessment methods and processes, and committee structures. In April 2006, the task force coordinated the pilot reporting and review of formal assessment plans. Task force subgroups reviewed a sample selection of plans using a worksheet with prespecified and articulated criteria addressing completeness and clarity.

Required Resources

The university provided resource support for faculty development, faculty travel to assessment conferences, and professional resources to enhance faculty understanding of assessment and best practices. A full-time administrator was hired to support and coordinate assessment of student learning across the institution and to work with academic units and working groups, such as the task force, to develop and implement ongoing assessment activities. Examples of resource support included conference attendance, campus presentations by assessment experts, and professional publications.

Findings

Results of the initial faculty needs questionnaire indicated that many faculty "are using assessment practices in their teaching, but not to the fullest potential; would like to learn more about how programs in their academic specialty area, at other universities, and in other departments and schools have assessed learning; would like to know more about ways to assess student learning, including tailoring their existing assessments; and would like to find out more about methods for analyzing and using assessment results" (Widener University Self-Study Report, 2006, p. 124). In addition, faculty identified a variety of barriers to engaging assessment. The second administration of the questionnaire reaffirmed the existence of these barriers.

Assessment inventory results indicated that all programs had stated objectives or outcomes, though they were not necessarily student centered, and that most programs provided some assessment criteria. As anticipated, programs varied greatly in their assessment processes and documentation of how results were used. Additional inventory feedback highlighted the need to develop consistent assessment terminology, cross-disciplinary examples of assessment elements, and assessment exemplars. Based on the review of inventories, the task force identified the following areas for follow-up: developing student-centered learning outcomes, creating assessment criteria, reporting results, and using the results to improve teaching and learning.

Use of Findings

The task force used the assessment questionnaire and inventories to provide clear direction for faculty development workshops and presentations. In addition, the inventory responses assisted the task force in identifying effective assessment practices at the university. Schools and colleges used the task force findings to identify their priorities for planning and implementing ongoing assessment. Based on inventory feedback, common assessment terms were defined and communicated by the task force using multiple venues. Task force presentations to the university community addressed misperceptions and articulated assessment developments.

To bring institutional focus to student learning priorities, the task force crafted institutional learning objectives that were approved by the Faculty Council as overarching, shared learning expectations linked to the institution mission. All academic programs subsequently mapped their student learning outcomes to the institutional objectives. The task force collected and reviewed the mapped objectives to determine institutional gaps.

The pilot for assessment review identified areas for improvement in articulating the criteria in the review worksheet and communicating the process for review. To clarify the review process, deans and directors received training on the review process at the spring 2006 dean's retreat. All academic units had the opportunity to submit revised plans based on the adjusted criteria.

The concluding recommendation of the task force was to establish an ongoing university-wide committee to coordinate assessment of student learning and to address assessment issues. The committee was appointed by the provost and includes individuals with responsibility for assessment in each of the schools, colleges, and cocurricular programs. The assistant provost coordinates annual assessment reporting and reviews through the Implementation Committee for Assessment of Student Learning.

Impact of Using the Findings

Informed by the work of the early task force, the Implementation Committee reviewed a sample of assessment plans to understand various ways in which units report their student learning assessment activities and to explore ways to address coordination and integration of assessment. Program assessment coordinators shared formal structures and strategies for collecting and using assessment data. Using the task force worksheet criteria, the committee developed enhanced guidelines for annual assessment reporting, a reporting template, team review form, and annual time line. Informed by the task force assessment reporting pilot process, the committee established a team review process for assessment reporting.

The General Education Task Force has used the cumulative findings from the initial assessment task force to inform information gathering, faculty participation and acceptance, and development of an assessment framework. General education goals, approved in early 2006, correspond to and support the institutional learning objectives. Terminology pertinent to general education and its assessment were clarified. Institutional and program-level best practices for assessing general education were identified.

Success Factors

Much of the institutional progress and many of the assessment milestones can be attributed to cross-campus faculty leadership and ownership of assessment of student learning. Establishing a core group with expertise, long-term commitment, and campus influence contributed to the development of an institutional culture for assessment. Campuswide participation in assessment dialogues and decision making, along with ongoing feedback, provided the level of transparency needed to address barriers and advance ideas. Administrative support for assessment as a long-term institutional commitment provided necessary resources and helped to infuse assessment in formal and informal academic activities. Ongoing communication within academic units and across campus was necessary to develop common assessment language, vet issues and concerns, respond to feedback, and highlight local and national best practices. Recognition of local exemplary assessment models and practices as well as faculty scholarship in assessment has elevated assessment from "something we will have to do" to scholarly efforts that regularly inform teaching and learning.

Relevant Institutional Web Sites Pertaining to This Assessment Practice

Assessment at Widener University:

www.widener.edu/tasl/assessment.asp

CHAPTER EIGHT

USE OF TECHNOLOGY PROFILES

As faculty and staff are building comprehensive assessments, a major challenge has been to retrieve meaningful information on a timely basis and to keep track of multiple assessments and the results of administering them. Some academic leaders have turned to external companies and purchased databases to help keep track of their student assessments over time. The profiles shared in this chapter are not intended to endorse any particular company, but they serve as key illustrations about how technology can become a useful tool for organizing, implementing, and sustaining assessment. Other academic leaders have developed their own electronic portfolio systems that permit students to submit examples of their work, often from the freshman through the senior year, with reflections about their learning. Student affairs and academic units are increasingly using online surveys as a way to gather feedback from students. The following profiles demonstrate how useful technology is in maintaining an effective and efficient assessment system.

Faculty at Medgar Evers College of the City University of New York have focused serious attention on the major challenge of student retention. Gale Gibson-Ballah and Douglas Walcerz describe how they worked with TrueOutcomes staff to develop an innovative early warning system that identifies at-risk students and helps faculty determine strategies to assist these students. Multiple sources of student information (including demographics, courses they take, attendance, results on rubric-scored class assignments, and a survey for measuring psychological adjustment to the college environment) are used to calculate the attrition risk score for each student. The retention model includes these key predictors of success, which have been used by faculty in the first-year program. First-year instructors discuss the results and design intentional interventions to improve student retention.

Faculty and staff at Bellevue University found that they had no system in place to integrate large amounts of assessment information so that it could be used in a meaningful way. They also received feedback from their accrediting body that assessment of student learning was a weakness. Given these issues, they decided to use a Web-based system to organize the assessment process. Pat Artz tells us that although they initially wanted to design their own system, they found challenges associated with this effort. Eventually they purchased access to the system called WEAVEonline. Faculty and administrators have reported that this system has greatly facilitated their organization of assessment. In their environment, this online system is crucial to sustaining and reporting assessments to both internal and external stakeholders and to making assessment more simplified and manageable.

Linda Anstendig and Sarah Burns Feyl report on the implementation of an electronic portfolio approach to assess student learning at Pace University. For the three required English courses in writing, students submit samples of their written work, which are assessed using a rubric based on learning outcomes developed by faculty. Instructional librarians collaborate with faculty on the part of the rubric that addresses information literacy competence standards. Since 2002, a portfolio review day has been held at Pace during which instructors and staff together assess student work. Instructors in other schools, including education and computer science, are now using versions of the electronic portfolio system. Nearly 80 percent of students want to continue using these electronic portfolios, and three-quarters of these students find them effective for documenting class and cocurricular activities.

Academic leaders and faculty were worried about the quality of their winter session distance education courses and program at Binghamton University (SUNY) and developed an online survey to ask faculty about their perceptions. Sean McKitrick describes the findings. Instructors reported success using the winter session to teach courses but they found challenges in creating community and dialogue within a distance education format and wanted support for implementing effective pedagogy. Students also completed an online survey and reported that they felt discussion groups were extremely important for enhancing student satisfaction and their learning. Both students and faculty were concerned about the fast pace in the six-week compressed format of the courses. The assessment results have been used to make changes, including giving faculty more time to plan their courses. More organizational units are now working together to develop a program to assist faculty members with online instruction and assessment.

These profiles illustrate how technology can be useful in implementing and maintaining assessment systems. When effectively designed, such systems can provide important information about key results that can be shared with internal and external stakeholders. These systems can also streamline assessment so that it becomes more efficient and helps synthesize evidence about student learning on a timely basis.

Institutions

Doctoral and Research
> Private
>> Pace University; New York, New York (13,000 students)
> Public
>> SUNY at Binghamton; Binghamton, New York (14,000 students)

Master's
> Private
>> Bellevue University; Bellevue, Nebraska (7,000 students)

Baccalaureate
> Public
>> CUNY Medgar Evers College; Brooklyn, New York (5,000 students)

Improving First-Year Student Retention and Success through a Networked Early-Warning System (NEWS)

Gale Gibson-Ballah, Douglas Walcerz, Medgar Evers College of the City University of New York

◆ ◆ ◆

Look for a database early-warning system that identifies at-risk students and strategies to assist them. Multiple sources of student information and assessment results are used to calculate the attrition risk score for each student.

Background and Purpose(s) of Assessment

Student retention is a significant issue at Medgar Evers College, particularly during the first three semesters. The college worked with TrueOutcomes, a company devoted exclusively to assessment, to develop and implement a Web-based network early-warning system (NEWS) to calculate an "attrition risk score" for each student. NEWS is based on demographics, the courses students take, whether they paid a late registration fee, attendance, entrance exam scores, rubric-scored class assignments, and a measure of psychological adjustment to the college environment (the College Adjustment Scales from Psychological Assessment Resources, Inc.) The attrition risk score is the probability that the student will not return the following semester based on a logistic regression model. The primary purpose of the electronic network early warning system is to assess and identify at-risk students, especially first- and second-semester freshmen, in time to provide the necessary assistance and enhance the likelihood of their persistence in college. The conceptual dimensions that determine student persistence at MEC are well known—academic and social integration and commitment. Thus MEC's attrition risk score includes key variables that appear to have significant effects on retention.

Assessment Method(s) and Year(s) of Implementation

The Network Early Warning System collects several types of assessment data: (1) student attendance in the Freshman Seminar and in developmental courses (math, reading, writing); (2) student performance on the first assignment in the Freshman Seminar and developmental courses; (3) student responses to the College Adjustment Scales; (4) scores on the CUNY entrance exams; (5) student demographics (gender and race or ethnicity); and (6) student schedules and late registrants. Student attendance was collected directly from faculty who entered the information into the attendance book of the TrueOutcomes Assessment Manager. Student performance was assessed using faculty-developed rubrics, and data from different courses and rubrics were aggregated by aligning rows in the rubrics to the first-year program learning outcomes and combining scores for a common outcome. All performance assessment activities were collected in the TrueOutcomes Assessment Manager and data were aggregated automatically. Student responses to the College Adjustment Scales (CAS) were collected using the TrueOutcomes Survey Module. Students accessed the survey online from a computer lab during class time. Analysis of the CAS followed guidelines from the publishers that were programmed into TrueOutcomes. Student demographics, scores on CUNY entrance exams, student schedules, and late registration were stored in the TrueOutcomes Assessment Manager via a link between it and the college's student information management system. Development and implementation of NEWS began in the summer of 2004 with workshops on rubric development and use of the TrueOutcomes Assessment Manager. In 2005–06 the system was implemented with fewer than 100 students as a pilot to establish standard procedures for data collection. In 2006–07 the system was scaled up to the entire first-year program, including about 1,350 students. In 2007–08 the system continued with incremental improvements to the process.

Required Resources

The implementation of a retention alert system is a nontrivial process that requires significant consultation between TrueOutcomes and the faculty and staff of the college. Consultations involve determination of the predictors that should be included in a retention model; development of outcomes and instruments to support the retention model including learning outcomes, surveys, and rubrics; and analysis to build a multivariable regression model. The TrueOutcomes Assessment Manager, Survey Module, Student Information System Integration, and Retention Alert System are available from TrueOutcomes, a Cengage Learning company. The TrueOutcomes software is hosted by TrueOutcomes, so there are no hardware requirements.

Findings

Data from 2006–07 were collected from approximately 1,350 students. We examined the effect of 37 separate factors on fall-spring student retention:

1. Demographics
   a. Gender
   b. Race or ethnicity
2. CUNY entrance exam scores
   a. Reading
   b. Writing
   c. Pre-Algebra
   d. Algebra
3. Type of freshman seminar course
   a. Freshman Seminar (the standard course, FS 101, is a freshman orientation/first-year student survival course)
   b. SP/C (Special Programs Courses for students who are categorized as academically and economically disadvantaged)

   c. AIM (Academic Improvement Seminar for students on academic warning and/or probation)
4. Level of remediation in math
   a. First level
   b. Second level
   c. No remediation
5. Level of remediation in reading
   a. First level
   b. Second level
   c. No remediation
6. Level of remediation in writing
   a. First level
   b. Second level
   c. No remediation
7. Attendance
   a. Attendance in Freshman Seminar (all three types)
   b. Attendance in Developmental Reading (both levels)
   c. Attendance in Developmental Writing (both levels)
   d. Attendance in Developmental Math (both levels)
8. Adjustment to the college environment (CAS)
   a. Academic problems
   b. Anxiety
   c. Interpersonal problems
   d. Depression
   e. Career problems
   f. Suicidal ideation
   g. Substance abuse
   h. Self-esteem
   i. Family problems
9. Student performance aggregated by first-year program outcomes
   a. Academic skills
   b. Social skills
   c. Life skills
   d. Self development
   e. Personal skills
10. Registration
   a. Late fee assessed

We determined which factors had the largest correlation with fall-spring retention by a multistep process. We began by fitting a univariable logistic regression model to find candidates for the multivariable model. We then fit the multivariable model and eliminated variables that lacked significance or suffered from incomplete data. We did not consider factor interactions due to the lack of a theoretical basis for such interactions. The final model is based on about 1,000 students. (About 350 of the original 1,350 students did not have complete data for the final model.) The factors in the multivariable model, in order of significance are:

1. Attendance: percentage of missed classes in the first three weeks of the semester in the freshman seminar course
2. Late registration
3. Level of remediation in math
4. Type of first-year seminar course

Several factors that were significant in the univariable analysis were not included in the multivariable model because of incomplete data reporting. These factors may prove to be valuable predictors of attrition in the future:

1. Attendance: percentage of missed classes in the first three weeks of the semester in remedial math, reading and writing.
2. Adjustment to the college environment: scores for depression and career problems.
3. CUNY entrance exam scores for pre-algebra and algebra.

The usefulness of a logistic regression model depends on its power to discriminate; this means avoiding both false positives and false negatives. The model based on data from 2006–07 has a discrimination index of 0.67. As a reference, an index of 0.5 is a useless model (no better than a coin flip), whereas an index of 0.9 is a virtually perfect model. An index of 0.7 is considered the threshold of a useful model. We are slightly below the threshold, but the fact that we are approaching the threshold provides motivation for improving our data collection to obtain a better model. Data from 2007–08 may improve the discrimination index; they are still being analyzed.

Use of Findings

Faculty in the First Year Program, who also serve as academic advisors to their students, reviewed the NEWS findings and discussed intentional interventions to improve student retention. Mandatory tutoring was implemented for students who missed classes within the first four weeks of the semester. Students who were identified with issues of depression, career problems, and interpersonal problems were referred to the counseling unit for further follow-up. Students who were in jeopardy of receiving a failing grade by the middle of the semester were advised to officially withdraw from courses in order to salvage their grade point averages and not be placed on academic warning. Finally, a number of students were identified as registered but never attended the courses. As a result, the First Year Program instituted a no-show list of freshmen each semester and contacted those students to encourage them to officially withdraw from courses and to advise them on readmission procedures and financial aid implications. Some of the no-show students with valid reasons for not attending were advised to submit academic petitions with supporting documentation.

Impact of Using the Findings

The primary impact of NEWS is to give the faculty, who are also academic advisors, tools for identifying at-risk students and determining the types of interventions that will be most effective. The immediate impact is that faculty advisors have remarked that NEWS largely supports their qualitative observations of their advisees and provides a rich source of information to enable them to assist their advisees. Though we expect this will lead to increased student retention, we are still collecting data and will not be able to prove the impact until we have data for an additional year.

Success Factors

Numerous success factors benefit students, faculty, and the institution. Some of these are: identification of first-year students who require early academic and nonacademic intervention; decreased number of freshman students who are placed on academic warning or probation; enhanced coordination of academic and student affairs efforts; student awareness of college policies and procedures; better assessment of student needs early in the process in order to implement and engage the appropriate student support services that have implications for increased freshman retention.

Relevant Institutional Web Sites Pertaining to This Assessment Practice

For more information regarding the Learning Outcomes Web-Based Management System, see the Web sites below:

www.trueoutcomes.com/
www.centerdigitaled.com/conference.php?confid=263&past=1
www.govtech.com/cde/conference.php?confid=327&past=1

Organizing the Chaos: Moving from Word to the Web

Patrick Artz, Bellevue University

◆ ◆ ◆

Look for how a university implemented a Web-based system to organize the entire assessment process, including reporting assessment results to internal and external stakeholders.

Background and Purpose(s) of Assessment

In 2005 we received preliminary feedback from our accrediting body that our assessment of student learning was a serious weakness that "rises to the level of an accreditation issue." The academic alarm bells sounded. We needed to get our academic assessment house in order, and our deliverable needed to be concise, accurate, and substantive.

The feedback was especially frustrating because we had been working diligently on academic assessment for some time. We thought we had made steady progress, but very little of that progress was visible to outside accreditors. We had no way of pulling the vast amounts of assessment information together in a coherent way for outside stakeholders to view and understand. Our records were formatted as Microsoft Word documents and scattered throughout the campus. Faculty and administrators, already somewhat jaded by the complexity of academic assessment, viewed the task of reorganizing our assessment information with trepidation.

Assessment Method(s) and Year(s) of Implementation

We made the decision in September 2005 to move academic assessment for the entire university from Word files to a Web-based system. This decision was outside the comfort zone for most direct stakeholders. However, everyone also realized that the current system simply was not providing the answers we needed for institution-wide assessment of student learning. We needed to move outside our departments and colleges to embrace a more efficient system or else run the risk of drowning in our own paperwork.

The main goal of moving to a Web-based system was to simplify the process for everyone. We wanted an easier way for academic program directors to enter information as well as an easier way for administrators to run reports.

We planned the change during the 2005–06 academic year. We moved to the new system in 2006–07 and have continued to use it for 2007–08.

Required Resources

We initially thought we could build our own Web-based system. This would have afforded us maximum flexibility in tailoring the system to our current assessment processes. However, it would have taken a full year to be operational, and then another year to debug the first version to make sure things were running well. With our backs against the wall, we did not have that sort of time.

Instead, we purchased access to a system from Virginia Commonwealth University (VCU). The system is called WEAVEonline. It cost approximately $25,000 for the initial contract and then $2,500 or so for each subsequent yearly contract. VCU hosts the system and maintains the database and server software. We simply use our Internet browsers to access the system.

It took several days to assemble the necessary information to submit to VCU for the initial start-up. Then it required several hours of faculty in-service time to train everyone to use the Web interface. Now one of our system administrators occasionally is asked to update a feature or user or program in the system. All in all, it is a fairly low-budget solution for a university assessment system.

Findings

The preliminary report from our accreditors, compiled before we implemented our Web-based system, stated that our lack of coherent evidence for assessment of student learning rose to the level of an accreditation issue. The official report from the accreditors, compiled after we implemented our Web-based system, expressed satisfaction with our assessment of student learning. The sigh of relief was audible across the campus.

Equally important, faculty members, program directors, and administrators alike report satisfaction with the Web interface, the reports, and the overall ease of our assessment processes. We now have one place to go for critical assessment information. In other words, the new system appears to be appropriate and sustainable for both internal and external stakeholders.

Information is now available for various reports that the Web-based system can generate on demand. These reports highlight gaps in our assessment information and identify the personnel responsible for filling those gaps.

Use of Findings

Perhaps the most valuable use of our findings has been a clearer articulation of our general education requirements in an assessment format. General education has been notoriously hard to assess because it spans many departments and has many course options for students. A Web-based system, with its visible interface, encouraged our College of Arts and Sciences to pin down the objectives for the general education requirements and then select measures for those objectives. Basically, we moved from discussion to consensus in a difficult area.

The most public sign of our commitment to assessment has been the creation of the Writing Center. Faculty members discovered a campuswide problem with the quality of student writing. Our best students as well as our struggling students were not producing the quality of writing we wanted to see in our assessment measures. In response, the university funded the creation of the Writing Center and staffed it with trained, full-time professionals. Students and instructors now have a one-stop shop for everything from basic writing advice to tips on how to craft documents for academic conferences or publication.

Impact of Using the Findings

Implementing action plans was one of the weaknesses in our previous assessment system. We often compiled lots of information but then either failed to act or acted but failed to document our actions. With our Web-based system, we are able to enter and track action plans quite easily. The elusive goal of "closing the gap" has finally become part of our routine.

With the basics of assessment in place, we have been able to move to the next level, which, for us, is curriculum mapping. We have put all courses into the system, and now each college is moving forward with pilot programs to map those courses to program objectives.

Curriculum mapping allows for a flexible approach. We decided to use Bloom's Taxonomy (1956) and a category called "depth of instruction" as our analysis approaches. We may add other approaches as we become more comfortable with curriculum mapping. For now, analysis via Bloom's Taxonomy has focused our attention on challenging students with application-level assignments, which is a key part of our mission statement. And we discovered important academic skills that were introduced repeatedly in some programs but never mastered. Everyone has always been in favor of "depth of instruction," and now we can address gaps in our approach.

Success Factors

The main success factor was a willingness on the part of faculty and administration to move beyond discussions about why we do assessment and the various ways that we might do assessment into the phase of agreeing on a framework for actually implementing assessment. Another success factor was the simplification of assessment processes. Our Web-based system focuses attention on the basic questions of what we are assessing, how we are assessing it, and what we are doing with the results. Our mantra became, "What are your objectives, what are your measures, and what are your action plans?" Focused attention on crucial dimensions of the assessment process is a critical success factor.

A third success factor was collaboration between faculty and administration in implementing the new system. When an initiative spans the divide between faculty and administrators, open and ongoing communication is critical for success. The faculty Academic Assessment Committee invited a dean to attend committee meetings. Also, the administration funded release time for the faculty chair of the committee to focus on academic assessment. Open lines of communication enabled a potentially wild herd to move in a calm, orderly fashion toward the goal of a simplified assessment system.

Relevant Institutional Web Sites Pertaining to This Assessment Practice

The WEAVEonline Web Site:

www.weaveonline.com/

Bellevue University's Assessment Information Web Site:

www.weaveonline.net/subscriber/bellevue/

Multifaceted Portfolio Assessment: Writing Program Collaboration with Instructional Librarians and Electronic Portfolio Initiative

Linda Anstendig, Sarah Burns Feyl, Pace University

◆ ◆ ◆

Look for the implementation of an electronic portfolio approach to assess student learning and the use of rubrics to judge the levels of student performance.

Background and Purpose(s) of Assessment

The beginning of our two-pronged portfolio assessment initiative coincided with the redesign of Pace University's core curriculum in 2002, which is anchored by twelve learning outcomes, including communication, analysis, information literacy, and civic engagement (see www.pace.edu/page.cfm?doc_id=18384). We found that using portfolios enabled students to integrate their learning, demonstrate achievement in their general education courses, facilitate self-assessment, and prepare students for their future careers. We began a department-level portfolio assessment program that has been sustained over the past six years, and an electronic portfolio program that was meant to include many disciplines as well as our Co-op and Career Services Department.

We developed a team of colleagues who, after seeing the potential for portfolio assessment, applied for and were awarded the first Pace Presidential Learning Assessment Grant for a pilot e-portfolio initiative. The director of career services, our instructional librarian, the director of our Center for Teaching, Learning and Technology, as well as several English professors, including the director of the writing program, are some of the members who have collaborated and built bridges among various departments and disciplines. The funding we received for the e-portfolio initiative enabled us to move forward, and provided incentives for faculty to become involved.

We feature the English department's efforts here because the electronic portfolio initiative has not gained full administrative or faculty support, even though over the past six years pockets of progress have been made and some schools, including our School of Education, have been using e-portfolio assessment more widely.

Assessment Method(s) and Year(s) of Implementation

Portfolio review for the Pleasantville Writing Program encompasses three required courses (ENG 110, ENG 120, and ENG 201). During finals week portfolio review day is held, attended by faculty who pair up and read a sampling of each others' course portfolios and evaluate them using a rubric based on course learning outcomes. Instructional librarians join the faculty to review and evaluate the research papers and reflective essays that are required components of the portfolios; they use their own rubric, based on information literacy standards. Students' reflective essays address their research and writing processes and demonstrate how both have evolved throughout the semester. Librarians and professors who have helped to shape the prompts for these reflective statements gain further insight into the students' research processes and mastery of information literacy outcomes. Over the past six years, the writing faculty have convened to read a variety of portfolio essays and holistically grade them. The first portfolio review day was held in spring 2002 and has been held every semester since then.

In addition, some faculty have incorporated e-portfolio assessment in their courses. Faculty development workshops have been held each semester so that interested faculty and students learn how to create the e-portfolio cover page and use the Pace Web file system (wfs.pace.edu), where students can upload their files, share them with faculty, and link them to their e-portfolio covers. We have a robust e-portfolio Web site (www.pace.edu/page.cfm?doc_id=18384) that features a tutorial for uploading files and a template for developing the e-portfolio cover page.

Faculty in other schools, including the Seidenberg School of Computer Science and the School of Education, are using different versions of the electronic portfolio for more widespread assessment. Many of the English department students are including their resumes as part of their e-portfolios and are submitting them to employers and internship supervisors. A rubric has been developed to evaluate student e-portfolios according to four of the core curriculum learning outcomes—communications, analysis, information literacy, and civic engagement—and faculty can send e-mail feedback to students about these portfolios.

Required Resources

Rubrics, student course portfolios, guidelines for evaluating portfolios, and lunch for all faculty involved in portfolio review days are some of the resources used. Faculty development workshops and trainers are needed for faculty wishing to use electronic portfolio assessment. In the past, incentives such as stipends have been given to faculty who undertake electronic portfolio assessment.

Findings

We ask writing faculty to bring a representative sample of student portfolios to the portfolio review day. Then we identify clear patterns of strength and weakness evident in the samples of student work (see Table 8.1).

Even when quality sources are used throughout the portfolios, we find that students have difficulty correctly citing their references. Writing faculty share good practices for designing assignments, teaching the research process,

TABLE 8.1. INFORMATION LITERACY SKILLS, 2002–2007: SUMMARY OF PAPERS RECEIVING A RATING OF "2" OR HIGHER.

Spring 2002	Fall 2002	Spring 2003	Fall 2003	Spring 2004	Fall 2004	Spring 2005	Fall 2005	Spring 2006	Fall 2006	Spring 2007
72%	72%	85%	81%	82%	79%	91%	61%	71%	60%	77%

addressing grammar issues, and evaluating student writing as a result of sharing portfolios, completing checklists, and discussing results.

The results have been pretty consistent: over 75 percent of students rate 2 or higher, but attention to documentation has improved considerably. Through our survey, we found that 78 percent of students wanted to continue using e-portfolios and 81 percent found the in-house e-portfolio template and online file system easy to use. Seventy-five percent found e-portfolios effective for documenting class and cocurricular activities

Use of Findings

Each semester librarians attend writing faculty workshops to report their results and discuss new ways to improve student research skills. Portfolio review findings have led to the development of handouts and learning activities to teach information literacy, including evaluating and citing information sources. Writing faculty have developed new strategies for improving student research skills, such as the use of annotated bibliographies. An online guidebook of models, handouts, and materials for all stages of the research process is now available to writing faculty. Based on early portfolio reviews, guidelines for student reflective statements changed to include more specific attention to the research process. This year, we have begun a learning outcomes initiative in the Dyson College of Arts and Sciences, with an emphasis on redesigning and assessing the senior capstone experience. We expect to work with a number of departments to incorporate electronic portfolios in the capstone courses. We have worked with faculty across disciplines and schools to find the best approach to implementing and assessing electronic portfolios. This is an ongoing effort.

Impact of Using the Findings

Library instruction sessions have evolved to emphasize evaluation and citing of information sources, and now incorporate more active and hands-on learning activities. Collaboration and partnerships between writing faculty and librarians are strengthened each semester. Because of participation in portfolio review day, writing faculty share assignments, which have become more explicit. Faculty are now able to break down the research paper process into multiple assignments throughout the semester. Writing program administrators are better equipped to maintain the standards of the program; there is more consistency, because many sections are taught by adjuncts, and assignments can be monitored more effectively. Based on the recommendations of our instructional librarians, we meet with certain adjuncts who need additional help in overseeing the research process.

More departments are getting involved with electronic portfolios. Faculty development has begun with the communications studies and political science departments. Collaboration with other schools—Computer Science and School of Education—is under way.

Success Factors

Collaboration between faculty and librarians and consistent participation by 90 percent of writing faculty are evident, as well as a willingness on the part of librarians and faculty to attend faculty development activities where assessment findings are addressed.

Most of those who have used e-portfolios want to continue using them. In the past, we conducted an e-portfolio contest for students from all disciplines and now we hope to institute incentives for faculty development.

Pace faculty and administrators involved in our portfolio and electronic portfolio assessment have published about these initiatives and presented at many conferences, including the American Association of Colleges and Universities, Conference on College Composition and Communication, International Writing across the Curriculum, and Learning Community Conference at Wagner College.

Relevant Institutional Web Sites Pertaining to This Assessment Practice

Core Curriculum:

www.pace.edu/page.cfm?doc_id=5203

E-portfolio:

http://www.pace.edu/page.cfm?doc_id=18384

Information Literacy at Pace:

www.pace.edu/page.cfm?doc_id=20608

Using Surveys to Enhance Student Learning, Teaching, and Program Performance of a Three-Week Winter Session

Sean McKitrick, Thomas Kowalik, Donna Fish, Binghamton University, State University of New York

◆ ◆ ◆

Look for faculty and student responses to online surveys regarding their experiences with distance education courses in a six-week compressed format. Results from these surveys have been used to make targeted changes.

Background and Purpose(s) of Assessment

The importance of assessing winter session distance education course programs (courses taught during the break period between the end of the fall semester and beginning of the winter semester, usually a six-week period) has been a continual focus, not only for the university, but also for regional accreditors and, for us, the New York State Education Department (NYSED). Although the university does not have distance education programs that require accreditation approval (those that include 50 percent or more of instruction at a distance) during the winter session or anywhere else throughout the university, it does offer many distance education courses that need to be assessed, especially those offered in the winter session. Unfortunately, there is still an impression that winter session courses are easier courses or require less student commitment than traditional courses taught during fall or winter semesters. In addition, the university needed to assess NYSED's distance education standard: "The means chosen for assessing student learning are appropriate to the content, learning design, technologies, and characteristics of the learners" (see www.highered.nysed .gov/ocue/ded/outcomes.html). We therefore determined that we had to assess student access, student satisfaction with services provided by the university, perceptions of academic challenge associated with winter session courses, as well as the appropriateness of content, in order to comply with state regulation and accreditation criteria regarding distance education services.

Assessment Method(s) and Year(s) of Implementation

We wanted to determine to what extent distance education winter session courses offered an academic challenge when compared to distance education courses taught during the fall and winter semesters, and to what extent any disparities existed with regard to technical support and services provided to students during the winter session.

The university's Continuing Education and Outreach Division designed two forms of an electronic survey, to be completed by e-mail, in order to assess academic challenge, student services, and technological services for the university's winter session. The first survey asked faculty about any issues that they perceived with regard to their own access to the library, student services, and instructional and technological services, as well as their own impressions about the level to which they feel students were academically challenged, as compared to comparable traditional courses taught in the classroom. The second survey asked students who participated in the winter session to answer the same questions, but to report on their own perceptions with regard to instruction, technical support, advisement, library resources, and other services provided to students. Students enrolled in the winter session were e-mailed the survey and respondents had a chance to win one of four iPods. The procedure and the text of all student contacts were approved by the university Human Subjects Office prior to sending the surveys to students. Seventy-seven percent of winter session faculty responded to the survey, as did 45 percent of winter session students.

Required Resources

The implementation of the survey required the expertise of a consultant who was already on staff at the Division of Continuing Education and Outreach and in the Academic Affairs Assessment Office. The Division of Continuing Education and Outreach also utilized the services of an electronic survey utility program, sponsored primarily by the university's Division of Student Affairs. In addition, the Division of Continuing Education and Outreach provided the funding to purchase the four iPods.

Findings

When asked about their primary reason for attending winter session, the majority of students responded that they were either making up or getting ahead with regard to credit requirements. The vast majority of students indicated that they did not have problems with registration—of the 11 percent who did have problems, they indicated that there was confusion about where to register for courses, or finding out where and how to pay for the courses they registered for. Most (92 percent) stated that they were able to navigate the technical requirements, and 88 percent were satisfied with their overall experience. Fifty percent of students indicated that they lived at their primary residence (off campus) while taking winter session courses, and only 10 percent lived on campus while doing so. Student survey results also indicated that students felt strongly that discussion groups were a very important mechanism for enhancing student satisfaction and learning, both in traditional course formats and in online learning during the winter session.

Sixty percent of faculty felt that students taking winter session courses performed about the same as students taking courses during the fall and winter semesters, whereas 33 percent felt that winter session students performed better. Faculty also felt that teaching a winter session course requires careful syllabus construction and instructional pacing to cover all of the necessary material. Forty percent of faculty felt that instructional and technical services were very good or good, and 27 percent rated them as average, poor, or very poor. Ninety-three percent of faculty felt that students' level of engagement in their courses was adequate and compared well to courses taught during fall and winter semesters.

Overall, the survey data revealed satisfaction with support and advisement services for the winter session and with the level of academic challenge for students taking winter session courses. However, the results also revealed that we must recognize that the compressed format of special sessions, such as the winter session, as well as the challenges of creating community and dialogue within a distance education format, require support for effective pedagogy. Regular assessment of special sessions, we found, provides an opportunity for faculty and student feedback to continually improve our course offerings and delivery of services.

Use of Findings

The finding of greatest concern from both surveys was that some faculty and students were worried about the fast pace of courses. The faculty were especially concerned that the compressed format required careful lesson planning. As a result, winter session 2008 dates were changed to start a few weeks after the end of the fall semester in order to allow students time to travel back home to get settled, based on the survey results showing that a majority of students take courses from home (usually, their parents' home). This action also gave faculty more time to plan their courses, syllabi, and lesson plans.

Because the survey results indicated concerns with lesson plans, the university's Technology Services Division, Technology Training Center, and Office of Curriculum, Instruction, and Assessment are exploring the development of a program to assist faculty with course design, the nuances of teaching distance education classes using various technologies, and assessing distance education courses. Numerous offices are seeking to improve faculty access to Blackboard before the beginning of the winter session to allow course building and to improve and speed up the process of hiring and appointing winter session instructors.

The registrar's staff, technology staff, and admissions staff also discussed how to establish protocols to contact nonmatriculated students electronically with information necessary to access Blackboard and classes at a distance.

Impact of Using the Findings

The findings of the survey have affected the tenor of conversations regarding support services, advisement, and technical support. The findings have brought to our attention a greater need to support faculty, especially those new to winter session, and to expand the time necessary for them to prepare and plan for courses. The results have also enabled winter (and summer) session staff to collaborate more effectively and proactively with registrar, financial aid, and academic staff to ensure that students receive the support they need to succeed.

Success Factors

We have found that two factors in particular are significant. First, it is essential to have staff and administrators who support assessment and the use of assessment findings to improve the program. Second, we have found that it is quite important to use the findings once they are aggregated in useful form. If they are not used, then those who initially participated in the assessment are less motivated the second time around.

Relevant Institutional Web Sites Pertaining to This Assessment Practice

Principles of Good Practice in Distance Education:

www.apa.org/ed/graduate/distance_ed.pdf

Evaluation of Distance Education:

www.learnerassociates.net/debook/evaluate.pdf

New York State Education Department Office of College and University Evaluation Distance Education, Outcomes and Assessment:

www.highered.nysed.gov/ocue/ded/outcomes.html

CHAPTER NINE

PROGRAM REVIEW PROFILES

At many colleges and universities, faculty and administrators have integrated outcomes assessment with an established program review process. This can be an effective strategy for several reasons. First, as faculty are quite familiar with peer review of their research, they value a process of peer review of their academic programs, especially when the review team includes respected colleagues in the discipline from other institutions. The self-study for a program review has long focused on resources (books in the library collection for the department, credentials of faculty, characteristics of entering students) and processes (approaches to curriculum and pedagogy, service to the community, and publications of faculty). When assessment is added as a component to be addressed in the self-study, student learning outcomes receive added emphasis in the review. The fact that program review is understood and accepted by faculty and is even considered a valuable institutional process by many makes it a good vehicle for strengthening outcomes assessment.

Another reason for linking assessment to program review is that it is such a comprehensive process. On many campuses, it is applied not just to academic units but also to student affairs and other academic support and administrative programs and offices. The review incorporates the history of the unit, its current status, and its aspirations for the future. It looks at personnel, achievements, and needs. The addition of outcomes to the traditional look at resources and processes is viewed by many in the academy as a logical step. Preparing the self-study and undergoing a review by internal and/or external peers may be conducted under the auspices of the institution itself or by a disciplinary or regional accreditor.

Finally, program review usually has a follow-up component that is helpful in maintaining the focus on assessment. Reviewers typically submit a written report. Then the faculty and administrators associated with the unit being reviewed have an opportunity to respond to observations, conclusions, and recommendations in that report. Many colleges and universities as well as accrediting bodies subsequently follow up at some point in the future to see what actions have been taken to address the contents of the report. A team of decision-makers in the institution may convene a meeting for this purpose; the next accreditation team to visit the program will expect to discuss responses to the last review team's report. If it is made clear to the reviewers that the written report should contain an appraisal of the assessment of student learning, program review can help to ensure a long-term focus on this topic.

Ronald Terry, Kristie Seawright, and Larry Seawright describe a decade-old comprehensive program review process at Brigham Young University that is being applied to 58 academic units and 65 support units. Disciplinary experts from outside the university and members of an internal team conduct a joint visit to the unit being reviewed but prepare separate reports. According to the authors of this profile, the self-study, the reviewers' reports, and the subsequent planning meeting between the appropriate vice president and unit leaders for the purpose of incorporating review findings in future plans "encourage and establish effective assessment practices and processes across campus."

As a means of complying with assessment expectations set by the Illinois Board of Higher Education, members of the Assessment Advisory Council (AAC) at Illinois State University have integrated review of assessment plans with an established seven-year program review cycle. During the fall semester each year, AAC members use a rubric to rate unit assessment plans as "undeveloped," "developing," "established," or "exemplary." Program chairs are strongly encouraged to improve their assessment plan ratings before the self-study for program review is completed. Mardell A. Wilson and Matthew B. Fuller observe that "for those departments or schools that have cycled through the (program review process) there has been an increased awareness in and development of more systematic, meaningful, and pragmatic assessment practices."

Philip I. Kramer of the College of Saint Benedict and Saint John's University reminds those of us in academic administration that we may be asking our colleagues for too many reports! During a periodic examination of program review policies, a recommendation was made to integrate three previously unconnected reports: annual departmental reports on faculty accomplishments, annual program assessment reports, and program review reports submitted every seven years. Now an online reporting system has been created that Kramer says "keeps the faculty and academic leaders apprised of ongoing efforts to improve student learning through a more immediate and clearer understanding of institutional policies and procedures, the role and success of the faculty, and the achievements of our students."

College Park Scholars is a group of twelve living-learning programs for academically talented first- and second-year students at the University of Maryland. Though each of the twelve programs underwent a traditional program review between 2003 and 2005, Grieg M. Stewart reports that the reviewers' recommendations did not address assessment of learning. This prompted leaders of College Park Scholars to develop a new plan for assessment that requires students to formulate a "big question" and develop a narrative illustrating what they have learned about that question, as well as what they consider to be the value of their Scholars experience. The narratives may be submitted in paper format, in an electronic portfolio, or on the student's own Web site. Program directors review narratives annually; triennially a sample of the narratives is reviewed by the program's Faculty Advisory Council. Observations about the quality of student work, as well as students' comments about the Scholars program, are used to improve the program continuously. In this illustration, the failure of program review to address outcomes assessment satisfactorily provided the impetus for program leaders to develop a new approach to assessment.

Susan D. Johnson, Victor M. H. Borden, and Susan Sciame-Giesecke from Indiana University describe a multicampus review of approaches to "infusing diversity and equity into the higher education curriculum and enhancing the underrepresented populations of students, faculty, and staff." Faculty on each of the eight Indiana University (IU) campuses were asked to develop a self-study using a common template. Then the campuses were paired for purposes of peer review. Faculty in each pair of institutions exchanged self-studies, site visits, and written evaluations following the visits. As a result of the information exchange across all eight campuses, the state of diversity within the IU system was gauged and faculty and staff were more aware of good practice as they undertook the next step: creating campus diversity plans with realistic goals and benchmarks.

Each of the profiles selected for this section illustrates a different focus for program review or for some aspect of the process for conducting it.

Institutions

Doctoral and Research
    Private
        Brigham Young University; Provo, Utah (34,000 students)

Public
> Illinois State University; Normal, Illinois (20,000 students)
> Indiana University Bloomington; Bloomington, Indiana (39,000 students)
> University of Maryland–College Park; College Park, Maryland (36,000 students)

Baccalaureate
> Private
> College of Saint Benedict; St. Joseph, Minnesota, and
> Saint John's University; Collegeville, Minnesota (3,800 students; combined enrollment)

Ongoing Systematic Assessment: One Unit at a Time

Ronald Terry, Kristie Seawright, Larry Seawright, Brigham Young University

◆ ◆ ◆

Look for a well-established, comprehensive program review process for academic and educational support units. Both internal and external reviewers participate in the campus visit, but the two groups prepare separate reports.

Background and Purpose(s) of Assessment

In the spirit of systematic ongoing assessment, Brigham Young University (BYU) initiated Unit Review in 1997 for 58 academic units (degree granting) and in 1999 for 65 educational support units (non-degree granting). As of 2008, 87 academic and 68 educational support unit reviews had been conducted. All units at BYU have now been reviewed at least once, with 50 percent of the academic units reviewed twice.

Reporting to the university president, the Office of the Assistant to the President for Planning and Assessment supervises a University Academic Unit Review Committee (UARC) composed of faculty, and a University Educational Support Review Committee (UESRC) composed of faculty and staff. These two university committees are charged with organizing and conducting unit reviews, that is, unit assessment procedures and evidence, with recent increased emphasis on student outcome measures. These process and outcome metrics also inform the university's annual resource planning and facilitate benchmarking with external entities. These processes also promote unit strategic planning and accountability.

Primary goals of the Unit Review process include:

- Improving teaching, learning, campus services
- Facilitating regular comprehensive self-study by each unit
- Facilitating college/division and university processes of evaluation and strategic planning
- Providing information and documentation for BYU institutional and disciplinary accreditation
- Encouraging use of effective assessment practices and processes relative to university and unit goals and performances as established in BYU's mission, aims, and institutional objectives

The Unit Review process includes the following elements:

- Self-assessment conducted by the unit resulting in a written self-study by unit personnel
- On-site visit by invited external reviewers teamed with university internal reviewers, culminating in written reports by the external reviewers and BYU's internal review team
- Presentation of final report to either the academic vice president or line vice president for the specific educational support unit being reviewed
- Planning meeting between appropriate vice president and unit leaders (chairs, directors, deans, division heads) to incorporate review findings in future institutional planning

Assessment Method(s) and Year(s) of Implementation

This review process consolidates all former university-wide reviews into a single review (for example, undergraduate education, graduate studies, general education, and so on), which requires collaboration with varying entities across campus. Campus feedback over the years has led to iterative changes in this review process and the self-study templates.

Campus units provide their own assessment in written self-study reports. The on-site visit explores and validates the unit's self-study from the perspective of qualified disciplinary experts (external specialists) and campus colleagues (UARC or UESRC members). The on-site visit also offers firsthand observations and data from staff, faculty, and students; promotes a university-wide culture of assessment and continuous improvement; and demonstrates evidence of that culture.

Drawing on the unit self-study and the written reports by external reviewers and internal review colleagues, unit reviews encourage and establish effective assessment practices and processes across campus. This includes promoting connections between the unit review and strategic planning, decision-making, and resource allocation processes at unit, division, and university levels. Involvement of university-level administrators helps ensure meaningful and effective follow-up for each unit review as part of the unit's and university's commitment to continuous improvement and renewal.

Required Resources

Two Office of Planning and Assessment associates supervise academic and education support unit reviews. Both associates are faculty members on half-time multi-year assignment. Internal reviewers on three-year appointment are faculty members (currently 26) assigned to the UARC or faculty and staff members (currently 18) assigned to the UESRC. The respective units nominate a pool of possible external reviewers. One or two of the candidates are selected and scheduled by the associates and invited to come on behalf of the university.

Findings

A meta-analysis was conducted of the 26 unit reviews completed between fall semester 2002 and winter semester 2005. This analysis used only the official, public-domain internal team reports.

For academic unit reviews, each of the cited strengths and challenges, as well as each recommendation, was systematically coded in the NVivo qualitative data handling and analysis software package, using a standard open-coding system. A summary of most commonly cited strengths and challenges, and most commonly cited recommendations, follows.

Strengths. Table 9.1 presents in rank order the five most commonly cited strengths, each of which is found in more than half of the internal reports (62–85 percent).

The quality of undergraduate students at BYU was cited as a strength in 62 percent of the internal reports. Given the university's focus on undergraduate education, this pattern is seen as encouraging.

Challenges. Table 9.2 presents in rank order the five most commonly cited challenges. Though undergraduate education is BYU's principal focus, "selected graduate programs of real consequence" (BYU Mission Statement, November 4, 1981) play a critical role in defining and sustaining campus academic climate. Issues related to the quality, distinctiveness, role, and function of graduate

TABLE 9.1. FIVE MOST COMMONLY CITED STRENGTHS—ACADEMIC UNIT REVIEWS.

Item	Rank	Times Cited/Reviews
Overall quality of faculty	1 (T)	22/26
Faculty research and scholarship	1 (T)	22/26
Faculty collegiality	3	20/26
Quality of teaching	4	18/26
Quality of undergraduate students	5	16/26

TABLE 9.2. FIVE MOST COMMONLY CITED CHALLENGES—ACADEMIC UNIT REVIEWS.

Item	Rank	Times Cited/Reviews
Graduate program issues	1	15/26
Faculty research and scholarship	2	14/26
Faculty diversity	3 (T)	12/26
Faculty recruiting	3 (T)	12/26
Facilities and physical resources	3 (T)	12/26

education and culture at BYU were the most commonly cited challenges in the academic reviews.

For education support units, a similar meta-analysis was conducted of the 25 unit reviews completed between January 2003 and December 2005. A summary of the most commonly cited strengths and challenges, as well as the most commonly cited recommendations, follows.

Strengths. Table 9.3 presents in rank order the five most commonly cited strengths. Each of the five most commonly cited strengths is found in nearly half

TABLE 9.3. FIVE MOST COMMONLY CITED STRENGTHS—EDUCATIONAL SUPPORT UNIT REVIEWS.

Item	Rank	Times Cited/Reviews
Overall quality of the leadership	1	22/25
Overall quality of the staff	2	19/25
Services that are provided	3	15/25
Mentoring of student employees	4	12/25
Working relationships with customers	5	11/25

of the internal reports (44–88 percent). The top three strengths relate directly to overall leadership quality, staff, and the services they provide.

Challenges. Table 9.4 presents in rank order the seven most commonly cited challenges. These include issues related to the facilities, use of technology, adequate funding, and relationships with both internal and external individuals.

Use of Findings

Unit review includes follow-up with unit leaders and line vice presidents regarding review recommendations. Recent academic unit reviews have helped improve use of student learning outcome measures, communication among faculty and staff in several units, and college and department leadership. Recent education support unit reviews have contributed to changes in safety requirements for several campus units, reallocation of FTEs, and improved internal and external unit communication. Where appropriate, unit review recommendations inform the university's annual strategic resource planning. This process includes presentations by college deans and area directors to the president's council to review unit circumstances and resource requests consistent with institutional and unit objectives and university metrics and data elements. The planning effort also includes review of resource implications related to recommendations coming from unit reviews—all part of aligning institutional purpose with practice, planning with assessment, and accountability with stewardship.

Impact of Using the Findings

Unit leader attitudes toward the review process dramatically influence unit review. Most unit leaders view unit review as helping their units improve and fulfill their mission. Seen in this light, unit review becomes positive and

TABLE 9.4. SEVEN MOST COMMONLY CITED CHALLENGES—EDUCATIONAL SUPPORT UNIT REVIEWS.

Item	Rank	Times Cited/Reviews
Adequate facilities (including space)	1	15/25
Use of technology	2 (T)	13/25
External working relationships	2 (T)	13/25
Adequate funding	4	12/25
External communication	5 (T)	8/25
Clear statement of goals and objectives	5 (T)	8/25
Cyclical and heavy workloads	5 (T)	8/25

constructive. For example, the unit leader for Undergraduate Education (UE), responsible for diverse university-wide programs, organized two retreats for full-time employees. One brainstormed and planned the unit self-study; the other invited diverse UE elements to share program information. As employees became more knowledgeable about UE's strengths and challenges, they contributed more to information and problem solving such that UE now uses this process in its own annual strategic resource planning. Indeed, UE areas frequently reference their self-study reviews in their resource planning.

Success Factors

- BYU has developed trust for proven constructive processes at the institutional, college, department, and individual faculty and staff levels for academic and educational support unit review; the process itself furthers a climate of assessment and continuous improvement on campus.
- BYU has informed its strategic resource planning process and other campuswide efforts to demonstrate educational quality and to foster continuous improvement by a now-established process of strategic planning and preparation for institutional and discipline accreditation "one unit at a time."

Relevant Institutional Web Sites Pertaining to This Assessment Practice

Office of Planning and Assessment Home Page:

> http://home.byu.edu/webapp/assess/

Academic Unit Review Web Page:

> http://home.byu.edu/webapp/assess/content/page/academic_review/index.html

Educational Support Unit Review Web Page:

> http://home.byu.edu/webapp/assess/content/page/support_review/educational_review_committee.html

Connecting Assessment to Program Review

Mardell A. Wilson, Matthew B. Fuller, Illinois State University

◆ ◆ ◆

Look for incorporation of assessment of student learning in a state-mandated program review process. Members of an assessment advisory council use a rubric to gauge the effectiveness of assessment plans. Then assessment professionals offer appropriate advice and faculty development experiences for departments that need assistance.

Background and Purpose(s) of Assessment

In February 1999, the Illinois Board of Higher Education (IBHE) adopted *The Illinois Commitment*. This collection of six policy frameworks guides the majority of Illinois college and university dealings with the IBHE and the Illinois state legislature. Goal five of *The Illinois Commitment* states, "Illinois colleges and universities will hold students to even higher expectations for learning and will be accountable for the quality of academic programs and the assessment of learning" (Illinois Board of Higher Education, 2004).

The IBHE has articulated three beliefs that support Illinois colleges and universities as they engage in assessment for the sake of student learning:

- "Assessment should include multiple qualitative and quantitative measures of student learning."
- "Assessment measures should not be reduced to a single instrument such as a standardized test."
- "The IBHE has recognized the need for specific assessment plans and processes to originate locally ... and quality processes should reflect the missions of each institution." (Illinois Board of Higher Education Faculty Advisory Committee, 2003)

By fall 2004, each academic department or school at Illinois State University was required to have on file for annual review an academic assessment plan, containing the critical elements consistent with effective educational practice as well as with goal five of the IBHE *Illinois Commitment*. The Assessment Advisory Council (AAC), populated by faculty and staff representatives drawn from across campus, reviewed the documents during the 2004–05 academic year and recommended an annual process that both satisfied the requirement of the IBHE and facilitated a reasonable and appropriate exercise for chairs, directors, and faculty.

It was determined that the assessment plans would be reviewed annually by the AAC in conjunction with the seven-year program review cycle. The focus of the review was to ensure evidence of an assessment process for each degree program that is systematic and dynamic. Faculty and administrators are guided through the Program Review for Academic Assessment Plan process (PRAAP) by the University Assessment Office (UAO), which provides the necessary support for academic departments and schools to begin the process of engaging in student learning assessment, making use of results, and potentially refining their originally submitted assessment plan(s).

Assessment Method(s) and Year(s) of Implementation

Since the 2005 academic year, members of the Assessment Advisory Council (AAC) have used a rubric in reviewing the assessment plans for degree programs during the fall semester. Assessment plans that are reviewed are from programs that will be completing the self-study process one year prior to their review, with submission of program documents two years from the date of the review. Program review has an institutionally defined seven-year cycle that is recognized by the Illinois Board of Higher Education. The rubric used by AAC members includes basic elements of a quality assessment plan and a range of sophistication. Following the two- or three-person review, the director of the UAO contacts the chair or director to discuss the feedback provided by the AAC peer-review team. The results may necessitate revisions or additions to the public plan. This meeting occurs approximately 18 to 20 months prior to the deadline for submission of program review materials. The UAO provides consultation to the chairs or directors in the development of any suggested modifications. It is recommended that changes be finalized 14 to 16 months before the program review deadline and a final report of "Academic Assessment Plan Status" is submitted to the appropriate dean's office 12 months prior to the department's or school's scheduled program review. The director of the UAO serves as one of three permanent appointments on the Academic Planning Committee, a subcommittee of the Academic Senate that evaluates the program review documents and makes appropriate recommendations. During the review process, the UAO director shares the PRAAP results for each degree program being examined and indicates whether or not the department or school responded to the outcomes of the Process for Review of Academic Assessment Plans as required in the program review guidelines. Once degree programs have cycled through the process, chairs or directors submit an annual update each year outlining which data collection methods were employed, what actions were taken if any, and whether or not any changes to the assessment plan have been made. The annual update is intended to support systematic assessment that will result in evidence-based decision making. At the end of the next seven-year program review cycle, it will be easy to summarize advancements that have been made based on solid assessment practices.

Required Resources

The primary resources required for the Process for Review of Academic Assessment Plans (PRAAP) include the expertise and time of AAC members and UAO staff. AAC members are given two to three months to review assessment plans and provide feedback. Although UAO staff time and operational funds are allocated for preparing the assessment plans for review, collecting feedback from reviewers and organizing the final documents, meeting with department chairs or school directors to offer feedback and support, and maintaining a database of all review practices, the resources are minimal relative to the campuswide benefits.

In addition to directing the PRAAP, the UAO also supports departments through the provision of data from students and alumni. Three primary sources of data used in the program review process include (1) annual alumni survey results, (2) surveys of student engagement, and (3) locally developed surveys. The UAO staff produce reports of alumni survey data for each department, school, and college on campus every year. Undergraduate and graduate alumni are surveyed one, five, and nine years post graduation. In addition, departments and schools are given the option of including department- or school-specific questions in addition to the core alumni survey items. Departments and schools also have access to National Survey of Student Engagement, Beginning College Survey of Student Engagement, and Faculty Survey of Student Engagement data. Finally, UAO supports departments and schools as they develop surveys, focus groups, and review processes that are locally meaningful.

Findings

For program review purposes, as well as continuous annual assessment, department and school leadership often make use of data from one or more of the sources identified to triangulate a range of student experiences or outcomes with multiple, locally meaningful measures. However, the UAO has learned that many departments and schools still perform in the *developing* ranges of the PRAAP rubric with respect to program assessment. In the 2007 academic year approximately 70 percent (n = 35) of the degree plans being reviewed had learning outcomes that AAC reviewers estimated as *developing*, 25 percent were *established*, and only 5 percent were *exemplary*. In terms of feedback from stakeholders, analysis of results and use of results, degree program assessment plans were primarily designated as *undeveloped* or *developing*. The institution-level results maintain a general trend that is consistent with the prior two years of PRAAP data. Although the results of the review indicate a large margin for improvement, the process has certainly increased conversations campuswide regarding what constitutes a meaningful and manageable assessment process for degree programs. The initiation of the annual update has also helped to sustain momentum among departments and schools regarding assessment and its relationship to the program review process on the Illinois State University campus.

Use of Findings

The University Assessment Office has used results from the PRAAP to offer specific, solutions-based programs and consultations for faculty and administration. In addition, Barbara Walvoord, noted assessment practitioner and consultant, provided a half-day workshop at ISU for faculty and staff titled "Assessment Clear and Simple," which was tailored to the PRAAP. Ninety-two percent of participants at the well-attended event (n = 52) found the workshop to be an effective use of their time and felt that it resulted in an improved assessment plan. In addition to these efforts, the UAO has begun creating a self-paced online training module to support departments and schools in their efforts to develop improved assessment plans that more clearly meet the parameters of PRAAP. Finally, the Academic Planning Committee clearly understands PRAAP and has a better set of guidelines from which to formulate recommendations regarding assessment as it relates to the program review process.

Impact of Use of Findings

For those departments and schools that have cycled through the Process for Review of Academic Assessment Plans (PRAAP) there has been an increased awareness in and development of more systematic, meaningful, and pragmatic assessment practices. UAO staff and members of the Assessment Advisory Council have also generally concurred that PRAAP and the follow-up annual updates have resulted in improved evidence of student learning and the subsequent identification of strengths and weaknesses on which to base curricular decisions. In general, engagement in the PRAAP has provided faculty and staff with a clear and direct vision for quality in assessment at ISU, and provided for increased engagement in evidence-based program improvement.

Success Factors

Primary factors in the success of the PRAAP include:

- A philosophy of assessment as a systematic, valuable process supports the individuality of departments and schools at ISU while seeking evidence-based improvements. This philosophy is illustrated in the working documents of the Illinois Board of Higher Education and the Office of the Provost at Illinois State University.

- Realizations that "more assessment" can oftentimes be less meaningful than "planned assessment."
- A focus on the use of results to formulate solutions and services that support instruction and learning in higher education.
- Staff commitment and administrative support for managing difficult situations and logistical issues.

Relevant Institutional Web Sites Pertaining to This Assessment Practice

Program Review and Assessment Web Site—Office of the Provost:

www.provost.ilstu.edu/resources/assessment.shtml

University Assessment Program Assessment Web Site:

www.assessment.ilstu.edu/program/

Integrating Assessment, Program Review, and Disciplinary Reports

Philip I. Kramer, College of Saint Benedict and Saint John's University

◆ ◆ ◆

Look for a faculty review that produced a new online reporting system which integrates three previously unconnected reports: annual assessment reports, annual department reports, and program review reports submitted every seven years.

Background and Purpose(s) of Assessment

Historically, at the College of Saint Benedict and Saint John's University (CSBSJU) little consideration was given to the possible interrelatedness of three important academic reports. Annual academic departmental and program assessment reports were submitted at the end of the calendar year to the Office of Academic Assessment and the faculty governance committee responsible for overseeing academic assessment and program review activities on campus. Annual departmental reports, highlighting faculty accomplishments in teaching, scholarship, and service, were submitted in the summer to the academic dean. Program review reports were only submitted to the Office of the Provost either when a department or program completed its self-study (once every seven years) or when the provost requested a formal midcycle program review update. While most campus stakeholders realized the content of all three reports overlapped, there had never been an attempt to link the reports coherently. During a periodic review of our program review policy and in conjunction with work on our institutional reaccreditation self-study, academic administrators and members of the aforementioned faculty governance committee considered integrating all three reports. Integrating the reports was appealing for a number of reasons, including the possibility of further elucidating the similar purposes of the reports; increasing coherence to improve academic excellence; and reducing the workload of faculty members, department chairs, and academic administrators.

Assessment Method(s) and Year(s) of Implementation

In late 2007, the faculty committee, at the request of and in concert with the provost, the academic dean, and the director of academic assessment, began an extensive evaluation of the assessment, departmental, and program review purposes, policies, and report systems. Members of the committee contacted individual faculty members, including department chairs and department assessment coordinators, for their input. The evaluation concluded in the spring of 2008.

Required Resources

No resources were required beyond faculty time to conceive the plan.

Findings

The faculty committee drew the following conclusions:

First, there was significant overlap between the three reports. This overlap was confusing and frustrating to those compiling data and writing reports. Indeed the same assessment coordinators or department chairs frequently would write all three reports for their respective departments. Second, an overwhelming number of the coordinators and chairs complained that large portions of the three reports were redundant. Third, many coordinators and chairs believed they were being asked to gather data and write reports that were never used by the administration to improve teaching and learning or to make strategic fiscal or academic policy goals or plans. According to coordinators and chairs the reports were essentially "busywork" and a waste of time.

Use of Findings

Because of the committee's conclusions, the policies and practices of campuswide peer review and reporting were completely reconfigured. To simplify matters, committee members decided to create a tailored, homegrown online reporting system. This new online system was initially implemented in spring 2008.

Impact of Using the Findings

The results of the committee's work have clarified the expectations of academic administrators for the faculty, integrated the function and format of three previously disparate reports, eliminated the redundant workload of key internal quality assurance and quality improvement stakeholders, and helped all institutional stakeholders appreciate the importance of collegial and collaborative conversations between members of the faculty and academic administrators.

Success Factors

The effort to integrate formerly disparate reports has resulted in a new online system that keeps the faculty and academic leaders apprised of ongoing efforts to improve student learning through a more immediate and clearer understanding of institutional policies and procedures, the role and success of the faculty, and the achievement of our students.

Relevant Institutional Web Sites Pertaining to This Assessment Practice

> www.csbsju.edu/
> www.csbsju.edu/cac/webassessmentgrid.aspx

A New Plan for College Park Scholars Assessment

Greig M. Stewart, University of Maryland

◆ ◆ ◆

Look for an assessment plan for twelve living-learning programs for academically talented first- and second-year students. This plan was designed to focus on the assessment of student learning after reviews of the twelve programs had failed to do so.

Background and Purpose(s) of Assessment

Between 2003 and 2005, College Park Scholars, a class of twelve living-learning programs for academically talented first- and second-year students, underwent individual program assessments. Drawing from Angelo's principles of assessment (1995), the Scholars Faculty Advisory Council (SFAC) adopted an assessment model similar to those implemented by professional accreditation associations. Descriptive analyses (Lalli et al., 1993)—or self-studies—were compiled by each of the twelve faculty directors, using criteria established by the SFAC. An "outside" panel of two to four faculty examined the self-study and conducted supplemental research, such as focus groups of alumni, instructors, and resident life staff. Special attention was devoted to surveying and interviewing current students. Reports were generated, then reviewed by the program directors. Final reports were synthesized and presented to the SFAC at a meeting to which all faculty directors were invited to discuss findings and recommendations. Those assessments resulted in the following list of ten best practices (see Table 9.5).

Though the Scholars' program assessments proved valuable, they did not directly address Angelo's primary theme of assessment—improving student learning. In 2005, a university-wide learning outcomes initiative, prompted by a forthcoming accreditation review, opened the door for Scholars to take that next assessment step. Scholars faculty directors were eager to participate in this campus initiative as it would provide an opportunity to demonstrate how the Scholars program goes beyond delivering positive retention rates, graduation rates, student satisfaction, and grade point averages; and it would provide an opportunity to design and implement a cycle of assessment and renewal of its scholastic endeavors.

Faculty recognized that to understand the value of their Scholars experience fully, students needed to formulate a "Scholars narrative" (see Ibarra & Lineback, 2005). Using Bain's concept (2004) of the "big question," each faculty director articulated a big question for students to focus on in their narratives.

TABLE 9.5. BEST PRACTICES—COLLEGE PARK SCHOLARS.

Program Content and Culture	Organization and Systems
Intentional community building	Strong Web presence
Qualitatively unique and strong academic rigor	Advisory councils
Active learning	Full-time staff presence
Reflective learning	Leadership stability and effective transition
Diversity	Support and clarity of responsibilities

Assessment Method(s) and Year(s) of Implementation

College Park Scholars finalized its learning outcomes assessment plan in 2005 and initiated it in the 2006–07 academic year. The plan follows (see Table 9.6):

TABLE 9.6. COLLEGE PARK SCHOLARS ASSESSMENT PLAN.

Student Learning Outcomes	Assessment Measures and Criteria	Assessment Schedule
(list the three to five most important)	(describe one or more measures for each outcome and criteria for success)	(initial year, and subsequent cycle)
1. (Knowing) Students will articulate what they learned in Scholars, as prompted by their Scholars program "big question."	**Measure**: Part one of the students' Scholars narrative that addresses the specific program's "big question." **Criteria**: Narratives will be reviewed based on an evaluation rubric developed by program director.	**Annually**: Program directors will review narratives and evaluations of all citation-reviewed students. Program directors will write a two-page analysis that will (a) determine whether the class achieved the learning outcomes set; (b) identify major contributions to that learning within the curriculum and cocurriculum; and (c) make recommendations for curricular and cocurricular modifications to the program, as well as for appropriate adjustments to future portfolio inclusions. These reports will be submitted to the Scholars executive director and the program's sponsoring dean. **Triennially**: Each program's faculty advisory council will review a sample of narratives from each of the past three years, together with the program director's analysis. Any additional observations and recommendations will be reported in writing to the program director and copied to the Scholars executive director and the program's sponsoring dean.

TABLE 9.6. *(continued)*

Student Learning Outcomes	Assessment Measures and Criteria	Assessment Schedule
2. (Understanding) Students will be able to articulate the value of their Scholars experience, as it relates to their junior and senior years, even beyond their undergraduate experience.	**Measure**: Part two of the students' Scholars narrative. **Criteria**: Narratives will be reviewed based on an evaluation rubric developed by program director.	
3. (Doing) Students will be able to provide concrete evidence of their Scholars learning.	**Measure**: One or more of the following portfolio artifacts: (a) résumé; (b) academic showcase poster; (c) PowerPoint presentation (or video of verbal presentation); (d) video or other artifact documenting artistic or other learning outcomes; (e) internship supervisor evaluation; (f) other (as mutually agreed to by the student and his or her program director). **Criteria**: Each program will set criteria for acceptable portfolio artifacts and provide feedback to each student, based on those criteria.	

Required Resources

Faculty in each of the twelve programs implement their big-question assessments differently. Some use portfolios, such as the *KEEP Toolkit*, produced by the Carnegie Foundation for the Advancement of Teaching (March 2004). Others require students to develop their own Web sites. Still others ask students to submit paper copies of their big-question responses. Some program faculty review the students' responses themselves. Others hire junior or senior graduates from their programs to assist with the reviews.

Findings

Having only completed one academic year cycle, findings are preliminary. An example follows:

The Advocates for Children program piloted a portfolio project. Using a rubric that addressed academic excellence, active contribution to the learning community, advocating for children, a personal road map, and composition, portfolios were rated on a scale of 0 to 3 in each of the areas. An overall average was computed. Based on a pilot of 20 portfolios, most students scored in the 2 to 3 range.

Use of Findings

Though the example provided above represents a labor- and time-intensive process, it provides a unique opportunity for faculty directors to assess how students make meaning of their Scholars experience. From these findings, directors can validate or modify their curricular, pedagogical, and community development efforts.

Impact of Using the Findings

Costs for higher education are outpacing inflation and gains in financial aid, resulting in limited resources for enhancement and enrichment programs. More and more, resource decision makers are demanding data to inform their programmatic investments. With respect to College Park Scholars, current and future students deserve a quality program, requiring faculty to have effective tools to measure outcomes. Through program and learning outcomes assessments, together with participation in national studies such as the Boyer Partnership Assessment Project (Nesheim et al., 2007) and the National Study of Living-Learning Programs (www.livelearnstudy.net, 2007), Scholars faculty and staff leaders systematically gather, analyze, and interpret data to inform program enhancement and renewal.

Success Factors

Golde and Pribbenow (2000) lead us to believe that the success of this initiative is predicated on faculty buy-in to the process. Their buy-in results from:

a. the unique "big questions" developed by the program directors
b. the flexibility to allow faculty to revise their big questions, should they not be measuring what they are purported to measure
c. faculty analysis of student responses to their big questions and consequent recommendations
d. review of faculty analyses by their deans, the dean for undergraduate studies, and the College Park Scholars executive director

Relevant Institutional Web Sites Pertaining to This Assessment Practice

College Park Scholars Assessment:

www.scholars.umd.edu/execdir/assessment.cfm

Assessing Diversity and Equity at a Multicampus Institution

Susan D. Johnson, Victor M. H. Borden, Susan Sciame-Giesecke, Indiana University Bloomington

◆ ◆ ◆

Look for a systemwide review of diversity and equity efforts on eight campuses. The campuses were paired for purposes of exchanging self-studies, site visits, and peer critique. A systemwide conference encouraged the exchange of ideas for planning, implementation, and improvement of campus diversity.

Background and Purpose(s) of Assessment

In 2000, Indiana University (IU) began a multicampus exploration of infusing diversity and equity into the higher education curriculum and enhancing the underrepresented populations of students, faculty, and staff. Since then, via a two-day Enhancing Minority Attainment (EMA) conference, faculty and staff have worked to develop and test a range of strategies to enhance teaching and learning and to transform the existing curriculum.

Assessment Method(s) and Year(s) of Implementation

In 2006, as a mechanism to assess the current status of diversity and equity efforts, each of the eight IU campuses received a diversity portfolio template and partnered with another campus to engage in an exchange of self-study, site visits, and peer feedback. The peer-review process was intended to give campuses with similar characteristics an opportunity to have open conversations, share effective practices, and provide feedback that would facilitate future action at the campus and system levels. The purpose of the self-study and review was to enable campus teams to converse about the diversity work on partner campuses leading to a judgment about campus- and systemwide strengths and challenges.

The Campus Diversity Portfolio Self-Study and Review Process entailed four steps:

1. Assembling the Campus Diversity Portfolio for review by the partner campus
2. Planning, scheduling, and conducting site visits between partner campuses
3. Providing the partner campus with constructive, evaluative feedback
4. Developing a reflective response on the process and partner campus feedback for a later EMA presentation

The Campus Diversity Portfolio Self-Study and Review focused on the following four dimensions of diversity and equity:

1. *Institutional leadership and commitment*—the clarity of expectations, investment of human and fiscal resources, and accountability as demonstrated through the words and actions of campus leadership at all levels
2. *Curricular and cocurricular transformation*—the extent to which principles of multiculturalism, pluralism, equity, and diversity are currently incorporated into the curriculum and cocurriculum, as well as ongoing efforts to further infuse them into same
3. *Campus climate*—the degree to which the events, messages, symbols, and values of the campus make it a welcoming and inclusive environment for all students, faculty, staff, and members of the broader community
4. *Representational diversity*—the degree to which the campus attracts, retains, and develops students, faculty, and staff of color, commensurate with the campus mission and service region

From this exercise, campuses were asked to develop a diversity plan with institutionally integrated, campus-specific approaches toward advancing the broad context of diversity (race, ethnicity, gender, age, social class, religion, sexual orientation, disability) and equity, with the intention of doubling the enrollments of underrepresented minority students in the coming years.

Required Resources

The assessment process required each campus to create a team consisting of approximately eight to ten members, including senior administrators, staff, and faculty, and to assign a team leader to manage the overall process, for example, by scheduling partner site visits or assembling the diversity portfolio. In addition, an EMA leadership team served as an additional resource to campuses seeking information and assistance during the peer-review process.

Findings

The Indiana University Diversity Portfolio Project enabled faculty and staff from across eight campuses to reflect on and evaluate their diversity efforts over a five-year period, review their campus goals, engage a variety of constituents from their campuses in the review process, particularly senior leadership, and move beyond traditional approaches to evaluation, using a self-study and peer-review process to evaluate diversity efforts. The information gleaned from the project provided campus representatives with a better sense of the current state of diversity across the university as well as direction toward a more comprehensive and intentional plan to gauge institutional progress.

Emergent themes included:

- *Curricular transformation*: All campuses reported having a general education diversity requirement with some of that work being continued in a student's major, yet no campus had an existing process to assess whether curricular transformation has an impact on student learning.
- *Cultural transformation*: Campuses were asked to reexamine the effect of current diversity and equity efforts on the campus climate and the extent to which faculty, staff, and administrators were held accountable for policy and practices related to diversity. Campus leaders expressed the need to improve accountability and prioritize and revamp less-effective diversity programs through the use of both quantitative and qualitative assessment tools. By doing so, campuses could determine whether existing initiatives were in sync with the institutional mission and strategic plan.

- *Recruitment and retention*: Several campuses shared information about recruitment programs and collaborative efforts with Historically Black Colleges and Universities (HBCUs) in an attempt to increase the number of underrepresented minority faculty, students, and staff at IU. EMA participants also encouraged greater use of the existing pool of individuals on the IU campuses and in surrounding communities.
- *Leadership and commitment*: Although participants on most campuses praised their administrations for incorporating diversity into strategic plans and review processes, it was less clear how well distributed responsibility and accountability were throughout the university.

Use of Findings

Findings were used to create campus diversity plans with a series of action items based on the four university-wide EMA constructs. The plans were intended to complement current and future activities campuses might undertake and to provide benchmarks for progress.

Impact of Using the Findings

By December 2007, each campus had submitted a diversity plan to the vice president for Diversity, Equity, and Multiculturalism for review. Currently, the EMA leadership team is working to assist in monitoring campus progress on the specific goals, measures, and targets outlined in the plans.

Success Factors

The EMA process was aligned with an organizational learning framework as it was self-imposed rather than mandated by external sources, took into consideration both internal and external influences, and concentrated on *diversity progress* rather than merely *diversity activity*. Campuses were asked to be candid in their self-evaluations and reminded to value substance over quantity; by doing so, the process generated useful information and allowed for future collaboration between partner campuses.

Relevant Institutional Web Sites Pertaining to This Assessment Practice

For background documents, full report, and other pertinent resources, see:

www.indiana.edu/~dema/confl13007.shtml

CHAPTER TEN

FIRST-YEAR EXPERIENCES, CIVIC ENGAGEMENT OPPORTUNITIES, AND INTERNATIONAL LEARNING EXPERIENCES PROFILES

The Association of American Colleges and Universities (AACU, 2007) has identified the types of college learning that are crucial for students to be prepared for the "new global century." In order to enhance personal and social responsibility, AACU asserts that the following capabilities should be developed: civic knowledge and engagement (both local and global), intercultural knowledge and competence, and ethical reasoning and action. Increasingly, faculty and student affairs professionals are transforming the curriculum by creating initiatives designed to foster greater student engagement and address the learning needs identified by AACU. These initiatives include building first-year experiences, developing civic and community opportunities, and designing international learning experiences.

Often faculty and staff develop new formal courses and other types of interventions—all designed to help college students develop the necessary skills and knowledge that will enable them to adjust to college and to be more successful in achieving their academic goals and fulfilling their personal lives (Schrader & Brown, 2008). Some first-year experiences are referred to as programs because they tend to be campuswide initiatives that include explicit and measurable goals, "program design, instructional and developmental strategies, and assessment" (Troxel & Cutright, 2008, p. viii). In a similar manner, other learning experiences can be designed by the faculty to cultivate undergraduates' civic engagement as well as to enhance their global awareness and international learning.

Formal assessments can provide meaningful information about student engagement and achievement of key learning outcomes. Kuh, Kinzie, Buckley, Bridges, and Hayek (2007, p. 45) have found that "student engagement in educationally purposeful activities is positively related to both grades and persistence." In addition, Pascarella and Terenzini (2005, pp. 307–308) report that student participation in community service activities has "substantial positive effects on a wide array of civic values and attitudes." The profiles presented in this chapter reveal that assessments can be designed to determine the levels of student engagement in college as well as changes in their attitudes or values.

At St. Mary's College in Maryland, results from NSSE and locally developed instruments revealed that students considered general education the weakest part of the curriculum and that they saw little connection between general education courses and the courses required for their majors. Students also reported that longer research papers assigned in general education courses were less useful than shorter and more frequent writing activities. Ben Click et al. describe how new first-year seminars were designed to address shortcomings that students reported. Faculty implemented these seminars, which reinforced and emphasized four key general education outcomes, including critical thinking, information literacy, and written and oral communication. In addition, new resources were provided to hire liberal arts associates who work with the writing center director to design useful course materials for instructors. Professional development also was instrumental in helping faculty identify assignments and develop their course syllabi. As these first-year seminars continue to unfold over time, the faculty will be implementing a portfolio system to gain further evidence about student learning and development.

At North Carolina State University, faculty and staff have designed a program of intensive major and career exploration for undecided first-year students. According to Kim Outing and Karen Hauschild, undergraduates participate in a year-long required First Year College (FYC) course as well as the First Year College residential learning community, and receive individual advising. The overall goal for these initiatives is to help students enhance their personal and academic success by encouraging them to use campus resources and engage with a diverse community. The FYC Village Advisory Council developed its own Student Experiences Survey (SES) to gauge students' involvement in college. Key results indicated that students living in the FYC residential learning community were more likely to engage in discussions with other students about diversity, religion, and current events than non-Village students. In addition, they were significantly more likely to use supplemental instruction. Based on these assessment results, the council decided to continue and expand programs such as walk-in tutoring and a leadership retreat for students. In addition, the FYC has integrated several diversity-related experiences for students.

Student engagement continues to be an important goal at Tufts University. Faculty members in the Tisch College of Citizenship and Public Service seek to advance student development through a variety of experiences designed to help students grow as leaders, provide quality work in communities, and make progress toward both academic and personal goals. A formal evaluation was conducted to assess the impact of activities and programs at Tufts that influence civic development through locally developed approaches, including surveys and interviews. Rachel Jin Bee Tan, Dawn Geronimo Terkla, and Stephanie Topping describe seven different measures of civic engagement, including: civic attitudes, community attitudes, political attitudes, participation in community service or civic activities, participation in political activities, participation in Tufts-sponsored activities, and the degree to which students understand and value the dynamics of difference. An added strength of this assessment is that the longitudinal design can determine changes in civic engagement to be tracked during the students' four years of college enrollment and two years post-graduation.

Another strategy for engaging students is to help them gain international learning experiences and to become more globally competent. Jill Wisniewski and Christa Olson at the American Council on Education created a consortium of six colleges and universities that worked together to improve student international learning. An e-portfolio system was designed so that student work developed in courses, programs, and other education experiences could be documented and then assessed by trained raters using detailed rubrics with criteria associated for each of the desired student international learning outcomes. This approach enabled faculty to glean concrete evidence of the positive impact of study abroad on enhancing students' knowledge, skills, and attitudes.

Although many colleges and universities use the National Survey of Student Engagement, it is challenging for individual faculty members to understand students' perceptions about levels of engagement within individual specific courses. Robert A. Smallwood and Judith Ouimet received permission to develop and pilot a classroom version of the National Survey of Student Engagement that is known as the Classroom Survey of Student Engagement (CLASSE). Students are asked questions about how frequently they engage in various educational practices and activities within a specific course. Instructors are asked how important each of the educational practices is for their students to be successful in the particular course. The benefit of these classroom-level surveys is that faculty members can gain useful information about students' perceptions that can supplement traditional end-of-course evaluations.

Across all of these profiles, faculty and staff worked on the common goal of promoting greater student engagement during their enrollment in college. Assessment findings document the effects that various curriculum transformations—including the first year of college, civic opportunities, and international learning experiences—have on enhancing student development.

Institutions

Doctoral and Research
Private
Tufts University; Medford, Massachusetts (8,500 students)
Public
North Carolina State University; Raleigh, North Carolina (31,000 students)

Baccalaureate
Public
St. Mary's College of Maryland; St. Mary's City, Maryland (1,900 students)

Organization

American Council on Education and Consortium of Colleges and Universities

Using Assessment Data to Improve Student Engagement and Develop Coherent Core Curriculum Learning Outcomes

Ben Click, Linda Coughlin, Brian O'Sullivan, Lois Stover, Elizabeth Nutt Williams, St. Mary's College of Maryland

◆ ◆ ◆

Look for use of assessment findings to provide a rationale for creating first-year seminars. These seminars were intentionally designed to reinforce and emphasize key general education outcomes, including information literacy, critical thinking, and oral and written communication.

Background and Purpose(s) of Assessment

In spring 2001, a steering committee was formed to review St. Mary's College's assessment practices and existing assessment data. The committee discovered that the college collects a substantial amount of data that assesses student learning as well as academic programs. The work of this committee led to the creation of a standing assessment committee and a General Education Curriculum (GEC) Review Committee. Over the next five years these committees gathered and generated information about student learning and engagement and discovered a common issue among faculty and students alike: the college lacked a shared and purposeful first-year experience, and the general education curriculum in general was perceived as lacking in cohesion and failing to spark intellectual engagement. To produce a variety of integrated curricular and extracurricular options to address this common issue, the college adopted a process that allowed individuals, groups of individuals, or departments to offer proposals for a GEC revision. Various proposals were presented to the faculty in spring 2006. The college adopted a core liberal arts curriculum and a Core Curriculum Implementation Committee was established. This core curriculum model is unique in the state of Maryland, and the new core curriculum represents the most extensive curriculum revision that St. Mary's College has undertaken since adopting the Western Heritage curriculum funded by the National Endowment for the Humanities in the mid-1980s.

The Core Curriculum Implementation Committee was composed of five subcommittees representing five areas in the new core. All subcommittees stressed the need for coherence between the mission of the college, the mission of the core curriculum, the definitions of the skills, the measurable learning outcomes of the skills (assessment), and sustained faculty support and development. This coherence was vital for the new core curriculum to develop and succeed in meaningful ways. Committee members produced a comprehensive report in June 2007, and the committee was disbanded. A new dean of the core curriculum and First Year Experience, hired in July 2007, established a standing committee (the Core Curriculum Committee) to finalize implementation details for launching the core curriculum.

Assessment Method(s) and Year(s) of Implementation

The college faculty examined several existing assessment methods supplied by the Office of Institutional Research to inform its reexamination of the general education curriculum. The main methods included alumni surveys from one, five, and ten years out, the senior exit survey and results, and the results of the 2004 National Survey of Student Engagement (NSSE).

In disparate form these various methods, coupled with numerous faculty and student surveys from 2001 to 2006, provided clear direction for the Core Curriculum Implementation Committee. Each of the five subcommittees developed a detailed list of student learning outcomes. In the fall of 2007 four pilot first-year seminars were assessed according to general learning outcomes under the new core's four fundamental skills (critical thinking, information literacy, written expression, and oral expression). All pilots incorporated selected outcomes from the detailed list; some of the outcomes were not applicable to a first-year seminar.

Required Resources

The Core Curriculum Implementation Committee identified several resources that would ensure a strong start to fully implementing first-year seminars. The elimination of the universal writing requirement and a new core curriculum with more student choice provided the flexibility to staff and fund 30 first-year seminar (FYS) sections by fall 2008. In addition, the college was able to hire a dean of the core curriculum and First Year Experience and two full-time liberal arts associates. The assistant director of the college's Writing Center was given a full-time staff position (previously this position was on a yearly contract). During the spring and summer of 2007, the five professors teaching in the pilot first-year seminars attended numerous training workshops on the four skills. Throughout the spring of 2008, the dean organized several training workshops for the 28 instructors who would be teaching the FYS in the fall semester. The five professors from the pilot FYSs participated and led some of these training workshops.

Finding

Assessment data taken from the 2000 survey of graduating seniors, summaries of five and ten years out surveys of the graduating class of 1990, and the 2004 National Survey of Student Engagement (NSSE) revealed that students felt that the college prepared them to succeed upon graduation and that the best learning experiences occurred in their major areas of study and in their senior capstone projects. In both NSSE and the five- and ten-year internal surveys, students overwhelmingly pointed to the weakest part of their education as courses taken to fulfill the general education curriculum. Students reported that they saw little connection between GEC courses and courses in their majors. And the 2004 NSSE results showed below average engagement with writing among first-year students. Students also commented that longer, research-oriented writing assigned in courses in the general education curriculum was less engaging and useful than shorter and more frequent writing.

The dean of the core also administered an assessment survey to students in the four pilot FYSs. The highest rating for an academic aspect of the course was about engagement. Results showed that students felt they improved in critical thinking and information skills more than in oral expression and writing skills.

The results also suggested that students felt they could have been challenged even more in the FYS experience.

Use of Findings

The Core Curriculum Committee and the dean of the core reviewed the findings of the FYS surveys. The dean will begin working with two new liberal arts associates, the librarians, and the director of the Writing Center to continue to provide support for the faculty teaching in FYS in the fall of 2008. Although student engagement improved, students did not feel as if their writing skill improved as much as it could have. Addressing this perception, along with the obvious instructor anxiety that writing will now be taught by all faculty members, the liberal arts associates and Writing Center director will begin designing ways to alleviate that anxiety and provide useful and usable material for instructors. In addition to numerous workshop opportunities, faculty can also access a growing list of online resources, such as sample syllabi and assignments designed to employ the four fundamental skills.

Impact of Using the Findings

The Core Curriculum Committee, the dean of the core, and the director of institutional research will continue to revise their instruments for assessing various aspects of the FYS and its relevance to the core curriculum as well as to the various majors. As each major begins to develop its own plan for making its learning outcomes connected to the numerous outcomes within the core, it will also make further use of the assessment results. All departments have already analyzed their majors to determine where the "holes" might be in terms of developing students' facility in the four liberal arts skills; their next step will be to engage in curricular revision to fill these gaps and thus ensure that students hone their skills to the point needed to complete of their senior projects. Implementation of a portfolio system will be piloted this fall within the first-year seminars, as will a pre-post assessment of writing, critical thinking, and information literacy. Proficiency in oral communication will be assessed and as students progress through their careers at the college, their development in this skill across time will continue to be assessed.

Success Factors

The entire process for developing a coherent core curriculum with measurable learning outcomes has succeeded initially because the college has made use of its existing assessment data, developed new assessment surveys, and involved the entire faculty in being responsible for addressing how learning outcomes will be achieved within each major as well as within the core. In addition, a new online teacher evaluation system will be used to administer assessment surveys that will augment methods developed and approved by individual majors.

Relevant Institutional Web Sites Pertaining to This Assessment Practice

At this time, the core curriculum information Web site (listed below) provides an overview of the curriculum, the catalog copy associated with the curriculum, and information about the First Year Experience. The core curriculum was fully launched in Fall 2008, and the Web site is updated regularly to reflect changes in each year (such as with the First Year Seminar topics and the composition of the Core Curriculum Committee).

www.smcm.edu/firstyear/index.html

Using Assessment to Enhance Student Resource Use, Engagement, and Connections in the First Year

Kim Outing, Karen Hauschild, North Carolina State University

◆ ◆ ◆

Look for use of assessment results from the First Year College and other related experiences to enhance students' awareness of their own values and worldviews by increasing their openness to different points of view.

Background and Purpose(s) of Assessments

The First Year College (FYC) at North Carolina State University is a program of intensive major and career exploration for undecided first-year students. In addition to the goal of transitioning to a major, the program seeks to encourage students to enhance their academic and personal success by utilizing campus resources, by seeking out opportunities for involvement, and by engaging with a diverse community. These goals are addressed through individual advising, the year-long required FYC course, and the First Year College Village residential learning community.

Some assessment of student knowledge of resources and awareness of diversity issues had been done through the FYC course evaluation and the assessment of student writings on diversity. Also, the university Sophomore Survey and the

FYC Graduating Senior Survey offered some insight into the level of involvement and resource use of former FYC students. Overall, however, the picture was incomplete. The program lacked data on levels of involvement for first-year students, specific resource use, engagement beyond the classroom on topics such as diversity, and level of faculty interaction outside the classroom. These data would inform all aspects of the program, but particularly programs in the FYC Village. The FYC Village supports the student learning outcomes through additional peer resources (FYC resident mentors) employed in both the residence halls and as TAs in the FYC course, through special programming, through opportunities to interact with a cross-section of university faculty in informal gatherings, and through opportunities to participate in and build community as part of special linked courses. How these efforts influence student learning, involvement, and engagement would be key in the planning for Village resources and programs.

Assessment Method(s) and Year(s) of Implementation

In fall 2005 a subgroup of the FYC Village Advisory Council with representatives from University Housing and the FYC assessment team began discussions on how to assess involvement, engagement, and use of resources for FYC students, both Village and non-Village residents. The FYC Student Experiences Survey (SES) was piloted at the end of the spring 2006 semester and has been administered during an FYC class period at the end of each semester since then. The initial three administrations used a paper-and-pencil instrument, and in fall 2007 the move was made to an online instrument in order to simplify administration and data collection and to reduce the time requirement. The online instrument takes approximately ten minutes to complete. The survey asks about the types of organizations students are involved in, the amount of time spent in certain types of activities, how frequently they use specific campus resources, and about interactions with faculty, peers, and resident mentors.

Required Resources

Data analysis is performed by a staff member in the Office of Assessment in the Division of Undergraduate Academic Programs, where FYC is housed. FYC staff and the Village Advisory Council discuss the results and recommend next steps. The online instrument is updated and monitored by an FYC staff member.

Findings

For the spring 2006 SES, FYC Village residents reported spending significantly more hours in residence hall programs and socializing with friends in the residence hall as compared to students not living in the Village. Village residents used walk-in tutoring offered in FYC classroom space in the residence hall more frequently than non-Village students, even though the resource was available to all FYC students. Village students also reported statistically higher use of supplemental instruction (offered through the University Tutorial Center for subjects such as calculus and chemistry). Village students were more likely to engage in discussions with other students about diversity, religion or spirituality, and current events. Non-Village students were more likely to have joined a fraternity or sorority by the end of the first year (17 percent, compared to 8 percent of Villagers). FYC and Housing staff also learned about the types of activities and organizations in which students were most likely to be involved. There was a near-significant tendency for Village students to have more informal discussions with faculty outside class.

Use of Findings

Based on the higher levels of engagement for Village students, the Village Advisory Council felt good about the community and programming. The council decided to continue and expand such programs as walk-in tutoring, cultural outings, informal faculty dinners and talks, and a leadership retreat for students who were not already involved in organizations and leadership activities. The positive SES data, along with evidence of higher academic achievement for students in the Village and a recommendation from the Boyer Partnership Assessment Project (completed in 2005), helped to build support for requiring all incoming FYC students living on campus to live in the FYC Village (up to this point the Village option had been "strongly recommended"). FYC also discussed ways to connect those students living off campus. Some of these ideas included more emphasis on involvement during individual advising sessions and classroom instruction, as well as offering more programs outside the Village. The FYC curriculum had just been modified to include a student portfolio as part of the program capstone requirement (based on other assessment findings) and a component of this new assignment was to be a section on "personal accomplishments." Including this in the curriculum would be another way to encourage students to consider leadership, campus activities, and service activities in order to enhance their personal and academic development.

Much of FYC's diversity effort is directed toward helping students become more aware of their own values and worldview as well as more open to understanding different points of view and experiences. Dinner discussions hosted by the FYC resident mentors, with speakers on such topics as religion and affirmative action, were popular draws in the Village and possibly contributed to discussions among peers on such issues. Attending cultural, educational, or service events outside the classroom is a required component of the FYC course. These events may be sponsored by FYC (as in the resident mentor dinner discussions) or by campus or community organizations. FYC staff compile a calendar of the events, known as "Forums," which may be used to satisfy this cocurricular requirement. Students must attend three Forums per semester, and must submit a brief reflective summary of each Forum to complete the requirement. A written reflective summary is part of the forum assignment. The assessment team recommended that the resident mentors plan at least one diversity-related dinner discussion topic each semester. The assessment team also decided to include a qualitative analysis of student reports of their diversity-related forum experiences to assess how these experiences contribute to the diversity learning outcomes.

Finally, FYC decided to incorporate focus groups into future assessment plans in order to gather more in-depth data on involvement, engagement, programs, and resources such as the resident mentors. The SES data provided a starting point for developing these focus-group topics and questions.

Impact of Using the Findings

Since its pilot administration in spring 2006, the SES has helped FYC staff understand how students are engaged outside class. The survey has generated much fruitful discussion around programming in the Village, student-faculty connections, and the role of the FYC resident mentors.

Students will attend programs offered in or near the Village residence. Funding has increased for such programs due to their demonstrated success. Service and leadership initiatives and more opportunities for informal student-faculty interactions are among the program enhancements undertaken since 2005–06.

Starting with the 2006–07 entering class, FYC students living on campus are now required to live in the FYC Village. The FYC mission statement was revised to reflect the role of the Village in delivering student learning outcomes.

The first focus groups were conducted in spring 2008 with the goal of gathering more information on how students view and use the resident mentor resource, what they think of the types of programs presented by FYC, and what types of programs they would like to see in the future.

Along with a continued emphasis on diversity programming in the Village, FYC is implementing a diversity certificate starting fall 2008, earned through attending a certain number of diversity-related forums and submitting a reflection on what was learned.

Success Factors

One crucial factor in the success of this assessment practice has been the ongoing collaboration between FYC and University Housing in developing and refining the survey as well as in implementing the decisions that have evolved as a result of the assessment. Decisions that included expanding programming could not go forward without the financial and staffing support of FYC's housing partners. FYC instructors have supported the classroom administration of the SES; and the brevity of the instrument and the ability to complete it online are a plus.

A second crucial factor in the success of this assessment has been the close, synergistic working relationship of the FYC assessment group, composed of members of key program committees—diversity, curriculum, advising, and the Village Advisory Council.

Relevant Institutional Web Sites Pertaining to This Assessment Practice

First Year College Assessment (links to plans and reports):

www.ncsu.edu/fyc/assessment/

First Year College Village:

www.ncsu.edu/fyc/village/

A Mixed-Method, Longitudinal Approach to Assessing Civic Learning Outcomes

Rachel Jin Bee Tan, Dawn Geronimo Terkla, Stephanie Topping, Tufts University

◆ ◆ ◆

Look for multiple methods used over time to gauge students' development of civic engagement, changes in attitudes, and the degree to which students understand and value the dynamics of difference.

Background and Purpose(s) of Assessment

Recently there has been an increased push for colleges and universities to prepare students for lives of active citizenship (Boyer, 1996; Checkoway, 2001;

Harkavy, 2006). The Tisch College of Citizenship and Public Service at Tufts University aims to embed civic knowledge, skills, and values into a liberal arts education through the Tisch College (TC) Scholars program. The TC Scholars program engages students, referred to as Scholars, in active citizenship projects while providing skills-based training and required academic course work. The program enables Scholars to grow as leaders, provide quality work in communities, and make progress toward both academic and developmental goals. Scholars serve as catalysts for change among their peers, engaging individual students and student groups in their project work. To understand whether and how Tisch College helps students become committed public citizens, stakeholders designed an evaluation examining the links among students' experiences at Tufts and the development of their civic and political activities and attitudes. This outcomes evaluation assesses both the impact of the TC Scholars program and identifies activities at Tufts that influence students' civic development.

Assessment Method(s) and Year(s) of Implementation

The longitudinal, mixed-method study began in 2003 and tracks four cohorts of undergraduates over their four years at Tufts University and two years post-graduation, which will result in nine years of data by the end of the study in 2012. Each cohort consists of approximately 65 students divided into research groups based on their levels of community service during high school: TC Scholars, highly involved participants, and minimally involved participants; the highly and minimally involved participants serve as controls for the Scholars groups. The evaluation design includes examination of student transcripts and financial status, civic engagement data collected from the entire student body on numerous surveys (orientation, sophomore, exiting, alumni), and an annual survey instrument administered only to the study participants—the TC Civic and Political Activities and Attitudes Survey (CPAAS)—along with supplemental interviews. The CPAAS provides a broad overview of student involvement each year in civic and political activities and of student attitudes toward local and global issues affecting themselves and the community. During their sophomore year, students are randomly selected within the three groups to participate in interviews to provide context for how and why they became civically and politically involved. These same students are interviewed again in their senior year to examine how their attitudes, activities, and sources of influence have changed. Through item response theory (IRT) analyses of CPAAS responses and coding of interview data, comparisons among groups and across time provide important information about the role of the TC Scholars program in promoting student civic engagement.

Required Resources

Tisch College and the Office of Institutional Research and Evaluation (OIR&E) at Tufts University work in conjunction to evaluate the TC Scholars program. The program's staff assistant at Tisch College helps to keep track of study participants while they are enrolled at Tufts and after graduation, a process that is facilitated by monetary rewards for participants. For every annual CPAAS completed, participants receive a $20 Barnes & Noble gift card, which is also the reward for participation in an interview (sophomore or senior). If, and only if, students complete all six annual administrations of the CPAAS, they receive a single $150 gift card for Barnes & Noble.

The design of the longitudinal, mixed-methods study, including the instrumentation, was the result of collaboration between the associate provost of institutional research, assessment, and evaluation, the assistant director of OIR&E, the director and associate dean of Tisch College, and an evaluation consultant at Tisch College. A research analyst at OIR&E is responsible for the bulk of the data collection — conducting and coding interviews, preparing the CPAAS for administration, collecting survey responses, and conducting item response analyses on the survey results. Results are presented to various stakeholders and to the larger research community by all team members from Tisch College and OIR&E.

Findings

IRT analyses of the four years of available data indicate that the CPAAS measures seven different aspects of civic engagement: civic attitudes (attitudes toward issues affecting the global community), community attitudes (attitudes toward issues affecting the local community), political attitudes, participation in community service or civic activities, participation in political activities, participation in Tufts-sponsored activities, and the degree to which students understand and value the dynamics of difference (for example, that individuals, regardless of where they begin life, do or do not all have the same opportunities). Comparisons among the TC Scholars, highly involved participants, and minimally involved participants indicate that there are significant differences between groups on all seven scales, with the TC Scholars scoring the highest, and minimally involved participants scoring the lowest. It also appears that among groups there are larger differences in civic and political attitudes than there are in actual participation in civic, political, and Tufts-sponsored activities — indicating that how students feel about issues does not translate directly into the actions they take to address these issues.

Coded interview data from the sophomore and senior interviews indicate the importance of pre-Tufts attitudes and activities in influencing civic engagement in college. The interviews conducted so far reveal that students chose to participate in particular activities and organizations at Tufts because they became interested in them while in high school, and students chose to participate in new activities because they related to interests they had before coming to college. However, TC Scholars did mention that participation in the Tufts University Education for Active Citizenship course affected their level of civic engagement. Though one cannot be certain that this course does enhance civic engagement because only TC Scholars have the opportunity to take the course, this finding warrants further investigation in future interviews.

Use of Findings

The expansion intent of this mixed-method study (Greene, Caracelli, & Graham, 1989) allows for an investigation into students' civic engagement as a program outcome measured by the survey, and also the process of how the TC Scholars program influences student civic engagement as gauged by the interviews. The longitudinal design allows for changes in civic engagement to be tracked over participants' four years of college and two years post-graduation, and permits results from each year to be used in a formative manner to improve the study design and program elements and to provide summative information to stakeholders.

Thus far, changes to the CPAAS, in the form of added and revised questions, have been made based on analyses of results from previous administrations. Such changes improve the ability to measure students' civic engagement using the CPAAS. After conducting the first interviews, questions were revised to improve the interview process in an effort to maximize information gathered from participants during a minimal amount of time. Changes to instrumentation based on each year's findings help to improve data collection efforts, which provide crucial information to Tisch College about which aspects of the TC Scholars program are effective and which need improvement. Improved instrumentation also helps provide the most accurate information about student civic engagement to the Tufts community and to the larger research community through dissemination of findings at conferences.

Impact of Using the Findings

The CPAAS is a unique instrument and a powerful tool for assessing civic engagement that, with minor tailoring, can be used at any higher education institution. In conjunction with supplemental interviews and other methods used to expand the breadth of data collected, levels of active citizenship can be measured along with the success of program elements designed to promote civic engagement. Using a standardized instrument such as the CPAAS will enable comparisons of student civic engagement levels to be made across various colleges and universities. Such a data collection effort would have a large impact on the civic education field, as it would supply summary information on how successful higher education institutions are at promoting civic engagement, and also provide diagnostic information on how to improve programs so as to prepare students for lives of active citizenship. In addition, cross-institution cooperation will serve to further improve the assessment process as new ideas are shared across diverse settings.

Success Factors

Several factors contributed to the success of this assessment effort. In maintaining participants in a longitudinal study, incentives were crucial, as were individuals to keep track of changed contact information; without the longitudinal component the study would not have been as powerful or informative. Both internal and external evaluators were necessary to help design a feasible evaluation plan and facilitate data collection, whereas the expert knowledge of civic education supplied from Tisch College was requisite for designing relevant and valid instrumentation. Extensive research into preexisting survey tools and the civic education literature provided vital information on what research had already been conducted and how to make a contribution to the field through this study.

Relevant Institutional Web Sites Pertaining to This Assessment Practice

Information on the TC Scholars program can be found at:

http://activecitizen.tufts.edu/?pid=19

Assessing International Learning Using a Student Survey and E-Portfolio Approach

Jill Wisniewski, Christa Olson, American Council on Education and Consortium of Colleges and Universities

◆ ◆ ◆

Look for a collaborative effort among colleges and universities to assess international learning among undergraduates and identify necessary improvements in curriculum and related programs.

Background and Purpose(s) of Assessment

Many institutions have articulated the goal of producing "globally competent graduates," but few have clearly defined what this means or how they will know when they have achieved this goal. Success is most often measured in terms of the level of activity, or the inputs, into international learning. Applying student learning outcomes and assessment to internationalization is a relatively recent practice. The institutional benefits of engaging in this work include: demonstrating student international learning, improving curriculum and programs, and bringing greater coherence and clearer direction to an institution's internationalization efforts.

With these objectives in mind, the American Council on Education engaged in a three-year project funded by the Fund for the Improvement of Postsecondary Education (FIPSE) to advance the assessment of international learning with the long-term goal of improving student international learning at U.S. higher education institutions. The project group comprised six institutions with a commitment to internationalization: Dickinson College, Kalamazoo College, Kapi'olani Community College, Michigan State University, Portland State University, and Palo Alto College.

Assessment Method(s) and Year(s) of Implementation

The student survey and e-portfolio approach, developed and piloted by the six project institutions from 2004 to 2007, involves student completion of an e-portfolio focused on international learning and of a survey called the Student Portfolio and Information Form (SPIF).

The e-portfolio is an electronic collection of student work developed in the context of courses, programs, and other educational experiences. Electronic portfolios are evaluated by trained raters using a detailed rubric with criteria for each of the desired student international learning outcomes. When used in combination with a rubric and rating process, the e-portfolio is a flexible, direct, and qualitative method of assessment.

The SPIF asks questions about the e-portfolio artifacts, student demographics, and international learning experiences. The answers to SPIF questions and portfolio ratings can be compared in the aggregate to see how specific international learning experiences or demographic factors affect the attainment of international learning outcomes. Some of the tools created to support the e-portfolio–SPIF approach include:

- a ranking document for prioritizing international learning outcomes
- a rubric that uses specific criteria and a rating scale to evaluate the e-portfolios

- anchor portfolios that demonstrate examples of low-, medium-, and high-scoring portfolios
- a rater training handbook that helps standardize the rater training process

The strengths of the SPIF and the e-portfolio approach—its flexibility in addressing multiple complex outcomes as well as its capacity to assemble significant student data for analysis—also presents some challenges for implementation. These challenges include:

- obtaining leadership support and commitment of sufficient resources
- appropriately familiarizing students and faculty with the approach and providing incentives for them to create and rate portfolios
- presenting the data collected through the assessment process in usable format and making good use of these data

Faculty at each institution selected a different set of students for their sample. Many institutions had difficulty in collecting data from their intended sample; the institution that had the most success collected almost 100 full data sets (consisting of data from a completed e-portfolio and SPIF).

Required Resources

The *minimum* infrastructure and funding required for the SPIF and the e-portfolio approach includes:

- an assessment coordinator (respected by faculty and able to conduct analysis)
- faculty or staff willing to invite students to complete a SPIF–e-portfolio
- funding for an e-portfolio platform, survey, and statistical applications for data collection, analysis, and retrieval
- rater teams (at least three faculty, staff, or graduate students and on-call language experts)
- space and support for orientation and training sessions

In addition to the above, the *ideal* infrastructure and funding for the SPIF and the e-portfolio approach includes:

- a technical assistant for data collection and retrieval (with assigned or released time)
- a survey specialist to review SPIF, conduct data analysis, and present findings
- multiple teams of faculty raters (offered stipends per portfolio rated)

- modern language raters (on or off campus for all likely languages to be included)
- student assistants (offered stipends to assist students with portfolio creation)
- professional development workshops for faculty and staff orientation to the approach, for rater training, and for discussions about how to interpret results

Findings

Several of the institutions in the ACE-FIPSE project gleaned important information through the implementation of the SPIF and the e-portfolio approach. Faculty at one institution, Portland State University, compiled sufficient comparative data to engage colleagues in meaningful discussions about the findings. These preliminary findings include:

- a general upward trend in the attainment of international learning outcomes as students move through the general education program, with the portfolios of students in the upper-division courses scoring higher on most outcomes than those produced by students enrolled at the first-year level
- clear evidence of the positive impact that study abroad has on all three types of learning outcomes (knowledge, attitudes, and skills)
- heritage learners (U.S. residents whose first language is not English) scored lower in the attitudinal ratings than both monolingual and international students
- international studies majors generally outperformed nonmajors in knowledge and skills learning outcomes, but international studies majors generally scored *lower* on the attitudes outcomes than other students
- monolingual English students who reported numerous trips abroad of short duration unconnected with study actually scored lower than the norm on most of the attitudes outcomes

Use of Findings

Faculty at the project institutions are using their findings to start conversations with key constituents including students, faculty, administrators, and assessment personnel. These conversations address both specific findings such as those listed above and on some campuses address the larger goal of internationalizing the curriculum and cocurriculum. Faculty at Kapi'olani Community College are using the tools to assess their Asian Studies and International Studies Departments' general education certificates and are leveraging their findings to create connections and articulation between their international studies programs and the programs at the four-year institutions in their system.

On an individual level, many faculty engaged in the rater training experience have realized opportunities to revise courses they teach to more effectively assist students in achieving the specified learning outcomes. This assignment alignment between stated international learning outcomes and specific course assignments is a direct result of their participation in the assessment process.

Impact of Using the Findings

It is too early to evaluate the full impact of the findings at the project institutions.

However, many project institutions have made plans to continue the assessment of international learning. The project institutions that are continuing to use the SPIF and the e-portfolio approach are revisiting the tools to create buy-in with their faculty and administration and make them most appropriate to their own institutional context. And as discussed above, many individual faculty members have undertaken improvements in their own courses to align more effectively with international learning outcomes.

Ultimately, the international learning outcomes and assessment process is intended to assist faculty and staff in making data-informed improvements in their international learning experiences. If after an additional round of assessment, the hypotheses that were developed initially are confirmed, then there is sound evidence to suggest appropriate revision of programs and courses.

Success Factors

Several important lessons were learned through the successes and mistakes made in the pilot stages of the ACE-FIPSE project. Many of these lessons are important in ensuring success in future rounds of assessment.

An international learning outcomes and assessment process should be endorsed by campus leadership, situated in the broader institutional context for assessment, and supported by key stakeholders. Before plunging into the implementation of the SPIF and the e-portfolio approach, it is advisable to evaluate the institutional context for assessment, form a team, and develop an assessment plan.

The assessment process flows most smoothly when a holistic assessment package is developed that includes explicit instructions for students, and how faculty can guide students with the submission of their data. If multiple assessment tools are used, such as the SPIF and the e-portfolio, they should be coordinated at the beginning.

The assessment process should be embedded in a course or required for program completion; otherwise students will not be motivated to participate. In addition, the assessment process should be a meaningful learning experience for students; they should be provided with authentic feedback on their performance. The institution that had the greatest success in attracting students to participate in the ACE-FIPSE project was able to build in the e-portfolio as a course requirement.

Each institution is likely to develop different international learning outcomes. Because it is important that the assessment instruments align with the outcomes, preexisting rubrics like those created for the ACE-FIPSE project should be adapted rather than adopted by institutions interested in using them. As the project institutions move forward with assessment, some institutions are revising the learning outcomes and rubrics to align better with their institutional mission.

Relevant Institutional Web Sites Pertaining to This Assessment Practice

The ACE Web site has extensive information about preparing for assessment, the e-portfolio and the SPIF approach, and other methods for assessing international learning. It is available at:

www.acenet.edu/Content/NavigationMenu/ProgramsServices/cii/res/assess/index.htm

CLASSE: Measuring Student Engagement at the Classroom Level

Robert A. Smallwood, Judith Ouimet, University of Alabama

◆ ◆ ◆

Look for the Classroom Survey of Student Engagement that provides individual instructors with useful information about how their own students perceive their levels of involvement within specific courses.

Background and Purpose(s) of Assessment

It is not uncommon for institutions participating in the administration of the National Survey of Student Engagement (NSSE) to subsequently disaggregate institutional results into smaller units of analysis, usually at the college or academic department levels, to localize variation in levels of student engagement, and target corresponding improvement initiatives. When doing so, it is often the case that deans, academic department chairs, or faculty will suggest that less-desirable engagement findings are the result of shortcomings in other colleges, other departments within the college, or other courses within the department rather than their own. "These less-engaged students are not *my* students" is a proclamation often advanced.

Until now, an approach to assessing variation in student engagement at the classroom level has not been available. In 2005, the authors received permission to develop and pilot-test a classroom adaptation of the NSSE that came to be called the CLASSE (Classroom Survey of Student Engagement). In addition to asking students in a particular class how frequently they engaged in various educational practices and activities in that class, the instructor of the course is asked how important each of the educational practices is for the students to be successful in that class. Copies of the CLASSE plus more detailed information can be found at http://assessment.ua.edu/CLASSE/Overview.htm.

Assessment Method(s) and Year(s) of Implementation

The CLASSE is being pilot-tested not only at the University of Alabama but at other institutions across the country. Most often it is administered toward the end of the semester (eleventh to thirteenth week) after students have had ample opportunity to engage. Its usefulness as a summative assessment tool is being explored as a supplement to the end-of-course student evaluation process.

Required Resources

A very simple five-step process is in place to seek permission to participate in the CLASSE pilot study (see http://assessment.ua.edu/CLASSE/Participation .htm). At this time there are no charges associated with an institution's participation. The institution assumes responsibility for administering the instruments, summarizing the results, and analyzing the findings.

Findings

The following three generalizations have emerged from preliminary results obtained from the pilot administrations of the CLASSE:

a. There is a positive correlation between the importance or value that faculty place on a given engagement practice and the frequency with which students report engaging in that practice. For example, in a given class, if faculty think it is important for students to collaborate on the completion of assignments outside class, there tend to be above-average levels of collaborative activity among the students enrolled in that class. If faculty think it is not so important for students to put together ideas or concepts from different courses when completing assignments, the frequency of occurrence of such activity by enrolled students tends to be below average.

b. In every course in which we have administered the CLASSE, there have been a small number of engagement practices that the instructor believes to be important, but which the students report not doing, or doing so at below-average frequency levels. Sometimes faculty have readily identified the causal factors responsible for these "disconnects," but more often than not, the disconnects have prompted the faculty member to think about and ponder what he or she is doing or not doing in the class that might be responsible. In addition to such introspections, the instructors often begin to talk about related best practices with their colleagues, and even with campus experts who are knowledgeable about effective instructional strategies.

c. Not only do CLASSE results vary between faculty but also within faculty. That is, the educational practices that faculty perceive to be especially important in one of their classes may be quite different from those they perceive to be important in another class they teach. This result is consistent with verbal reports received when student engagement results at the department and college levels have been discussed. Faculty frequently remark, "How much collaborative activity I encourage depends on the course," or "I have students give oral presentations in my upper-level class but not my lower-level class," or "I think class discussion is very important in my upper-level capstone course, but only somewhat important in my lower-level introductory course."

Use of Findings

Many faculty have reservations about the usefulness of typical end-of-course student feedback measures. They often question the appropriateness of comparing their results with those of their colleagues. Too often, they argue, the nature of the teaching-learning experience is so different from one course to another or from one instructor to another that comparative assessments are empirically unsound. With this backdrop in place, the CLASSE results, and the way in which they are derived, represent a desirable supplement, if not an alternative, to the more traditional approach to assessing instructional performance. The "opportunities for improvement" are not derived by contrasting results between and among faculty. The opportunities for improvement that surface from CLASSE results relate to those educational practices that faculty have indicated are particularly important in a designated class, but which students report not doing very often.

The inappropriateness of between-faculty comparisons is further accentuated by the fact that no two CLASSEs are necessarily the same. The faculty participant has the opportunity to add up to eight unique survey items that draw attention to practices or activities that he or she believes are important to success in the designated class.

CLASSE results, particularly when represented using the "quadrant analysis" approach to presenting results (see http://assessment.ua.edu/CLASSE/Results.htm), shift the focus of the assessment effort to improvement rather than accountability, and that emphasis is not only less threatening but much more constructive in facilitating student learning. "Working on strategies to be more successful in my class sounds like a worthwhile objective," said one of our faculty participants.

Impact of Using the Findings

Among the major points that have surfaced in follow-up focus groups with faculty participants using the CLASSE are:

- Faculty liked the positive, upbeat, noncompetitive approach to identifying areas for potential improvements.
- Faculty thought CLASSE would be an excellent replacement for or supplement to traditional end-of-course evaluations.
- Department chairs like the faculty development implications. It would be much easier to initiate conversations about improvements in teaching effectiveness when prompted by CLASSE results than from end-of-course student evaluations.
- Institutional leadership like the link between NSSE results and CLASSE results to prompt improvements in teaching and learning.
- Participating faculty would recommend participation to their colleagues and would themselves participate again.
- Faculty praised the shift in emphasis from instructional accountability to improvement in instructional practice.

Success Factors

The favorable reaction to CLASSE by participating faculty most often is linked to their dissatisfaction with existing measures of instructional effectiveness and the inappropriate comparisons that are made using the results from more traditional end-of-course student evaluations. Their CLASSE results do not compare and contrast their students' perceptions with those of their colleagues but rather provide this information for themselves—it is focused on how they are doing relative to what they think is important in their class rather than how their students' perceptions of a course contrast with those of other instructors.

Because there is such widespread awareness of the importance of student engagement in the learning process, there is a predisposition by faculty to consider exploring new measurement approaches to assess variation in levels of engagement and educational practice. The CLASSE results also lend themselves to serving as a means for prioritizing actions to improve. The faculty participant can examine his or her results and decide to work on one or two particularly important practices that are not occurring as frequently as would be needed for students to be maximally successful in the selected course. The diagnosis and opportunity for improvement is unique to the instructor and the respective class.

Relevant Institutional Web Sites Pertaining to This Assessment Practice

An overview of Classroom Survey of Student Engagement, including the survey instrument and the results:

http://assessment.ua.edu/CLASSE/Overview.htm

CHAPTER ELEVEN

STUDENT AFFAIRS PROFILES

Student affairs professionals have long recognized the need to move from counting the number of students who attend an event to collecting meaningful information about how effectively the goals of the event or program are being met. An intermediate step for many has been the assessment of student satisfaction. Now student affairs professionals are being explicit about developing program goals for promoting student development and using direct measures of student learning. Institutions represented in this section include three that have long-standing assessment programs employing well-respected measures and one where major changes have been made recently to the division assessment process.

Vickii Castillon and Lori Varlotta report that the vice president for student affairs at California State University, Sacramento initiated a new planning and assessment process that was intentionally centered on student learning. To begin the process, unit directors were asked to align department missions with the division's and university's mission statements, then to identify planning goals. Next, directors defined student learning outcomes. This process called for the units to use data beyond student satisfaction, and several measurement instruments were developed, including questionnaires, report-writing exercises, and direct observations. Changes in the delivery of programs, instrument design, and training for staff are among the improvements being undertaken by student affairs staff based on results obtained from these measures.

Student affairs professionals at the Pennsylvania State University have a long history of measuring student satisfaction and learning through the Penn State Pulse program—a series of telephone and Web-based surveys in which staff ask students about such topics as health and wellness issues, in- and out-of-class experiences, and community service. According to Andrea Dowhower and Philip Burlingame, Career Services employees surveyed random samples of students in 1998, 2002, 2003, and 2007 and have used the data to make changes to services, educate students about the services provided, and support requests for additional resources.

Joan Harms tells us that University of Hawaii at Manoa student affairs staff have employed locally developed satisfaction and usage surveys for several years in conjunction with the College Student Experiences Questionnaire (CSEQ). As a result, the health center staff have been able to use reports of high student satisfaction with the center's services to strengthen grant proposals and their accreditation self-study. To assist directors and to provide staff development, the student affairs assessment office staff develop a survey report that includes the results and guidance on how to read and interpret both aggregated and subgroup data. Student affairs staff, campuswide committees, and other campus stakeholders are continually informed of assessment findings and responsive actions through additional reports.

Yet another well-established assessment process is one developed at Truman State University, where students who have violated the alcohol policy are required as a part of the sanctions to write a reflective essay that is rated by students on the student conduct board. David A. Hoffman reports that students write in their essays about the sanction assignment experience and their learning outcomes. Student raters look for evidence that suggests whether or not the sanction experiences were positive, the information received was useful, and the student writers learned from the experiences. Student raters also seek evidence that writers are using reflective judgment as they complete the essays; that is, are they taking responsibility for their actions, and will they alter their actions based on their experience?

Institutions

Doctoral and Research
    Public
        The Pennsylvania State University; University Park, Pennsylvania (43,000 students)
        University of Hawaii at Manoa; Honolulu, Hawaii (19,000 students)

Master's
> Public
>> California State University, Sacramento; Sacramento, California (28,000 students)
>> Truman State University; Kirksville, Missouri (6,000 students)

Creating and Implementing a Comprehensive Student Affairs Assessment Program

Vickii Castillon, Lori Varlotta, California State University, Sacramento

◆ ◆ ◆

Look for the focus on student learning and attention to the appropriateness of assessment instruments as well as the transparence of assessment results that encourage collaboration among units.

Background and Purpose(s) of Your Assessment

Sacramento State's Student Affairs planning and assessment process was revitalized approximately two years ago when staff in the division made a genuine and explicit agreement to become a data-driven organization. With a new vice president at the helm, a Western Association of Schools and Colleges (WASC) reaccreditation process unfolding, and enrollment and budget challenges at hand, there was no better time to start replacing anecdotes and assumptions with data and evidence.

Throughout the late 1990s and early 2000s the planning and assessment programs within Sacramento State's Division of Student Affairs, for those departments that had initiated them, focused primarily on student satisfaction and program improvement. Realizing that the former foci were a bit askew from the student learning emphasis that was taking center stage nationally, the vice president for student affairs (VPSA) redirected the planning and assessment processes. Along with external consultants from the University of Central Florida and campus colleagues from the Office of Institutional Research, the VPSA showed directors how they could move from a focus on student satisfaction and program improvement to a focus based on student learning outcomes. Two years later, changes are afoot. Though no final destination has been reached, significant progress has been made.

Assessment Method(s) and Year(s) of Implementation

Within the first year of implementation (2005–06), each student affairs director was charged with explicitly aligning his or her departmental mission with those of the division and the university. Next, directors were asked to identify the two or three overarching planning goals that would broadly frame their work during the upcoming years. Finally, directors were expected to articulate at least one significant student learning outcome (in 2007–08 they identified at least two) that they would like students who participate in their programs or utilize their services to achieve. It took approximately six months for directors to write all of the objectives in ways that were SMART—**S**pecific, **M**easurable, **A**ggressive yet attainable, **R**esults-oriented, and **T**imely.

Directors were charged during the second year of implementation (2006–07) with developing instruments and collecting data to measure the learning that occurred. Working with the vice president for student affairs or staff within the Office of Institutional Research, the directors designed or borrowed instrument(s) that could measure the student learning outcomes associated with their respective programs or services. As expected, in this initial data collection stage, some instruments and assessment approaches proved to be more reliable than others. Despite the necessary revisions to several pre- and posttests, observed competence exercises, and emerging rubrics, the leadership team and the directors celebrated the fact that within a two-year time frame, each department had laid the foundation for evidence-based decision making and outcome-based assessment.

A variety of measurement tools have been developed, including pre-post tests, multiple choice tests, essay rubrics, and observed skill assessments. Unit staff are now beginning the process of analyzing results to determine if they have met their criteria for success. For example, the University Union is using a direct observation skills assessment to determine if student assistants have developed the knowledge and skills required for their jobs. Associated Students Incorporated is comparing student perceptions and advisor ratings of critical leadership skills. Housing and Residential Life is testing resident advisors' skills in incident report writing by providing mock scenarios and assessing reports that resident advisors develop. The Office of Student Conduct is analyzing the learning that has occurred through essays students are required to write as a condition to reestablish good standing. Many other units such as the Student Athlete Resource Center (SARC), Office of Financial Aid, Student Health Center, Women's Resource Center (WRC), Multicultural Center, Academic Advising

Center, and the Career Center are developing tests to assess the knowledge and skills that students have attained in their programs about critical policies, procedures, and resources. Student Activities and the Psychological Counseling Services are joining national survey initiatives to address their student learning outcomes. The aim is to ensure that each and every unit within Student Affairs can, through their assessments, isolate and eliminate any programmatic weakness that affects expectations for student learning in student affairs.

Required Resources

The resources required to support the initiative have included a part-time assessment coordinator who assists directors in the development and implementation of their assessments, as well as external consultants who provide insight into successful assessment strategies. In addition, both Academic Affairs and Student Affairs invested in StudentVoice technology to support units in the implementation and analysis of their assessments through Web- and PDA-based methodologies.

Findings

Preliminary findings have been gathered by many units and others will not have results available until the end of the 2007–08 academic year. Some found that the criteria set for a particular SLO were met. These include the Career Center, SARC, University Union, Housing and Residential Life, Women's Resource Center and Student Conduct. Others found that students have not achieved the criteria set for a particular SLO. These units include Academic Advising and Student Activities. The assessment process also revealed some methodological problems. These include ineffective instruments or questions (Women's Resource Center and Health Center), low attendance or participation affecting assessment (Student Activities and Psychological Counseling Services), and logistical difficulties with the use of personal digital assistants (PDAs) at events with large attendance (for example, a collaborative effort between Union and Women's Resource Center).

Use of Findings

Units are using their assessment results to reconsider program delivery, measurement tools, and assessment processes. For example, Housing and Residential Life will deepen the "content" area of their incident report–writing training as a result of their findings. The Academic Advising Center is reviewing areas requiring greater emphasis in the orientation program and providing additional training to peer mentors to emphasize critical policy areas for students requiring understanding of college preparatory programs. Women's Resource Center staff are reformatting activities to allow for more discussion in film presentations because scores were higher when more time was given. The Women's Resource Center has also achieved great success with enhanced PowerPoint presentations. Student Activities and Psychological Counseling Services are developing strategies to increase participation in specific programs that they plan to assess.

Units are reevaluating their assessment tools as a result of their preliminary findings. For example, the Women's Resource Center is redesigning test items that they found were vague to students. The Student Health Center is redesigning their instruments to ensure that they incorporate direct measures of student learning. The University Union is developing a rubric to focus and streamline the assessment process and address key core skills that interns are expected to achieve.

Finally, several units (SARC, Associated Students, the Career Center and Student Conduct) are now preparing to readminister their instruments to collect and assess longitudinal data.

Impact of Using the Findings

As a result of this initiative the division as a whole will be able to use assessment findings to inform the impending educational effectiveness phase of the Western Association of Schools and Colleges (WASC) accreditation process as well as the emerging and revitalized university strategic planning process. This capability greatly enhances the division's ability to showcase its impact on student learning.

Furthermore, as directors become more confident in the process and their skills, assessment strategies have matured to explore more deeply direct measures of student learning. In the first year of implementation units relied heavily on student perceptions of learning (for example, indirect learning outcomes) that occurred in student affairs programs. In the most recent cycle, units have developed direct measures that prompt students to demonstrate—via role-play, pre-post tests, portfolios, and essays—the knowledge that they have acquired or the skills they have learned. The recent focus on direct learning outcomes is allowing units to make targeted and strategic changes to improve and enhance student learning.

Because the assessment process has been public from the very start (all assessment reports, instructional tools, and findings have been posted on the division's Web site), units are aware of and share their experiences and findings.

As a result they are beginning to perceive areas of overlap and to develop and implement collaborative assessment efforts. For example, the Women's Resource Center and the University Union collaborated with each other and faculty on an assessment of student learning that occurred during the fall 2007 Martin Luther King Jr. event. In the coming year, we expect to see a dramatic increase in collaborative efforts that more efficiently and effectively assess the student learning that occurs within student affairs and between academic and student affairs.

Success Factors

Leadership within the division is critical to the success and institutionalization of the student learning outcomes assessment initiative. The vice president, supported by the associate vice presidents, provides clear expectations, consistent guidance, and the resources required to sustain the process that was initially an alien endeavor for directors. Critical resources such as an assessment coordinator, external consultants, and StudentVoice technology create an essential support network that enables units to broaden and deepen assessment of their impact on student learning.

Relevant Institutional Web Sites Pertaining to This Assessment Practice

For information on the Student Affairs assessment plan see:

http://saweb.csus.edu/students/assessment.aspx

For information on creating a comprehensive assessment program see:

www.csus.edu/student/VPSAPresentation2.8.07.ppt

Career Services Assessment Using Telephone and Web-Based Surveys

Andrea Dowhower, Philip Burlingame, The Pennsylvania State University

◆ ◆ ◆

Look for the use of data and reporting of findings at all levels of the institution, including the board of trustees, that have led to provision of increased fiscal and human resources—which in turn has led to a broader array, and increased use, of services.

Background and Purpose(s) of Your Assessment

The Penn State Pulse program is an ongoing series of telephone and Web-based surveys eliciting student responses throughout the academic year. The surveys focus on such varied topics as personal health and wellness, out-of-class activities, the first-year experience, community service, and academic issues. The findings provide measures of self-reported learning outcomes, opinions, preferences, satisfaction, needs, and expectations. Initiated in the spring of 1995, and modeled after a similar program at the University of Massachusetts-Amherst, the Penn State Pulse program was first developed by a residence life assessment committee chaired by Lee Upcraft, an assistant vice president of student affairs. A full-time assessment office was created in student affairs, and the program developed into a more comprehensive effort to evaluate systematically various programs offered throughout the Division of Student Affairs and across the university. Through the Pulse program, Penn State faculty and staff learn more about the impact that policies, programs, services, and facilities have on student satisfaction, learning outcomes, and student success.

Though all Penn State student affairs units have been the subject of Pulse surveys, for the purpose of this profile the surveys about Career Services will be the focus. The Career Services Pulse Survey focused on undergraduate students' career planning needs along with their use of and satisfaction with services. The survey also examined strategies to inform students about services, programs, and events.

Assessment Method(s) and Year(s) of Implementation

Using a random sample from the student database, Pulse surveys are first administered by a group of approximately 30 student employees using scripted questions and computer-assisted telephone interviewing (CATI) software. Students not reached by phone and those who would prefer to take the survey online receive an invitation to participate in the Web survey. Students are called up to five times and e-mailed up to four times. Modest incentives are used to promote survey completion.

Career Services Pulse surveys were administered to undergraduates at Penn State's University Park campus in 1998, 2002, 2003, and 2007. In addition, surveys addressing career services needs of graduate students and of students at the commonwealth campuses were administered in spring of 2005.

Required Resources

Three full-time and two part-time employees support the Pulse program. This includes a director, two staff assistants, a graduate assistant, and an information technology specialist. The director has responsibility for overall leadership for the program, survey design, consultation with stakeholders, analysis, and presentation or publication of the findings summaries. The office staff assistant provides administrative support, project management, and survey testing. Another staff assistant is the Pulse evening supervisor for on-site supervision of the student employees. A doctoral-level graduate assistant serves as the data analyst, and a part-time information technology specialist programs the surveys in the CATI and Web software. Student employees (30 to 35) conduct pilot and full telephone surveys on selected Sunday and Wednesday evenings.

Other resources needed for the Pulse program include access to workstations, CATI and Web survey software, phone expenses, and funding for incentives.

Findings

For each Pulse survey, data are summarized utilizing frequencies, selected comparisons of student groups, coded open-ended responses, and an executive summary. When appropriate, the data are analyzed with methods of statistical analysis including correlation, regression, and factor analysis.

With the 2007 Career Services Pulse survey, University Park students were asked about their interest in a variety of career-related programs and services. Students expressed the greatest need for help in obtaining relevant work experience and searching for jobs after graduation. These needs were followed in priority by self-marketing skills such as resume preparation and interview skill development. Furthermore, women, students of color, and first- and second-year students expressed greater need for assistance with most facets of career planning when compared to their respective counterparts. When addressing where students are likely to seek assistance for their career planning needs, students indicated they are more likely to seek assistance from Career Services for the job search process, including preparing résumés, developing interview skills, and searching for jobs after graduation. They more frequently seek assistance from their college academic advising area for needs related to deciding on a major, identifying career options, understanding their career interests, and finding careers that best suit their personality and strengths, as well as identifying graduate or professional education options and preparing for standardized tests. Students also indicated that the Career Services listserv, college listservs, and ads in the campus newspaper were among the most effective ways to inform them about Career Services offerings.

Similar to University Park students, students at the commonwealth campuses identified as their greatest need obtaining relevant work experience and job placement and correspondingly reported being more likely to visit Career Services for assistance in these areas. In addition, the percentage of students who reported using the various programs and services was relatively low. Graduate students most frequently reported the need for assistance in developing job search strategies and identifying career options outside higher education. In relation to their professional development, graduate students expressed a need for assistance in improving their grant-writing skills and in improving their ability to publish.

Use of Findings

Pulse surveys are used in multiple ways within student affairs and across the university. Findings are used to create or refine programs and services; guide policy formation and funding initiatives, including grants; assess the value-added components of programs, services, and interventions; develop marketing campaigns; describe the experiences of students; assess needed student advocacy; and educate students on policies and services at Penn State.

Findings from career services surveys have been applied operationally in a number of areas. For example, the results showed that students perceive that the primary purpose of career services is to assist with job placement rather than a broader mission that includes career development and counseling. As a result of this finding, the department has stepped up its efforts to educate students and academic colleagues about this broader role. Working through their college-based staff liaisons, they have created new handouts and feedback forms to ensure that academic leaders in all colleges are receiving consistent information about the full range of services. Another finding showed low awareness of standardized testing preparation services. Department staff are now marketing these services through academic advising offices and academic departments. They have also increased advertising efforts for the graduate and professional career fairs through departments and other channels. The results confirm their strategies to develop comprehensive student listservs, and they have invested additional resources to advertise in the student newspaper. With Pulse findings at hand, staff negotiated with the newspaper staff to get a free weekly space featuring upcoming events in a section called "Career Corner."

For the commonwealth campuses, these data have led to the funding of several regional career services staff positions to support the campuses in that region. Central funding was allocated to enhance each campus career library, purchase eDiscover licenses, provide student travel to University Park for career fairs, and to deliver live Webcasts. In addition, online workshops and Web-based learning modules have been created to extend career development educational programs to all campuses.

The Graduate School and Career Services have collaborated to enhance the resources available to graduate students and to increase marketing efforts for services. New initiatives include a career management handbook for graduate students, educational programs for graduate students, and educational resources on grant writing.

Impact of Using the Findings

The general impact of Pulse is in promoting the value of assessment and enabling staff to make data-driven decisions about programs and services for students. Pulse provides directors, such as the director of Career Services, with an ongoing effort to collect sound, rigorous data from students over time.

More specifically, in the area of career services, undergraduate student demand for a broader array of services has increased. And, as a result of the increased marketing efforts and targeting of advising offices and colleges, attendance at graduate school events has increased this year.

Success Factors

The Pulse program is well established at Penn State and is generally well respected by university administrators. The executive summaries are regularly sent to the administration, the board of trustees, interested faculty members, student affairs staff, student leaders, and others. Because there is consistent fiscal support from the leadership of student affairs, the program has full-time staff, and assessment efforts are not wholly dependent on the efforts of frontline practitioners. Not only is this important in ensuring that the needed time, resources, and skills are available, but also that findings are consistently and publicly presented with a measure of impartiality. Another important success factor is in the requesters' commitment to understanding and using the data. Without that commitment, the work of collecting and analyzing the data is merely an academic exercise.

Relevant Institutional Web Sites Pertaining to This Assessment Practice

www.sa.psu.edu/sara/pulse.shtml

Assessing Satisfaction and Use of Student Support Services

Joan Harms, University of Hawaii at Manoa

◆ ◆ ◆

Look for improvements made as a result of student satisfaction with and use of student services in nine areas. Results also have been used to compete successfully for grant funding and to garner additional campus resources.

Background and Purpose(s) of Assessment

Student support programs routinely assess student satisfaction with services, usually by surveying students who use program services. As tuition rates continue to rise so do student expectations for quality programs and services, including effective and efficient online services. A central question to both student and academic support programs becomes, How well are all students being served—and not just those who frequent programs and use services? Do students know about certain programs and services, do they use these programs, and if they do are they satisfied with the services? How well are we serving different groups of students? In searching for an assessment tool that would be simple, cost effective, easily understood by different constituents, and useful in raising questions to direct change, administrators, directors, and the assessment specialist at the University of Hawaii at Manoa (UH-M) revisited and refined a performance indicator used in 1990 to measure satisfaction and use of services at the division and program levels. The 1990 survey was replicated in 1999 and 2002. In 2006 it was revised to reflect all the programs in student affairs after a reorganization of the division. Although the scope of the programs changed, the purpose of the survey did not.

Assessment Method(s) and Year(s) of Implementation

At the time of the first administration of the survey, it covered nine student services (admission and records, career services, counseling, financial aid, learning assistance center, service-learning, student activities, student employment, and health services). These programs were selected because they served all students as opposed to programs that served selected subgroups, such as the Women's Center and College Opportunities program. Students responded to the following items for each of the nine programs: (1) I used it and was satisfied, (2) I used it and was dissatisfied, (3) I knew about it but did not use it, and (4) I did not know about it. The nine programs were carefully described by each unit head to give an accurate representation of the programs. Student characteristics survey items were included to further analyses of student subpopulations such as class, start status, resident status, ethnicity, gender, and residence. Upon piloting and refining the survey using undergraduate students who were employed on campus, it was appended to the College Student Experiences Questionnaire (CSEQ) and administered in 1990, 1999, 2002, and 2006 (Web-based). It will be administered again in spring 2009 as a brief Web-based survey independent of the CSEQ. All survey results were based on a random sample drawn proportionately by class of undergraduates.

Required Resources

The greatest value of the satisfaction and use survey rests in its simplicity and cost-effectiveness in time, materials, and personnel, especially if it is administered online. Our institution first administered the survey by appending it to a national survey along with its related costs, but it can be administered independently at a more reasonable cost. The assessment specialist coordinated all aspects of planning, administering, analyzing, and reporting on the results for about one-quarter time and effort. Required resources will be significantly reduced when the Satisfaction and Use Survey is administered next spring independent of the CSEQ using Perseus Survey Solutions for the Web and the UH-M server.

Findings

The 2006 results revealed that undergraduates generally were satisfied with the services provided by student affairs, with especially high ratings in employment, student activities, and health services. On the one hand, first-time students from Hawaii as well as underrepresented Filipino, Hawaiian, and Pacific Island students were most satisfied. On the other hand, transfer students, especially those from the U.S. mainland, and international students, were less satisfied with nearly all services. Freshmen were least satisfied with career services. The counseling program was especially challenged with low satisfaction with services from U.S. mainland, international, and first-generation students. Men were less satisfied than women with all services, especially with career and counseling services. Of equal concern was the slow downward trend over time of student satisfaction with services for employment, career, and counseling programs. Health services, although experiencing a drop in satisfaction, still maintained a fairly high satisfaction rate.

Student use of services revealed several startling findings. On the one hand, student activities experienced a significant jump in student engagement. On the other hand, although more students were using counseling services, more students were dissatisfied with those services. Also, nearly 20 percent of undergraduates did not know about counseling and career services.

Use of Findings

The results, along with other indicators, have been used in multiple ways. Using the specific findings cited above, executive management has discussed the results with individual program directors in light of needed action. For example, in the counseling program, the director has been reporting more mental health cases with the staff "stretched thin." Thus, the survey results in the counseling area along with other findings helped to confirm the need for a number of new positions in the counseling center. In career services, marketing strategies helped to inform students of the programs, as a good many students did not know about them. In the counseling program, marketing to student segments was more selective until more staff support became available. The dissatisfaction of U.S. mainland students corroborates the findings from residence hall studies and a leavers study and has led to a strong focus on developing special programs for students living on campus, many of whom are from the U.S. mainland. Findings are also used by programs for needs assessment, intramural and extramural proposal and grant development, and external reviews. For example, health center staff used their consistently high satisfaction and use outcomes in a recent grant proposal in the health area and in their latest accreditation process. The bound survey report, a staff development tool, provided written and specific guidance for directors, especially in the use of subgroup information. The report can be found on the OSA Student Assessment Report Web site and the Academic Affairs accreditation site. The report was also used by the Understanding Student Services Committee, an institutional and cross-functional committee, in a review of all student affairs programs at the university. In addition, a "research briefs" on the topic has been widely circulated and is also on the Web site. Finally, through the years the results, in the form of bar charts displaying trend data, have been used to inform university constituents of the status and progress being made in the various student affairs programs and the division in general.

Impact of Using the Findings

The impact of improving services and providing access to these services for students, especially by addressing student subgroup needs, has been noted above. Another important impact of the process is the gradual realization by faculty and staff of the value of assessment results as evidence of progress or improvement. They now view results as information to act on rather than as a threat that may bring punitive action. When we first started the assessment in 1990, a few programs resisted assessment of their services. Staff were suspicious of administrative motives to use the results purely for budgetary or punitive purposes instead of as evidence needed to work toward constructive improvement of programs. In addition, financial aid staff were certain that they would always be rated very low because students never got the amount of financial aid they wanted. Staff were surprised by higher-than-expected baseline results, and they were again surprised three years later by the huge jump in ratings. Slowly they became comfortable in the use of performance indicators as a way of taking the pulse of the program and as a tool for further dialogue and improvement of programs. Finally, the overall division satisfaction score obtained by averaging all program satisfaction scores helped to promote cohesion and teamwork among programs to provide the highest possible quality of services to students.

Success Factors

The instrument is simple to understand and use by program directors and stakeholders. The findings can be combined easily with results from other studies to corroborate and substantiate conclusions. Students find the survey clear and easy to complete. The cost is minimal when developed and administered online by the division. Subgroup information allows for more program accountability and more focused and precise action plans for improvement of services. Replication of the study has provided trend data demonstrating program direction as well as program status at specific time intervals. Success can also be attributed to consistent support by leadership, the engagement of stakeholders in the development and refinement of the instrument, and the use of program results by unit heads to effect change.

Relevant Institutional Web Sites Pertaining to This Assessment Practice

The report on Indicators of Student Satisfaction and Use of Student Services can be found at:

www.hawaii.edu/osa/Assessment_Undergraduate.html

Research briefs on student satisfaction with student services increases from 1990 to 2002 at:

www.hawaii.edu/osa/Assessment_Research.html

Assessing Educational Sanctions That Facilitate Student Learning with First-Time Alcohol Policy Violators

David A. Hoffman, Truman State University

◆ ◆ ◆

Look for a process that involves student conduct board members in evaluating essays required of students who have violated university alcohol usage policy. The essay serves to encourage reflection and learning and to change behavior.

Background and Purpose(s) of Your Assessment

Motivated by *The Student Learning Imperative: Implications for Student Affairs* (American College Personnel Association, 1994) and an intensifying focus on learning outcomes assessment in the Division of Student Affairs at Truman State University, staff in the Office of Citizenship and Community Standards (OCCS) sought to develop a method for assessing the achievement of sanction assignment outcomes for first-time student alcohol policy violators. The sanction assignments were created and the assessment process began in the 2003–04 academic year. The sanctions were designed to facilitate student reflection, learning, and motivation for behavior change. The assignments and the assessment process have evolved. Since the 2005–06 academic year, first-time first-year student alcohol policy violators have been required to complete AlcoholEdu for Sanctions, participate in a 90-minute alcohol education discussion group facilitated by staff members of the university's Counseling Center, complete an assignment using Truman's Out-of-Class Experience Planning Map, read a stimulus essay written by another college student, and write a short reflective essay. First-time alcohol policy violators at the sophomore, junior, and senior levels are required to complete sanctions similar to those for first-year students, except that the Out-of-Class Planning Map assignment is replaced by an article review of the College Alcohol Study conducted by Henry Wechsler and colleagues at the Harvard School of Public Health. Stimulus essays written by other college students vary for first year–sophomore and junior-senior students.

Assessment Method(s) and Year(s) of Implementation

The alcohol reflection essays are evaluated by student conduct board members to determine if students were satisfied with AlcoholEdu for Sanctions and the alcohol discussion group. They assess whether students indicate in the essays if these sanction assignments were positive experiences and if the students report gaining useful knowledge or information from the sanctions. In addition, the raters are asked to evaluate the essay for evidence of reflective judgment. Does the essay demonstrate that the student is taking personal responsibility for his or her actions and behaviors during the incident? Does the essay demonstrate that the student gained useful knowledge or information from one or more of the educational sanctions? Does the essay demonstrate that the student will change his or her behavior? Each essay is assessed by two raters. If ratings differ, a staff member in OCCS reviews the essay and determines the rating. The data are then summarized based on the three areas: AlcoholEdu for Sanctions, alcohol discussion group, and the three reflective judgment questions. As noted above, during the 2003–04 academic year, the sanction assignments were created and an evaluation method developed that focused on the alcohol reflection essay and the Harvard review and reflection essay. During the 2005–06 academic year, the sanction assignments and assessment method were revised as described above.

Required Resources

Six student conduct board members reading roughly 20 essays each completed ratings for a sample of approximately 60–70 reflection essays. The OCCS student intern assists with project coordination, guaranteeing anonymous reviews, and summarizing the data (whether students answered yes or no to the questions, and listing the qualitative comments).

Findings

The assessments during the past two years have indicated that the majority of students completing the sanctions were satisfied with AlcoholEdu for Sanctions and the alcohol discussion group. The majority of students also indicated that they learned something from each of the sanction assignments. On the reflective judgment questions, between two-thirds and three-quarters of the students demonstrate taking responsibility for their behavior during the incident, gaining useful knowledge or information from one of the sanction assignments, and indicating a desire to change their behavior based on the incident.

Use of Findings

The findings from the essay evaluation demonstrate that the educational sanctions assigned to first-time alcohol policy violators result in the achievement of intended learning outcomes by a majority of the students. This assessment also assists with evaluating student satisfaction with two other sanction assignments provided to first-time alcohol policy violators. The assessment provides useful feedback to OCCS in determining whether the sanction assignments are effective as educational sanctions or if the sanction assignments need to be changed or revised to support student learning, reflection, and motivation for behavior change related to alcohol policy violations.

Impact of Using the Findings

The findings are made available each year on the OCCS Web site in an effort to be transparent to the university community with regard to student conduct code violations, sanctions, and assessment efforts. The findings are reported annually to the dean of student affairs in the OCCS director's performance portfolio. The dean shared results from the alcohol sanction assessment with the university board of governors in 2004–05 and has been asked to continue sharing the findings since that time. The assessment of the achievement of learning outcomes for alcohol policy violators demonstrates that even in a situation that is deemed undesirable by the institution and the student, student learning and reflection can be facilitated.

Success Factors

Student rater training with sample alcohol reflection essays has improved inter-rater agreement. Over the years, the rating evaluation form has been streamlined to focus on just a few essential satisfaction and reflective judgment questions, reducing the time spent by raters to evaluate each essay. Sampling essays, usually from fall semester, has also made the assessment process manageable.

Relevant Institutional Web Sites Pertaining to This Assessment Practice

Office of Citizenship and Community Standards:

> http://conduct.truman.edu/

Alcohol Sanction Essay Evaluation data:

> http://conduct.truman.edu/stats.asp

Out-of-Class Experience Planning Map:

> http://cocurricular.truman.edu/planning_map/purpose.asp

AlcoholEdu for Sanctions:

> www.outsidetheclassroom.com/

Stimulus Essays:

> "Academics Are the Easy Part of College" for first-year and sophomore students: www.collegevalues.org/reflections.cfm?id=322&a=1

"Figuring Out Life's Most Important Questions" for juniors and seniors:
www.collegevalues.org/reflections.cfm?id=676&a=1
2002 Harvard College Alcohol Study and Trends article by Henry
Wechsler and colleagues:
www.hsph.harvard.edu/cas/Documents/trends/Trends.pdf

CHAPTER TWELVE

COMMUNITY COLLEGES PROFILES

Faculty and staff assessing student learning in community colleges face unique challenges. Some scholars maintain that the missions of community colleges are broader than those of their four-year college or university counterparts and the student population is more diverse (Seybert, 2002). This chapter opens with a profile that describes an institution-wide mission-based assessment model. The next describes a campuswide program for assessing general education, and the last one describes a course-based assessment method.

John J. Cosgrove and Lawrence J. McDoniel describe a campuswide process at St. Louis Community College that involves 11 committees and over 100 faculty and staff who collect, analyze, interpret, and use data to assess student learning and institutional effectiveness. Each unit develops an assessment plan using one of the following approaches: **I**nquiry, **D**iscover, **I**nterpret, and **D**evelop (I DID) or **L**isten, look, and learn; **A**ct; **A**nother look; **S**hare the news; **I**mprove; **E**xcel and celebrate (LAASIE). The I DID approach is used by academic units, and the LAASIE approach is employed by service units to assess and improve processes and outcomes. Examples of improvements based on information collected using both the I DID and LAASIE methods are described.

Capstone courses have been a central component of the liberal arts and social sciences program at Tompkins Courtland Community College since 1998. In 2003 faculty developed a process by which capstone projects are collectively reviewed so that they could determine how well their rubrics assess the range of student performance and how consistently faculty interpret the rubrics. Jeanne A. Cameron reports that this process has resulted in continual revision of the rubrics and, most important, ongoing conversations about what faculty value and a recognition that meaningful assessment takes time and persistent attention.

When three community colleges merged in 1998 to form the multicampus Community College of Baltimore County, the three separate general education programs were also restructured and merged. The new general education program requires that all the program's courses cover and assess all the institution's general education goals. Multiple methods are used, including externally developed standardized instruments and locally developed processes. The focus of this profile by Rose Mince is on common graded assignments (CGAs), which disciplinary faculty teams develop to assess the six general education program goals. These common assignments incorporate team projects and individual written work that might include lab reports. Faculty select up to three CGAs and ask students to submit two copies of the assignment: one to be graded for the course and the other to be used to assess the curriculum.

Institutions

Associate
  Public
    St. Louis Community College; St. Louis, Missouri (23,000 students)
    Tompkins Cortland Community College; Dryden, New York (3,000 students)
    The Community College of Baltimore County; Baltimore, Maryland (19,000 students)

Mission-Based Assessment to Improve Student Learning and Institutional Effectiveness

John J. Cosgrove, Lawrence J. McDoniel, St. Louis Community College

◆ ◆ ◆

Look for a variety of rich examples of findings and uses of assessment results. Two locally developed models for gathering data have been used, resulting in significant participation by faculty and staff in improvement activities.

Background and Purpose(s) of Your Assessment

A community college's mission statement represents its promises to the community and therefore should play a significant role in its assessment processes. St. Louis Community College (SLCC) leaders have created a document that outlines the college's current mission-based assessment model and describes how the college moved from a classroom or course assessment approach to a more programmatic, mission-based model.

In 2006, SLCC began developing a mission-based, continuous-improvement process involving the systematic collection, analysis, interpretation, and use of data by faculty and staff to improve student learning outcomes and institutional effectiveness. Through assessment, the college seeks to develop a culture of inquiry in which faculty and staff can discover, interpret, and act on information. The thoughtful interpretation and use of assessment information by faculty and staff plays a central role in helping the college keep its promises to the community.

Assessment initiatives must be continually examined and modified to meet the changing needs of the college. To help guide such efforts, the college employs the following vision for assessment: "St. Louis Community College collects and uses assessment data to improve student learning, academic achievement, and overall institutional effectiveness. When combined with thoughtful interpretation by faculty and staff, assessment supports the overall decision-making needs of the college and the specific decision-making needs of individual units and programs."

Assessment is directed by the vice-chancellor for education and organized through a series of 11 collegewide committees comprising more than 100 faculty and staff. The assessment model is constructed within a framework that emphasizes teaching and learning as the college's most important processes. It is not a hierarchical model; no single committee is more important than any other committee, and no committee reports to any other committee. The model encourages faculty and staff to work collaboratively to enhance teaching, learning, and institutional effectiveness.

The Assessment Council includes 32 faculty and staff members and is responsible for promoting the design of appropriate assessment strategies and the collection, interpretation, and communication of data related to student academic achievement and institutional effectiveness. The council also continuously examines the college's assessment processes. Members provide campus and districtwide input, guidance, and coordination, which support assessment efforts aimed at improving student learning and related academic achievement, enhancing the college's effectiveness, and documenting outcomes related to the college mission.

Assessment Method(s) and Year(s) of Implementation

Beginning with the 2006–07 academic year, mission-based interest areas have been devising assessment plans to ascertain problems and develop solutions. Within each assessment plan, the academic or service area employs either the I DID or the LAASIE approach. I DID is a newly developed four-step process serving the academic areas of the college:

- *Inquire.* What do we want to know? This step focuses on defining the specific program, mission area(s), or student learning outcomes to be assessed.
- *Discover.* What do we know? This step focuses on identifying data sources and methods of assessment and collecting data.
- *Interpret.* What does the information tell us? This step focuses on analysis and the sharing of results of the data.
- *Develop.* What actions do we plan to take? This step focuses on using the results to design strategies for improving student learning and institutional effectiveness.

LAASIE, a six-step approach for assessing and improving college service operations, was derived from a series of examinations and modifications made to assessment practices following a focused visit by the North Central Association in 1997:

- L = Listen, look, and learn
- A = Act
- A = Another look
- S = Share the news
- I = Improve
- E = Excel and celebrate

Required Resources

The chancellor and the district leadership team fully support the college's ongoing assessment processes. In fall 2006 Chancellor Henry Shannon stated, "The thoughtful interpretation of assessment information by faculty and staff, and the use of such information to improve student learning outcomes and institutional effectiveness will play a key role in helping the college keep its promises to the community." The College Institutional Affairs Council and the College Academic Affairs Council have affirmed their support for assessment, and both councils have members on the Assessment Council and on the various assessment committees.

This support will be critical as the college seeks to more fully integrate its assessment, planning, and budget-development processes. In addition, leadership and institutional support for assessment are vital to the college's efforts associated with the current North Central Higher Learning Commission self-study process for accreditation.

When assessment committees, divisions, departments, and individual faculty and staff need assistance in the systematic collection and interpretation of assessment data, a primary resource is the college's Office of Institutional Research and Planning and Assessment (IRPA). IRPA staff have been working closely with the Assessment Council and the related assessment committees to develop a variety of research and information services related to student learning outcomes and service examination. A new Web-based assessment portal became operational in August 2006, and the college also provides access to an online, user-friendly survey development tool that assists in the evaluation of specific student learning outcomes or service areas. Divisions, departments, or individual faculty can quickly develop surveys to acquire information needed to make improvements.

Findings and Use of Findings

SLCC supports the use of assessment information to improve student learning outcomes and institutional effectiveness. The following list provides examples of several collegewide assessment efforts that have led to or are leading to improvements in student learning outcomes and student engagement.

2006–07

- Based on information comparing first-time student success with entering reading scores, the college implemented a reading requirement for certain 100-level courses. Early assessment results reveal that first-time students who successfully complete their developmental reading course achieve a higher GPA and return for the next semester at a higher rate.
- Assessment information obtained through LAASIE projects has been used to revise the college's new-student orientation program.
- Career and technical education programs have used information obtained through the developing a curriculum (DACUM) process to assess and revise the curriculum in a number of programs.
- Assessment information about the success of our transfer students has been used to develop new information exchange and research projects with the University of Missouri.

- Assessment information related to the general education goal of valuing has been used to improve the college's general education cornerstone courses.
- Based on information from clients and internal associates, the Center for Business, Industry, and Labor conducted several LAASIE projects creating better processes for staff hiring, an annual regional training survey, and a revitalized Web site.

2007–08

- General education faculty will explore student and faculty perceptions related to their experiences in speaking- and writing-intensive general education courses.
- Developmental education personnel are exploring how RDG 030 skills transfer to future college level courses in academic content areas.
- Career and technical education faculty will consider what factors affect student retention in CTE programs.
- Members of the Transfer Education Assessment Committee have conducted focus groups to determine the degree to which SLCC students who transfer to University of Missouri–St. Louis are using SLCC advisors and counselors to smooth their transfer experience.
- Continuing education and community development staff have studied the degree of student engagement in their seminars and examined the impact of such engagement on learning outcomes associated with such seminars.
- Institutional and student support services staff have opted to review the implementation process and effectiveness of a new tuition payment plan.
- Student affairs staff are monitoring the impact of late registration on instructional pedagogy, student learning outcomes, and credit-hour generation.

Impact of Using the Findings

The impact of using this mission-based model to generate assessment issues and projects has been considerable. The greatest impact is the shift in emphasis on the part of participants, for this approach has moved faculty, staff, and administrators beyond mere data collection to action based on the thoughtful interpretation of data. We are working on growing not only a culture of evidence, but also a culture of action.

Following are attributes that describe the SLCC assessment culture as it currently exists thanks to this mission-based approach:

- Greater collegewide participation in major elements of our mission
- Increased "thoughtful" interpretation of data

- More concrete steps taken based on data collection and interpretation
- More follow-up on identified surfacing issues and problems
- Greater interaction among shareholders
- Adoption and use of outside resources such as the Community College Student Experiences Questionnaire
- Greater support collegewide for implementing solutions to problems identified by assessment data

Success Factors

Because the model is not hierarchical, success obviously depends on the hard work and cooperation of the faculty, staff, and administrators involved. Buy-in throughout the college is a given, and a necessity. To work well, the model requires practitioners to address and study issues that they identify as crucial to student success. Having done so, success requires the institutional will to make improvements, and thus changes, for the sake of students and other shareholders.

Relevant Institutional Web Sites Pertaining to This Assessment Practice

SLCC Assessment Public Web Site:

www.stlcc.edu/Faculty_and_Staff_Resources/Assessment/

Living Rubrics: Sustaining Collective Reflection, Deliberation, and Revision of Program Outcomes

Jeanne A. Cameron, Tompkins Cortland Community College

◆ ◆ ◆

Look for faculty collaboration in the assessment of a required capstone project that leads to a broader understanding of the differences in disciplinary research as well as revision and improvement in the assessment process.

Background and Purpose(s) of Assessment

Faculty in the liberal arts and social sciences program at Tompkins Cortland Community College have been assessing student learning outcomes in a required capstone course since 1998. From the beginning, responsibility for facilitating our capstone has rotated from one faculty member to another, ensuring that each regularly and directly experiences the program's strengths and weaknesses. To further support this hands-on knowledge, in 2003 program faculty instituted annual collective assessment of student capstone projects. In this process, we assess (1) how well our rubrics capture the range of student performances, and (2) how consistently we interpret our rubric standards. This annual assessment has underscored a process of ongoing revision of our rubrics and deliberation about our goals.

Assessment Method(s) and Year(s) of Implementation

Faculty use collectively created outcomes rubrics to assess student capstone projects annually. This assessment practice began in 2003 and has occurred each year since.

Required Resources

Required resources include program outcomes statements, outcomes rubrics, student projects, and a collaborative faculty committed to student learning. This process can be facilitated by additional compensation for the time required for collective assessment, or by an institutional commitment to designating scheduled time for program assessment activities.

Findings

If meaningful assessment is a process requiring ongoing reflection, deliberation, and revision, then our work offers an exemplary model. As a liberal arts transfer program, our outcomes reflect the important general education competences of communication, information literacy, and analytical thinking. Such skills are multifaceted; their assessment is not reducible to test items. Rubrics offer a promising method for directly assessing complex performances.

The true test of a rubric is how well it meets seemingly contradictory goals. On the one hand, it should capture the complexity and authenticity of student performances. On the other hand, it must offer meaningful distinctions between performance levels in language that is clear and direct. In the assessment of program outcomes, there is the additional challenge that the rubrics must reflect a shared understanding of performance levels. In the case of a multidisciplinary program such as ours, performance standards as articulated in the rubrics must mean the same thing to faculty members in several distinct disciplines.

Our multiyear findings may be summarized with two observations. First, capturing the complexity of student performances in rubrics requires sustained attention and revision. Second, developing a consensus about what students should be able to do, and then translating that consensus into clear language that results in consistent interpretations of students' performances, requires ongoing deliberation. Really good assessment of complex skills is necessarily a work in progress.

Use of Findings

Each year we have revised some component(s) of our rubrics based on what we see in our students' concrete performances. For instance, we have added a paragraph development standard to our written communication rubric, based on our observations that the overall structure of a paper might satisfy our expectations, but that a pattern of poorly developed paragraphs compromises the paper's overall effectiveness. We have made a number of changes to our theory and methods rubrics over time; a key challenge has been to construct a rubric that speaks as effectively to the methods that historians use as to those used by sociologists and psychologists. Likewise, our information literacy rubric has undergone several transformations to capture what we are seeing on the ground.

The problem of interrater reliability has been a more significant challenge, resulting initially in minor modifications to our practice. For instance, in 2005 we distributed capstone projects two weeks in advance of our group assessment to promote more substantive and reflective reading of student papers. In 2006, we decided to conduct the assessment in June, rather than directly following submission of spring semester grades, to put some distance between the end-of-semester chaos and our program assessment. Though both of these modifications enhanced the overall quality of the group assessment, they did not resolve the interrater reliability problems we were seeing.

Based on continued interrater differences in 2007, we decided that we needed to make substantive changes to all the rubrics to enhance their clarity and specificity. We solicited detailed feedback from all faculty members about their current interpretations of each performance level on the rubrics and their recommendations for improving clarity. Feedback was used to revise and, in some cases, fundamentally transform rubrics. We are now engaging in norming sessions, using the revised rubrics to assess several papers that had received widely divergent assessments in 2007. We see this process as ongoing.

Impact of Using the Findings

Continued interrater reliability problems in 2007 resulted in the most ambitious revisions of our rubrics to date, but more important than this has been the recognition that our biggest challenge is reaching a working consensus about what matters most. In other words, the most profound impact of our findings has not been the particular rubric revisions from one year to the next, but rather the type of deliberative dialogue that this process promotes.

First, our process has raised substantive debate about what we value most in our students' work. For instance, on one end of the continuum, we have a faculty member who finds it difficult to recognize content in performances that have mechanical flaws: "I have zero tolerance for incorrect spelling, poor phrasing, awkward vocabulary choices, run-on sentences" (e-mail communication). On the other end of the continuum, we have a faculty member who has challenged us to consider how our expectations may be culturally biased: "In the writing traditions of many communities of color and communities where oral histories are valued, writing in unsynchronized, multi-thematic narratives is popular and valued" (e-mail communication). Through discussion, we have been able to reach a consensus that "flawless" writing is too high an expectation for sophomore-level students, and that a more meaningful approach is to look for evidence of careful proofreading and revision across multiple drafts of a paper. Moreover, we are in the process of determining how to value nonstandard discourses while at the same time promoting standard forms of communication that will be expected at most transfer institutions.

Second, through our dialogue, we have discovered that significant interrater disparities are often the result of cross-disciplinary misunderstandings. In some cases, student performances that have been especially rich in substance have been assessed as weak by a rater with an inadequate understanding of the theory and methods employed. These cross-disciplinary discussions have served to enhance everyone's awareness and appreciation of how research is conducted in other disciplines.

Overall, our process speaks to the complexity of meaningful assessment—it takes time and continuous deliberation. The most important impact of the repeated examination and subsequent revision of our rubrics has been to keep program outcomes front and center and to reinforce that if we want our students to achieve them, they must mean the same thing to each of us. Moreover, examining the inconsistencies in expectations each year has not only moved us in the direction of shared understanding but, more important, has also promoted a vibrant dialogue about what matters most.

Success Factors

The success factors involved in this process include faculty articulation and ownership of program outcomes, ongoing discussion and deliberation about what matters most, concrete student performances on which to base judgments, and persistence.

Relevant Institutional Web Sites Pertaining to This Assessment Practice

The relevant Web sites below are not from Tompkins Cortland Community College.

Academy of Art University—Faculty Resources, "Rubrics for Assessment and Grading":

> http://faculty.academyart.edu/resources/rubrics.asp

"Understanding Rubrics" by Heidi Goodrich Andrade:

> http://learnweb.harvard.edu/alps/thinking/docs/rubricar.htm

"Creating, Implementing, and Using Rubrics" by Marilee J. Bresciani:

> www.ncsu.edu/assessment/presentations/assess_process/creating
> _implementing.pdf

"Using Rubrics" by Michelle Christopherson of Modesto Junior College:

> http://virtual2.mjc.edu/mjcinstruction/CAI/Resources/index.htm

State Council of Higher Education for Virginia Web site:

> http://research.schev.edu/corecompetencies/VMI/comp_oral.asp

---

General Education Assessment Teams: A GREAT Project

Rose Mince, Lynne Mason, The Community College of Baltimore County

◆ ◆ ◆

Look for strong faculty involvement in merging three independent college general education programs with a multidimensional assessment process.

Background and Purpose(s) of Your Assessment

The general education program at the Community College of Baltimore County (CCBC) underwent a restructuring with the merger of three independent community colleges into one multicampus institution in 1998. Each college had its own well-established general education program that reflected the unique culture of its institution. A General Education Review Board was charged with creating one unified, cohesive general education program. In fall 2001, CCBC faculty implemented a new general education program with six goals focused on content knowledge; written, oral, or signed communication; critical thinking; technology as a learning tool; cultural appreciation; and independent learning. One hallmark of the CCBC program is that every general education course must address and assess *all* of the general education program goals.

The review board had the foresight to incorporate research on best practices in assessment in its new general education model. As a result, the review board designed not only a new general education program but also a multidimensional assessment model. This assessment model uses a three-pronged approach to include feedback from the SIR II faculty evaluation instrument, the Academic Profile test, and faculty-developed course-embedded assignments. The SIR II, a nationally normed instrument, was already in use at the college. Several questions were added to the SIR II evaluation instrument to assess students' satisfaction with the extent to which their general education courses actually increased their ability to demonstrate specified characteristics of the general education program goals. The Academic Profile, a standardized test of general education skills, was selected to provide a comparison against national norms based on scores from other community colleges. The Academic Profile was administered in 2001 and 2004 and will be replaced by the Measure of Academic Proficiency and Progress in 2008.

The third component of the CCBC general education assessment model is an internally administered project known as the GREAT (General Education Assessment Teams) Project. This element balances the external pieces and focuses on the unique aspects of the CCBC general education program not addressed in other aspects of the assessment model. The GREAT Project is faculty developed and faculty driven. This component of the CCBC general education assessment model is the focus of this profile.

Assessment Method(s) and Year(s) of Implementation

The purpose of the GREAT Project is to gather data to assess the first six general education program goals by implementing common graded assignments (CGAs) and accompanying scoring rubrics designed by faculty teams across the six general education disciplines: arts and humanities, social and behavioral sciences, mathematics, biological and physical sciences, English composition, and interdisciplinary and emerging issues. The project was piloted in spring 2002 using faculty volunteers. The first full-scale implementation occurred in fall 2003. The implementation schedule is on a three-year cycle, with one of the six disciplines participating each fall and spring semester. During the piloting phase, the General Education Review Board conducted extensive faculty development in the use of this assessment approach.

- CGAs are developed by faculty teams within a discipline and incorporate the six general education program goals. Each discipline may utilize up to three CGAs. Examples include a lab report, a paper, a team project, an annotated bibliography, and an analysis of a scholarly article. Discipline team leaders work with faculty to tighten existing assignments to incorporate greater specificity and detail. CGAs are approved by department chairs and academic deans.
- A six-point analytic rubric is utilized for each of the six general education program goals, with a 6 indicating evidence beyond the expectations of the assignment and a 1 indicating very little evidence the skill has been achieved. Students receive a copy of the rubric with the assignment. They submit two copies of the assignment—one with their name for faculty evaluation and one with only their student ID number for GREAT scoring.
- Faculty are invited to participate in scoring sessions at the end of each semester. They are trained and participate in a norming session. During the actual scoring session, each CGA is read by two scorers, and the scores for each general education category are averaged. A third scorer is used for any category where the scoring variance is greater than 1. The third reader's score is accepted for that category.

Required Resources

The most important resources are the faculty team leader and all of the faculty who participate in the GREAT project. Faculty are assisted by the GREAT coordinator, who receives six credits of reassigned time each semester. Further direction and support is provided by the college's Learning Outcomes Assessment Advisory Board (LOAAB). A number of written and electronic resources facilitate success, including the *CCBC Guide to Learning Outcomes Assessment and Classroom Learning Assessment* and the LOA Web page, which includes templates, forms, examples, and guidelines. Financial resources are needed to pay for scoring, supplies, and reassigned time for the coordinator. A critical resource is the assistance provided throughout all phases of data collection and analyses by the Office of Planning, Research, and Evaluation.

Findings

To ensure anonymity and to support the risk-free philosophy of assessment at CCBC, identifying student and faculty information was not included on the CGAs in the first six semesters. This encouraged faculty participation, but data analyses were limited to generalizations because there was no way to disaggregate the data based on population characteristics. Beginning in fall 2006, student identification data were captured for the purpose of disaggregating the data based on race, gender, age, number of credits completed, and GPA. This addition now allows faculty to have more salient information from which they can determine their interventions for improvement.

Although the purpose is not to compare courses across disciplines, and data have varied slightly among courses and semesters, a number of consistencies in scores have emerged among the six general education program goals.

- Across the board, on a 6-point rubric, the means are typically in the 3.0 to 4.0 range.
- Content scores are consistently the highest and align closely to a 4.0.
- There is often a high correlation between critical thinking and communication scores, but critical thinking scores vary widely.
- Information technology and cultural diversity scores are typically in the 2.0 to 3.5 range, which reflects the relative newness of these areas in some courses; similar results were found via the SIR II evaluation instrument.
- The disparate scores in critical thinking, information technology, and cultural diversity suggest that these goals are being incorporated into disciplines and defined by faculty in very different ways.
- There is a strong positive correlation between GPA and mean scores across all program goals.
- Mean scores usually increase with the number of credits completed, but this is not always the case; similar results were found using the Academic Profile.
- Most students in the samples have completed 0–20 credits, which reflects the introductory nature of many general education courses.
- Students in biological and physical sciences courses typically had completed more credits, and their scores are higher than scores from students in other disciplines.
- Students with more than 60 credits significantly outscored students with fewer credits.

Use of Findings

The purpose of the GREAT project is to identify areas of strength and areas that need improvement. The results are shared with team leaders, administrators, and faculty so that they can identify changes that should be implemented to further enhance student learning. Data are disaggregated to identify subpopulations of students who need special attention. For example, textbooks that specifically emphasize cultural diversity have been adopted. Numerous faculty development sessions on information literacy, critical thinking, and other general education program goals have been offered. Whenever possible, LOAAB links other collegewide initiatives and professional development opportunities with the needs of general education faculty, such as the annual Teaching-Learning Fair, Writing in the Disciplines and Across Communities, and Closing the Gap.

Impact of Using the Findings

The GREAT project has challenged faculty to examine and reexamine the prompts used in assessments to ensure that assessments are clearly written and support the six goals of the general education program. This focus has improved the overall quality of assignments in general education courses, which benefits students by providing the specificity and clarity required to optimize their skill levels as defined in the CCBC general education program goals.

Success Factors

The most essential factor is faculty buy-in, closely followed by administrator and institutional research support. The GREAT coordinator is also important to facilitate training; implementation; data collection, analysis, and review; and meetings. The sharing of CGAs and rubrics increases understanding and adoption, especially by new faculty, and the Web page enhances communication and accessibility to information and forms. Recognition of CCBC's assessment program by the Council for Higher Education Accreditation in 2006 with a national award for Institutional Progress in Student Learning Outcomes and by the Community College Futures Assembly with a 2008 Bellwether Award for High Impact Course-Level Assessment in the Instructional Programs and Services category greatly enhances faculty participation and leadership in assessment.

Relevant Institutional Web Sites Pertaining to This Assessment Practice

http://ccbcmd.edu/loa/genedindex.html

CHAPTER THIRTEEN

GRADUATE PROGRAMS PROFILES

In 1995 the National Research Council (NRC) issued a report on the status of research-doctorate programs (Goldberger, Maher, & Flattau, 1995) and another is expected in 2009. In preparation for the 2009 report, the council issued a methodology study (Ostriker & Kuh, 2003); one aspect of the methods used in the 1995 report criticized in the expected report was the emphasis on reputation as a measure of quality. The current study involves gathering data from institutional representatives, program faculty, and students. Included in the program questionnaire are items addressing admission requirements, completion rates, support provided to students, and courses taught by graduate students. New this time is a student questionnaire. Among the items are questions about the types and timeliness of evaluation and feedback and the types of engagement that students experience with faculty and advisors. These questions suggest that some attention may have been given to the wealth of assessment literature (admittedly the vast majority is on undergraduate student achievement), recommending that attention be paid to timely and frequent feedback for students and the importance of student engagement. Graduate faculty can use this national evaluation of graduate programs and the profiles presented in this chapter as they pursue improvements in graduate education. The profiles selected for this chapter include those written to evaluate complete programs and others that describe specific skills in graduate education.

Faculty at San Diego State University require a reflective learning portfolio for students in the master's and doctoral programs. Marilee Bresciani observes that results of analyzing learning portfolios have been used to improve the instruction and advising processes, including altering course sequences and requiring additional learning experiences. Further criteria used to evaluate the portfolios have been modified based on student feedback. Contributing to the success of this process is the time that external professionals and faculty devote to reviewing and commenting on the portfolios. Reports suggest that external professionals view this volunteer work as contributing to the overall quality of their profession by improving the learning of students bound for the field.

At Walden University, faculty have developed rubrics to evaluate and to make explicit the standards for quality dissertations and master's theses. According to Jordan Orzoff, data from 197 dissertations has shown that 10 percent of student work is rated as marginal or unacceptable. Responding to the finding that the dissertations were weakest in the area of qualitative methods, faculty continue to review the research curriculum. This evaluation process has become a model for others; faculty from other institutions are adapting or adopting Walden's rubrics.

Students in the Masters of Business Administration program at Johnson & Wales University complete coauthored capstone projects that are first evaluated by faculty for content and secondly for communication skills by tutors from the Professional Communications Center who are also adjunct instructors of communication. Joanne M. Crossman informs us that as a result of some of the findings, several initiatives have been undertaken. Senior faculty now mentor other full-time and adjunct faculty by leading discussions about teaching and learning. Faculty portfolios with shared assignments and rubrics have been developed. At-risk students are required to seek assistance from the Professional Communications Center. Finally, courses, outcomes, and capstone projects now are reviewed by the Graduate School Business Advisory Board.

Hugh A. Stoddard describes an online system used in the University of Nebraska College of Medicine to rate professional behaviors observed by faculty in classroom and clinical settings. The system helps to identify students who may need counseling or mentoring. Faculty speculate that the transparent and formative nature of this process may contribute to the fact that students generally change behaviors before the actions progress to become more serious problems; it is important that the behavior evaluations are used in tandem with students' academic scores to determine retention or termination decisions.

Institutions

Doctoral and Research
Private
Walden University; Minneapolis, Minnesota (28,000 students)
Public
San Diego State University; San Diego, California (37,000 students)

Master's
Private
Johnson & Wales University; Providence, Rhode Island (10,000 students)
Public
Special/medical
University of Nebraska Medical School; Omaha, Nebraska (2,900 students)

Using Reflective Learning Portfolio Reviews for Master's and Doctoral Students

Marilee J. Bresciani, San Diego State University

◆ ◆ ◆

Look for the use of student reflections in portfolios to reform curriculum and the advising process. Professionals in the fields volunteer each semester to review the portfolios and to offer feedback to students and faculty.

Background and Purpose(s) of Assessment

Faculty at San Diego State University implemented a reflective learning portfolio for the master's and doctoral programs to accomplish three goals: (1) to provide the student with a facilitated opportunity to reflect on his or her learning, therefore connecting curricular and cocurricular learning opportunities with intended program learning outcomes and with the student's personal and professional goals; (2) to use the reflective writings in advising sessions to provide academic and personal support interventions as well as additional alignment of courses to learning goals, and (3) to provide evidence of student learning that culminates in a 20-minute presentation of synthesized learning to program faculty and external professionals in the student's field as a part of the student's final oral examination.

Assessment Method(s) and Year(s) of Implementation

Although the portfolios have been used in the master's program for four years; the last two years have seen more significant use of the portfolio in the advising process. Thus, the full model in place at this point is only in its second year of use in the master's program and first year of use in the doctoral program.

Required Resources

Faculty collaboration and participation with students are the primary resources used. In addition, alumni volunteer to evaluate the portfolios for program review purposes. An external reviewer also volunteers to evaluate the quality of analysis for program review decisions. Other faculty and professionals volunteer to evaluate the student's oral and written presentations prior to graduation.

Findings

Findings indicate many areas for improvement in course outcomes, as well as in course sequencing. In addition, students report on their development progress cognitively and affectively. All students express surprise at how much they have learned and the many ways in which they can apply their learning to outside experiences. Students also report the desire to change some courses that are currently not required into requirements, as they believe these courses have been so valuable. Students also discuss how engagement in the reflective portfolio process helps them connect what they had thought were silly expected learning outcomes to their understanding of what was expected of them and why.

Use of Findings

The use of findings from the portfolio evaluations has led to improvement in course syllabi, rearrangement of course sequencing, and discussion of removing three program outcomes versus adding two courses in order to ensure student learning of those three outcomes. Students' reflections on their learning have also given faculty advisors rich information to use in providing additional learning opportunities or refinements to students' personal academic plans. Furthermore, when students are not able to recognize their learning in course reflections, faculty are able to offer further learning opportunities or to assist students in the identification of that learning. Faculty and external reviewers have provided feedback on the criteria used for overall evaluation of the portfolio, and improvements have been implemented. Students' suggestions for increasing the number of courses have not yet been implemented because faculty are considering the administrative and financial consequences of those decisions. Students have suggested improvements in the portfolio guidelines and directions, and these refinements and clarifications have been made.

Impact of Using the Findings

We have noticed an improvement in synthesis of learning and evidence of learning as a result of the change in course sequencing. In addition, students who graduated last year reported positive responses to their portfolio as evidence of learning from those interviewing them for professional positions. This year's cohort initially complained about the workload involved in completing the portfolio and expressed frustrations about the requirement of reflecting on the value of their courses to personal and professional growth. Their recently completed end-of-year reflections show a deeper understanding of why they were asked to reflect and an appreciation for the portfolio activity as well as other learning requirements.

Success Factors

The faculty in the program (adjuncts as well as full-time tenure-track faculty) are committed to student learning. They have been interested in the evidence contained in the portfolios and are collaborative in the discussions on improving learning. They have been willing to change how they teach and what they teach to create an improved student learning experience.

The professional volunteers who gather to review end-of-year learning presentations are generous with their time. They say that they do it because they care about the quality of the professionals in their field. They take the time to offer meaningful feedback to the students and to the program faculty about how to improve the program.

Our challenge now will be whether or not to drop some program learning outcomes or to add two courses. Given current budget cuts, this may be a difficult discussion.

Relevant Institutional Web Sites Pertaining to This Assessment Practice

Assessment plan and curriculum alignment matrix:

http://interwork.sdsu.edu/student_affairs/index.html

Details about the reflective learning portfolio:

http://interwork.sdsu.edu/student_affairs/current_students/
Reflective_Learning.html

Making Learning Outcomes Explicit through Dissertation Rubrics

Jordan Orzoff, Paula Peinovich, Eric Riedel, Walden University

◆ ◆ ◆

Look for use of a rubric to build consensus on evaluating dissertations and to link rubric items to PhD learning outcomes resulting in curriculum revision. Findings suggested that more emphasis needed to be placed on qualitative methods.

Background and Purpose(s) of Your Assessment

Walden University began a transformation of its doctoral programs' dissertation process in 2003. For at least a decade, faculty and accreditors had been concerned about inconsistent quality in student writing and research. Students, administrators, and faculty also complained that the standards applied by committees in mentoring, giving feedback, and evaluating student work were inconsistent. The main quality assurance strategy prior to 2003 was a retrospective anonymous review of the dissertations by a faculty member external to the committee after the committee had already approved the dissertation and the orals had been completed. The "anonymous reviewer" feedback sometimes contradicted the committee and generated hard feelings between faculty. Students who were caught in the middle were confused and understandably frustrated. Most important, the anonymous reviewer assessment strategy did not demonstrably improve the quality of the dissertations produced by the university.

Assessment Method(s) and Year(s) of Implementation

In 2003, the provost appointed a faculty committee to develop a rubric for evaluating dissertations. The intent of the rubric was to make explicit to both students and faculty the standards for a high-quality dissertation. For students, the rubric provided both a guideline for developing their dissertations and a structure for receiving formative feedback while revising the documents. For faculty, the rubric served as a starting point for committees to work toward consensus on evaluating dissertations and a mechanism for tracking students' progress. For students as well as faculty, the rubric made explicit a community standard for doctoral research at Walden University. Prior to its implementation, faculty standards were implicit and idiosyncratic, leading to the inconsistencies in quality and clashes between faculty noted earlier. The period of development, revision, implementation, and training in the use of the rubric lasted until 2005, by which point it was in use across the university. Following the implementation of the doctoral rubrics, faculty also developed rubrics for the master's theses.

Required Resources

The rubrics were developed over a period of three weeks by a committee of faculty drawn from all of Walden University's PhD programs. Once a draft of the rubric was completed, the committee solicited feedback from the entire faculty body through an online deliberative process, and successive drafts were developed and vetted. This process took approximately three months. Resources for this process included financial support for the committee and modest administrative support for document management and publishing. Once the faculty had approved the rubrics, all doctoral faculty had to be trained to use the rubric. This required resources for faculty trainers, faculty training, and the use of a service that facilitates conference calls. High-level, strong, and visible administrative support from the provost and deans was an essential resource for addressing concerns and maintaining the project's momentum. The university's Assessment Office completed all the data collection and analysis of the results and maintained a repository of rubric scores. Just to maintain the data collection for analysis required the addition of a paraprofessional position in the Assessment Office.

Findings

The dissertation and thesis rubrics allowed faculty to evaluate completed dissertations on ten separate indicators per chapter (assuming a five-chapter dissertation standard). Each indicator was given a rating ranging from 1 (unacceptable) to 5 (commendable), with ratings of 3 or above considered generally acceptable, though possibly still requiring some minor revision. Over the first two years of the rubrics' use, data were collected from 197 dissertation rubrics. Analysis of the data showed that about 70 percent of student work was rated as acceptable, with 20 percent somewhat commendable to highly commendable, and 10 percent marginal or unacceptable.

Use of Findings

Because the rating scores could be disaggregated to individual items on the rubrics, it was possible to see where specific strengths and weaknesses were found. For instance, the university learned that dissertations were weakest in qualitative methods. As part of the university's outcomes assessment plan, specific rubric items were linked to learning outcomes in the PhD programs. These data were used to validate accomplishment of certain learning outcomes or to indicate areas for program improvement. The rubric data were most useful in guiding a review of the content and effectiveness of programs' research curricula.

Impact of Using the Findings

Despite initial unease, the faculty have become quite comfortable with the use of rubrics and with improving their own communications on evaluating student work. Student-faculty conflicts and student complaints in these processes have been reduced significantly. The university followed up the dissertation rubrics with rubrics for masters' theses, developed using the same process outlined above for the dissertations, but modified based on lessons learned from the doctoral programs. In addition, faculty have also taken the initiative to develop specialized rubrics for some disciplines or methods and to adopt rubrics for course papers, online course threaded discussion postings, and student portfolios. A comprehensive review of the graduate programs' research curriculum began in 2007, using the rubric data as a major source of evidence. Rubric items continue to be a contributing data source for program learning outcomes assessment. Walden has been approached several times by doctoral programs at other institutions requesting permission to use or adapt the dissertation and thesis rubrics for their own quality improvement purposes.

Success Factors

Faculty involvement from the beginning was critical. There was considerable suspicion of administrative meddling in faculty oversight of dissertations, but having a faculty committee act as the agent of change defused some of that. Over the three-year period of the transition, strong and repeated messages of support from the provost and the deans kept this project alive and moving forward. Finally, having the central Assessment Office handle most of the paperwork and process steps freed faculty time and kept the transition on schedule and the rules consistently applied.

Relevant Institutional Web Sites Pertaining to This Assessment Practice

Dissertation process, forms, and rubrics:

http://inside.waldenu.edu/c/Student_Faculty/StudentFaculty_4276.htm

Thesis process, forms, and rubrics:

http://inside.waldenu.edu/c/Student_Faculty/StudentFaculty_4278.htm

Cross-Discipline Assessment of MBA Capstone Projects

Joanne M. Crossman, Johnson & Wales University Graduate School

◆ ◆ ◆

Look for cross-disciplinary assessment of student portfolios that lead to faculty development opportunities including senior faculty mentoring adjunct faculty and workshops to improve interrater reliability.

Background and Purpose(s) of Assessment

Johnson & Wales University Graduate School offers an MBA in global business leadership with concentrations in accounting, financial management, international trade, marketing, and organizational leadership. The MBA in hospitality features concentrations in event leadership, finance, and marketing.

In addition to course outcome assessments, program outcomes are assessed through students' performance in co-op and their career capstone courses: Business Policy and Strategy, or Hospitality and Tourism Business Policy and Strategy.

Therein, interdisciplinary, coauthored capstone projects center on strategic analyses and application of management, marketing, and financial practices essential to highly competitive career fields. Coauthoring teams are composed of three to four self-selected collaborators. The capstone project content is assessed by the course instructor, and a second reader assesses communication competence. The purpose of this cross-discipline assessment is to inform teaching and learning in the Global Business Leadership, Hospitality, and Strategic Communication courses.

Assessment Method(s) and Year(s) of Implementation

The cross-discipline assessment originated in 2004. Presently, the capstone project contributes 50 points (50 percent) of the career capstone course grade. The strategic communication competence assessment is valued at 20 of those 50 points.

Since 2004, several iterations of the strategic communication competence assessment rubric have led to its current format, which affords a maximum of 20 points for written communication skills assessed on: organization and unity; graphic representation; language, style, coherence, syntax, and mechanics; and APA style and format. From 2004 to 2006, executive summaries were also part of the strategic communication competence assessment.

Upon completion of their capstone project, students are required to submit two copies to the course professor, who assesses the projects for content. Initially, the second reader was a professor of communications who designed, piloted, and revised the rubric, and established interrater reliability with the present readers. Since that time, communication competence has been assessed by one or two Professional Communications Center tutors, who also serve as adjunct instructors of communication. They assess projects within a one-week period during which their other duties are secondary. Once assessed for communication competence, capstone projects are returned to the course professor for record keeping, and then to the students. Presently, in response to recommendations from the Graduate School's external Business Advisory Board, one professor plans to pilot a presentation assessment that would constitute 10 of the 20 points. This practice will afford assessment of collaboration and presentation skills, also essential to the MBA program outcomes.

Required Resources

Students must submit two copies of the capstone project to the course professor. Communication competence is assessed with the rubric and by a communications professional, as described in the section on assessment methods above.

Findings

Several revisions have been made to both the rubric and assessment procedures since the inception of the cross-discipline assessment of MBA capstone projects. The following logistical practices have proved essential:

- Time line: Project is due two weeks prior to the course end date and returned during the final class meeting. (Note: these are summative assessments.)

- Distribute and discuss the rubric with the assignment. Remind students that rubrics must be used to assist with preparation of the project and as instructive feedback about their assessed work.

Specific findings in communication competence include:

Executive Summaries

(1) Need more succinct explanations of the project purposes. (2) In general, summaries provided clear, correct, and succinct explanation of the project's major findings. (3) Occasionally confused findings with conclusions. (4) Need more specific language for recommendations geared to the reader, consistent with findings and conclusions.

Organization and Unity

(1) Headings and subheadings used to delineate and organize ideas must generally increase in number and specificity. (2) Bullet points or other succinct writing strategies captured and compared key information. (3) Information flowed logically, sequentially, categorically. (4) Need transitions that repeat key words or phrases, indicate supporting ideas, or announce shifts in position.

Graphic Representation

(1) Generally accurate and well-organized graphic representations of pertinent information, comparisons, trends, models, and analyses. (2) Need succinct definitions within the text and more definitive labels and titles. (3) Graphics were well placed in conjunction with supporting text. (4) Plentiful.

Language, Style, and Coherence

(1) As most of the students are nonnative speakers of English and new to the United States, the language was not consistently clear, concise, accurate, and readable. (2) Inconsistent use of active voice, parallel structure, and varied sentence structure. (3) Occasional obvious shifts in writing styles among coauthors. (4) Occasional use of first- and third-person narration. (5) Abundance of direct quotations. (6) Unsophisticated phraseology (such as "came up with"). (7) Generalizations (such as "lots of"). (8) Unprofessional tone.

Syntax and Mechanics

(1) Areas for improvement included verb tense, subject-verb agreement, sentence fragments, use of commas, missing articles, misplaced modifiers, spelling, possessives, commas, capitalization, and pronoun-antecedent agreement. (2) Items in a series were often not syntactically parallel to other series items.

APA Style and Format

(1) Errors of parenthetical format, particularly for electronic resources. (2) Reference lists required judicious editing. (3) Inconsistent match of parenthetical citations and reference lists. (4) Citations generally included as necessary. (5) Generally good manuscript format.

Use of Findings

The capstone course project executive summaries consistently needed improvement. Although the rubric clearly delineates the required indicators, ancillary references are provided, and assigned reviews of the literature illustrate these and other kinds of abstracts, a curriculum analysis indicated that the practice of writing executive summaries is not expressively taught in the programs' one requisite communication course. Therefore, the Curriculum Committee recommended that faculty include an executive summary assignment within one of the other core courses. In addition, from 2004 to 2006, executive summaries were assessed by the communication competence readers rather than capstone course content experts.

In 2006, the content professors assumed that responsibility. The Graduate School faculty recognize that communication and collaboration are highly valued career skills. To that end, the capstone course project assessment findings—based on organization and unity; graphic representation; language, style, coherence; syntax and mechanics; and APA style and format—are regularly reported to the faculty and dean. Subsequently, these are among many professional development activities and initiatives that transpired:

- Three senior faculty currently mentor all full-time and adjunct faculty to discuss how they uniquely teach to and measure course and program outcomes. Faculty then report assessment findings and refinement of assignments and andragogy.
- Faculty participate in workshops on interrater consistency, rubric design, and writing across the curriculum.
- Faculty portfolios are developed to collect and share assignments and rubrics.
- "Closing the Loop" discussions and activities take place at monthly Curriculum Committee meetings.
- Standardization of APA style and format is accomplished through the *JWU APA Basics Handbook*.
- Curriculum review and revision is occurring.
- Refinements are being made to course sequencing; particularly for the required Strategic Communications course and the Career Capstone courses.
- The Research and Analysis course will be reinstated in the core curriculum beginning in 2008–09.

- Multifaceted marketing campaigns have been mounted for the Graduate School's award-winning Toastmasters Club.
- Requisite tutoring at the Professional Communications Center is offered for students at risk.
- Effective communication is now required as a foundation course for students who earned an undergraduate degree from a non-English-speaking university.
- The Graduate School Business Advisory Board reviews courses, outcomes, and capstone projects.
- Plans are being made to invite advisory board members to capstone project presentations.

Impact of Using the Findings

The impact of using some findings has yet to be realized. However, the faculty mentoring and discussions have surprisingly created an esprit de corps, perhaps because assessment is more transparent through the capstone project, therefore illuminating the need for improved communication prowess, and shared responsibility for assessing communication skills across the curriculum. The Curriculum Committee is presently considering assessing these critical skill sets at interim points in the program.

Moreover, the faculty have committed to refining program and course outcomes and curriculum in collaboration with the Advisory Board for relevance to alternative-delivery and future distance education.

In addition, there is a steady increase in membership in the JWU Voice of Leadership Toastmasters Club, and many students have earned international certifications of *Competent Communicator* and *Competent Leader*. Since 2001, the Graduate School has followed the JWU *APA Basics Handbook*, a faculty-designed guide updated annually to help students understand and follow the requisite APA style and format, and more recently, student and faculty workshops have facilitated greater consistency.

Success Factors

Among the greatest successes of the cross-discipline assessment of MBA capstone projects has been faculty's realization that communication skills are not the sole purview of communications professors. Consequently, our faculty have begun to set more rigorous standards for written and verbal communications and collaboration.

Moreover, the ardent assessment practitioners agree that it is heartening to overhear students and faculty say "It's all right there, in the rubric."

Relevant Institutional Web Sites Pertaining to This Assessment Practice

www.jwu.edu/grad/resources.htm
www.jwu.edu/grad/index.htm
www.jwu.edu/sas/catalog/0809/pdf/ri_grad.pdf
jwu.freetoasthost.us

Measuring the Professionalism of Medical Students

Hugh A. Stoddard, University of Nebraska College of Medicine

◆ ◆ ◆

Look for the use of a professionalism rating scale as a formative assessment tool. The Professional Rating Form (PRF) has made expectations for professional behavior transparent to students.

Background and Purpose(s) of Assessment

Medical schools in the United States have been under increasing pressure from accrediting agencies, licensing boards, and professional academic societies to ensure that medical school graduates have acquired the attitudes and behaviors that are expected of a physician (American Board of Internal Medicine Foundation, 2002; Liaison Committee on Medical Education, 2007; and National Board of Medical Examiners, 2002). Medical professionalism is a topic of concern at all levels, from practicing physicians to medical school applicants, and medical schools are obligated to select and prepare students who will fit the mold of professional behavior that a medical doctor needs. A series of licensing exams has been used for many years to guarantee that persons with an MD degree will have sufficient scientific knowledge to be licensed to care for patients. The renewed emphasis on noncognitive factors, specifically professionalism, necessitates a novel approach to assessment for medical schools.

At the national level, since 2005 the United States Medical Licensure Exam series has included a performance assessment of students' clinical skills and patient communication skills (USMLE Step 2 Clinical Skills Exam). The challenge to medical schools has been to define, teach, and assess professionalism for medical students in preparation for the licensure process and to prepare students to become competent health care providers.

Assessment Method(s) and Year(s) of Implementation

In 2004 the University of Nebraska College of Medicine (UNCOM) implemented a professionalism assessment system by which faculty used an online system to rate the professionalism of behaviors exhibited by medical students during required classes, labs, and clinical courses. Faculty used a locally developed online rating form to assess the professionalism of each student in each course through the first three years of medical school. The process included at least nineteen different ratings assigned on the basis of observations in both classroom and clinical environments.

The first step to develop this professionalism assessment system was to define the traits of professionalism that are relevant to medical students and to design the rating form that would be used. Several professional medical organizations have defined professionalism; however, many of these were defined in relation to licensed physicians or residents (American Board of Internal Medicine Foundation, 2002; National Board of Medical Examiners, 2002; and Accreditation Council for Graduate Medical Education, 2007). Selecting appropriate traits on which to assess medical students at UNCOM was accomplished by identifying the traits that were considered relevant across the continuum of medical education and then modifying that list of traits to include only those that were relevant to students. This was accomplished through reviews of medical education literature (Ginsburg et al., 2000; Phelan, Obenshain, & Galey, 1993) and subsequent analysis by physician or educators.

The rating scale needed to be succinct and clear enough to be used by part-time clinical faculty and it had to be psychometrically defensible for use in student promotion or termination decisions. The solution was a professionalism rating form (PRF) that had six discrete traits and a seven-point rating scale for each trait. Behavioral anchors for each trait were developed and included on the form. The anchors were written and vetted by experienced medical educators from both the clinical and classroom realms who were familiar with the behavior of both medical professionals and students in training. Behaviors that were common and acceptable among medical students were the anchors at the center of the seven-point scale. Examples of extreme behaviors, both desirable and undesirable, were used for the anchors at either end of the rating scale. Based on reasoned judgment and past experience, we predicted that the faculty who assigned scores using the PRF would assume a normal distribution of scores and would therefore assign ratings with most scores falling in the middle range of the scale. Reported incidents of unprofessional behavior were rare and even minor offenses were uncommon, so the distribution of scores was expected to exhibit high positive kurtosis.

A critical element of the professionalism assessment system was that faculty needed to rate all students and not just report the outliers. Previous professionalism reporting systems at UNCOM had relied on exception reporting with the eventual result that very few violations were recorded. The new professionalism assessment system incorporated periodic, longitudinal ratings of students.

To compensate for an anticipated "grade inflation" phenomenon, raters were not allowed to assign ratings that were on either tail of the distribution without submitting written comments to justify the rating. On the seven-point scale outliers were defined as ratings in the lowest two or the highest two categories. Mandating extra labor for raters to assign an extreme score was intended to enforce the inclusion of formative feedback to those students who merited extreme scores and to discourage capricious use of the highest and lowest rating categories. Because the PRF was administered online, the requirement to include comments with extreme ratings was enforced automatically.

Required Resources

The three most critical resources needed to develop, implement, and evaluate the professionalism rating form at UNCOM were: the time needed to research and create the form, the time and expertise to train faculty on its use, and computer programming expertise to devise the Web-based data collection, storage, and reporting system. The funding to make these available was provided by the dean of the College of Medicine. Oversight for creation of the PRF was delegated to the UNCOM Curriculum Development Office, which is entirely funded by the dean and reports to the associate dean for academic affairs. The director of this office was charged with oversight of all steps of developing and implementing the system. The onus for data entry was delegated to departmental support personnel who did the work in conjunction with their other responsibilities regarding student data management.

Findings

The most important utilization of PRF data is by the associate dean of students who downloads periodic reports from the database. These reports are used to identify students whose behavior indicates a need for counseling or mentoring. Because the expectations for a medical student are dramatically different from those for a physician, many students exhibit behaviors early in their medical school career that may be typical for students but are not appropriate for health care providers. The PRF gave faculty members a means to single out students who were behaving inappropriately and offered the dean of students an opportunity to assist deficient students in reforming their attitudes.

The PRF reporting system has also been used in conjunction with academic scores to summarize individual student performance when making promotion, retention, or termination decisions. Faculty on the UNCOM Scholastic Evaluation Committee reported that the PRF data were helpful in garnering a comprehensive picture of medical students who were under review. Previously, decisions could only be made based on personal experience or anecdotal evidence.

Over the four years of active use of the PRF, the dean of students and other faculty leaders found that instances of unprofessional behavior were uncommon among the medical students. As had been anticipated, 95.2 percent of the ratings submitted were in the middle three categories. Only .6 percent of the submitted scores indicated professionalism problems. The formative nature of PRF and the manner in which it was used by the dean of students may have played a part in encouraging students to rectify inappropriate behaviors before more serious transgressions occurred. On the occasions when grossly unprofessional behavior occurred, a durable record of the incident was stored in the PRF database.

Use of Findings

The finding that the PRF had utility for both formative and summative assessments of student behavior has led to continued use of the system. Currently, PRF results are employed both for internal student evaluations and for composing recommendation letters for students when they apply for residence programs. Preliminary studies of the psychometric properties of the PRF indicate that additional training for raters would be helpful in improving the statistical properties.

After two years of data collection with PRF had been completed, a reconsideration of the traits, behavioral anchors, and the seven-point rating scale on the form was initiated. Based on feedback from current and former students, faculty members, and curriculum leaders, some minor changes were made in the wording of the behavioral anchors and the titles of the traits on the PRF. Although the PRF was developed as a compromise between the competing demands of faculty who teach in widely divergent contexts, users who have reviewed the reports have concluded that the existing PRF has sufficient validity.

Impact of Using the Findings

Because faculty found the PRF useful in assessing students' professionalism, the program has also increased awareness among students of the behaviors that are expected of medical students. The attitudes and behaviors that are expected of medical professionals are well documented; however, the PRF has made those expectations more transparent to medical students who are training to join the profession. The continued use of the PRF for assessment of students by faculty is also motivating implementation of self and peer ratings by students.

Success Factors

The most critical success factor for PRF was a core of faculty members who were dedicated to ensuring that students understand and practice professional behavior. This included the faculty who were involved in creating the system as well as the student affairs dean who employed the data in order to conduct his job. Students also understood the necessity of having a professionalism system that would fairly reward or discipline students for their conduct.

Relevant Institutional Web Sites Pertaining to This Assessment Practice

http://webmedia.unmc.edu/medicine/kdybdall/webpage/ ProfessionalismRatingForm2007.pdf

CHAPTER FOURTEEN

GOOD PRACTICE IN IMPROVING AND SUSTAINING ASSESSMENT

As many outcomes assessment programs enter a second or third decade, interest in improving and sustaining assessment initiatives is increasing. All of the principles cited previously in this volume as guides for planning and implementing an assessment program must be considered in improving and sustaining it. In this section we focus on a variety of ways in which assessment can be built into a culture that values evidence. Specifically, assessment at the institutions identified here is connected fundamentally to processes that faculty, staff, and top administrators value.

Assessment of the liberal studies program (LSP) at DePaul University uses the time-honored process of peer review to improve, strengthen, and sustain assessment. Faculty in each of thirteen areas contributing to the LSP prepare unit reports on their assessment activities and findings. Then a subcommittee of the Liberal Studies Council—compensated for summer work on the project—reviews each of the thirteen reports and offers constructive commentary on the learning outcomes selected, the assessment processes employed, and potential uses of findings. Katherine A. Cermak, Jodi Cressman, and Midge Wilson report that "the subcommittee makes recommendations for ways to improve assessments through the construction of better research questions, outcomes, and rubrics, and identifies where on campus help can be found." These authors observe that general education faculty are more engaged in assessment as they meet subsequently to consider the recommendations contained in the peer review for their unit. Moreover, as the recommendations for using the findings in the peer reports are implemented, staff in the writing and faculty development centers at DePaul have seen increases in the number of faculty seeking assistance with their approaches to teaching.

At Hocking College, faculty have developed exit competences in both general education and occupational areas for each associate degree program. Peer review of program outcomes, which takes place every four years, involves not only faculty but also employers in the relevant occupational areas. Every year since 1993 the college calendar has included an assessment work day, which helps to sustain outcomes assessment at Hocking. All faculty spend that day "analyzing the data collected during the past year and planning program improvements for the current year based on assessment evidence," according to Judith A. Maxson and Bonnie Allen Smith.

Connecting outcomes assessment to an institution's mission is an effective strategy for sustaining assessment. According to Warren Rosenberg, Iona College "has a clear and visible statement of mission that guides the college in all that it does and provides, as a statement to external stakeholders, the expectations that Iona holds for its graduates." To track progress on all elements of the mission, the Advisory Committee on Assessment has constructed 25 key performance indicators (KPIs) that draw on internal and externally benchmarked assessment instruments and practices. The KPI summary provides a report card on mission progress that is shared with trustees, accreditors, and the public, and forms a basis for annual performance objectives for deans, department heads, and other academic administrators.

At Colorado State University (CSU), outcomes assessment has been integrated with a long-standing process of program review. Each department completes an online self-study using a uniform template, and now student learning outcomes are included along with outcomes for faculty research and service. Using the online self-study, external review team members "can view a department's assessment planning activity over a six-year period," says Kim K. Bender. The online database permits faculty in each department to check boxes that link goals in the department's action plan to CSU strategic planning goals and metrics. According to Bender, "Aggregated data from this activity reveal what parts of the strategic plan are receiving strong planning activity and what parts are receiving little or no planning activity." The same database structure is now being used at the University of Nebraska-Lincoln in a collaborative assessment project with CSU.

Jackie Snell at San Jose State University (SJSU) describes a multicomponent process for building and sustaining a culture of assessment. These components include assessment specialists in each college who are available for consultation with departments; funding for faculty development; individual and group awards for best practices in assessment given at a spring forum where various kinds of faculty achievement are recognized; giving credit for assessment in the promotion and tenure process; incorporating student learning outcomes in each department's five-year development plan; and collecting departmental assessment reports annually as part of the program planning self-study that will be read by at least one external reviewer as well as a team of SJSU administrators. Snell believes that the success of outcomes assessment at SJSU is due primarily to three factors: (1) establishing a schedule for assessment that includes activities every semester, (2) integrating assessment with the institution's program planning and review process, and (3) employing multiple approaches to provide for learning about assessment and for bringing attention and rewards to assessment activities.

Institutions

Doctoral and Research
    Private
      DePaul University; Chicago, Illinois (23,000 students)
    Public
      Colorado State University; Fort Collins, Colorado (25,000 students)

Master's
    Private
      Iona College; New Rochelle, New York (4,300 students)
    Public
      San Jose State University; San Jose, California (30,000 students)

Associate
    Public
      Hocking College; Nelsonville, Ohio (6,000 students)

Peer Review of Assessment Plans in Liberal Studies

Katherine A. Cermak, Jodi Cressman, Midge Wilson, DePaul University

◆ ◆ ◆

Look for a subcommittee of the Liberal Studies Council whose members earn summer salary for reviewing, discussing, and providing suggestions about annual unit assessment reports. Not only have assessment methods been improved, but faculty now are more frequently taking advantage of on-campus resources for strengthening instruction.

Background and Purpose(s) of Assessment

Formative assessment processes can strengthen interdisciplinary communities within general education. DePaul University's Liberal Studies Program (LSP) comprises thirteen units, each of which annually conducts and reports on its own assessment of student learning. Although the assessment process was designed to recognize and strengthen faculty ownership, the annual studies alone were insufficient for building a broader culture of assessment that would include both routine evaluations of assessment practices and improvements in teaching and learning. To facilitate a greater sense of shared purpose and to strengthen the connection between program assessment and teaching practices, the LSP created a system of peer review, which provides not only concrete feedback to assessment committees but also suggests ways for the findings to be transformed into actionable plans to improve student learning.

Assessment Method(s) and Year(s) of Implementation

For the past five years, a subcommittee of the Liberal Studies Council (LSC), which governs the LSP, has met annually to review, discuss, and provide concrete and constructive feedback to all 13 areas within general education. Moreover, LSP faculty act on their assessment findings each year by holding annual developmental meetings and workshops in which all faculty who teach in a given area (including full-time tenure track, full-time non-tenure track, and contingent faculty) from across the university are invited to attend and discuss the previous year's assessment findings and the subcommittee's feedback on them. At that time learning outcomes are reviewed, best practices for teaching are discussed, and effective ways to implement proposed changes are identified.

Required Resources

The greatest resource is perhaps faculty time, as this peer-review process requires not only that the LSP unit advisory committees within each domain conduct and write up the assessment projects, but also that a separate subcommittee made up of faculty members from the LSC read and respond to each of the unit's findings. As this intensive review process takes place over the summer, another resource is funding, as the subcommittee faculty members are paid $1,000 each for their extra service.

Findings

Involving large numbers of faculty in assessment through the LSP unit advisory committees and the LSC assessment subcommittee has clarified and strengthened expectations about what authentic assessment entails, how projects can be improved, and how findings can guide action. LSC subcommittee members have found that the peer feedback provided to assessment committees within the different LSP units has indeed been integrated into future assessment activities. In part this may have resulted from increasing faculty awareness of local resources, including experts in writing, teaching, and assessment techniques available at DePaul. In addition, advisory committees at the unit level appear to be carefully reviewing the prior year's assessment feedback from their peers, and making adjustments accordingly. Finally, most areas of the LSP now hold annual meetings at which assessment findings are disseminated to full- and part-time faculty who teach in the relevant areas. These discussions often lead faculty to move toward actionable plans for enhancing student learning and teaching.

Use of Findings

Assessment reports have noted that information provided through peer feedback and advice regarding the use of local resources have been used to improve assessment. Often the subcommittee makes recommendations for improvements through constructing better research questions, outcomes, and rubrics, and identifies where help can be found on campus. In addition, it has been noted frequently by staff from the University Center for Writing-Based Learning and the Office for Teaching, Learning, and Assessment that their resources are being used more frequently by faculty associated with the LSP. The best-practices meetings and workshops that stem from assessment have attracted more involvement of faculty teaching in the various LSP units.

Impact of Using the Findings

Examples of concrete actions taken following peer review of assessments include the following:

- Based on its initial assessment and peer feedback the Religious Dimensions Learning Domain Advisory Committee decided to extend its assessment to address issues about the use of an imprecise rubric. The committee developed a detailed rubric that provided examples of what work within each criterion looks like and this proved to be a great improvement over the rubric used the previous year. Sampling was also improved and the student work reviewed was from a broader selection of courses taught within the domain.

- Faculty in the LSP units, and presumably those in the departments that feed into them, have become aware of the University Center for Writing-Based Learning as a valuable resource.
- With the Center for Writing-Based Learning, the Mathematics and Technological Literacy Advisory Committee held a writing workshop to develop a rubric for the final data analysis project in the first course of this component's two-course sequence.
- The Focal Point Seminar Advisory Committee reports plans to hold a best-practices meeting about how to teach students to revise their work, stressing that not only should revision opportunities be made available, but that students should be taught how to do revisions.
- As a result of feedback provided to the Philosophical Inquiry Learning Domain and members' own discussions, this area's advisory committee decided to hold a meeting to identify ways to clarify and assess critical thinking ability in writing with participation from the Writing Center.
- The Discover/Explore Chicago Advisory Committee plans to hold a series of writing improvement workshops with the Center for Writing-Based Learning that will include assignment design, revision processes, and sequencing assignments to build a larger project.

Relevant Institutional Web Sites Pertaining to This Assessment Practice

Liberal Studies Program:

http://liberalstudies.depaul.edu/

Office for Teaching, Learning and Assessment:

http://condor.depaul.edu/~tla/

Assessment of Student Academic Achievement in Technical Programs

Judith A. Maxson, Bonnie Allen Smith, Hocking College

◆ ◆ ◆

Look for multiple sources of direct evidence of student competence in eight general education outcomes at a technical college. During annual Assessment

Days faculty review assessment findings and make plans to undertake responsive actions to improve curriculum and instruction.

Background and Purpose(s) of Assessment

Hocking College is an innovative, experience-based technical college that nurtures learning and learner success. A plan for Academic Affairs ReVISIONing Learning challenged the campus community to reconsider each academic program in a new learner-centered paradigm. The ReVISIONing Learning process ensures that each academic area examines curriculum and instruction and evaluates adherence to nine criteria for excellence, our learning expectations for all associate degree programs. Early in the ReVISIONing Learning process, program exit competences representing entry-level knowledge, skills, and attitudes in occupational and general areas were identified through a Developing a Curriculum (DACUM) process. In 2002, we shifted to program outcomes using an outcomes-based educational process. Experts in the field and faculty members convene and respond to the question, "What do students need to be able to do 'out there' that we are responsible for 'in here'?" This process allows us to design our curricula with the end in mind. We update these program learning outcomes every four years so that we stay current. Program learning outcomes plus our institutional outcomes (Success Skills) are clearly articulated in the program handbooks for each academic area and form the basis of program and institutional assessment.

Assessment Method(s) and Year(s) of Implementation

For many years Hocking College faculty have utilized assessment tools and strategies in determining students' levels of academic success; for example, use of a rubric-scored departmental essay test for communications courses, and entry assessment for determination of initial placement in reading, writing, and math courses. In 1989, faculty identified and approved eight institutional general education outcomes representing work and life skills necessary for all associate degree recipients to be successful in the workplace, in transfer education, and in life. These competences, now known as Success Skills, include: communicates effectively; demonstrates math skills; demonstrates learning and critical thinking skills; maintains professional skills and attitudes; practices human relations skills; demonstrates knowledge of science and the environment; demonstrates community, cultural, and global awareness; and maintains a code of ethics.

A formal program of assessment was initiated in 1991 when faculty began the process of identifying missions, goal statements, and exit competences for each academic program. In 1993, a half-time assessment coordinator was appointed to assist with the development of the college's assessment plan. On the first annual Assessment Day, program faculty developed outcomes and measures of student academic success. Assessment work days have continued each year, resulting in modification of curriculum and instruction in response to assessment results. Responsibility for the assessment of student academic achievement was added to the job descriptions of faculty, coordinating instructors, deans, directors, and the vice president for academic affairs in 1996. In 1998, the assessment process became an essential part of the Academic Affairs ReVISIONing Learning process. Program exit competences derived from industry standards, DACUM panels, consultation with advisory groups, outcomes published by professional accreditation organizations, and work experience of Hocking College educators were reviewed and revised. We began using outcomes-based education in 2002. In February 2007, past assessment reports for each program were added to the college's Assessment Center Web site (www.hocking.edu/assessment_center) and may be reviewed by any interested stakeholder. The site is kept current by adding annual reports.

Required Resources

Faculty members communicate assessment evidence on two forms: the individual plan and the annual summary. The individual plan, unique to each program, has three sections: (1) mission statement and central objectives, (2) institutional Success Skills and program learning outcomes, and (3) criteria for assessment and reporting of results. Each plan also includes analysis of the data and program changes planned for the next year as a result of this analysis. The annual summary report requires information related to: (1) improvements to the program in the previous year brought about by the study of assessment results; (2) expenditures of time, money, and materials for the assessment program; (3) requests for assistance in implementing assessments; and (4) recommendations for altering the institution's assessment process. A full-time faculty member serves as the coordinator of assessment of student academic achievement. We set aside one day during fall quarter as an assessment work day.

Findings

Criteria and measures have been developed and modified over time to meet the college goal of preparing students for entry-level work in their chosen disciplines. Program faculty are encouraged to employ multiple assessment measures and strive for triangulation of data. Evidence of student learning often includes common direct internal measures such as capstone projects and products, portfolio assessment, standardized tests, and locally developed tests. Examples of direct external measures frequently include performance on national licensure or certification exams; external review of comprehensive capstone projects; and evaluation of performance during practicum, externship, or cooperative work experiences. Indirect measures reflected in assessment reports include graduate and employer surveys, exit interviews, and job placement data.

Use of Findings

Faculty in all academic programs report annually on the assessment of student learning outcomes. Faculty members in each technology program have developed assessment criteria and instruments to measure each criterion outlined in the program's individual plan of assessment. A variety of approaches is used to collect assessment data throughout the academic year. The college calendar specifies an annual assessment work day. Faculty spend this day analyzing the data collected during the past year and planning program improvements for the current year based on assessment evidence.

Impact of Using the Findings

As a result of the assessment of student learning outcomes we have many examples of curriculum changes leading to quality improvement. For example, in the wildlife management program, the instructors found that students were having difficulty performing mathematical calculations in the field (such as calculating acreage, supplies needed, or water depth). They reviewed the assessment report from the mathematics department, paying close attention to the scores their students received on the math exam taken by all students in the Introduction to Algebra course. The math test was developed by Hocking College faculty and addresses specific subskills of the math outcome. The scores for the wildlife management students were noted to be at or above the scores for other technologies and indicated that the students were satisfactorily meeting the math outcome. Because students were having difficulty applying math to their field of study, wildlife management faculty decided to increase the opportunities for students to practice math skills in their wildlife management classes, and provided more opportunities for application of these skills in field assignments. Wildlife faculty members have been pleased with the growth students now exhibit in their math skills.

The capstone course in each technical program is being redesigned to integrate summative assessment of the program and institutional outcomes learned throughout the course of study. Many programs require students to complete capstone projects. For example, drafting and design students choose a capstone project, work with an external mentor during the project, and prepare oral presentations and written technical papers related to their projects. The oral presentations are evaluated by internal evaluators from other areas of the college and external evaluators who are considered experts in the field of study. The ReVISIONing Learning Criteria for Excellence described earlier require that capstone experiences be included and used both as a synthesis-building learning situation and as an opportunity for end-of-program assessment. Assessment of all or many of the Success Skills is often incorporated in the evaluation of student performance.

Success Factors

Faculty members play the largest role in Hocking College's program of assessment. They have contributed at every stage of assessment program development. A full-time assessment coordinator meets throughout the year with faculty to educate and coach faculty about assessment practices, discuss assessment reporting, and assist in the development of assessment measures and tools. Proactive leadership by the provost and senior vice president for academic affairs in all initiatives related to the assessment of student academic achievement (curriculum development, professional development, ReVISIONing, course design, and hiring of personnel) has been critical to the success of Hocking's assessment process.

Relevant Institutional Web Sites Pertaining to This Assessment Practice

Assessment Center Web Site:

www.hocking.edu/assessment_center

Assessing Achievement of the Mission as a Measure of Institutional Effectiveness

Warren Rosenberg, Iona College

◆ ◆ ◆

Look for 25 indicators of mission effectiveness that are based on internal data as well as student responses to both national and locally developed surveys. Over three years continuing improvement has been noted on 18 of the 25 indicators.

Background and Purpose(s) of Assessment

Iona College has a clear and visible statement of mission that guides the college in all that it does and provides, as a statement to external stakeholders about the expectations that Iona faculty hold for graduates and for which we accept accountability. Developed by the collegewide Advisory Committee on Assessment, Iona faculty and staff have implemented a 25-item set of indicators that track our progress on all elements of the institution's mission using key performance indicators (KPI) drawn from a number of internal and externally benchmarked assessment instruments and practices.

Assessment Method(s) and Year(s) of Implementation

Referred to as the Mission KPI Summary, this collegewide assessment instrument has tracked three years of data and was initially released in AY 2007–08 as a three-year comparative summary. The KPI summary tracks 25 key indicators in five distinct categories of mission effectiveness. The data are drawn from multiple sources, which include Iona's Office of Institutional Research, the National Survey of Student Engagement, and the Iona College Senior Survey.

Required Resources

The assessment is compiled by the Office of Academic Affairs using data points collected from the sources just identified.

Findings

Deficiencies were noted in 4 of the 25 indicators, 18 demonstrated continuing improvement, and 2 indicated neither improvement nor decline. One of the selected indicators did not have multiple years of measurement and thus no comparison could be made. In sum, the findings indicate that Iona has successfully carried out its mission-related goals of being a diverse community of learners and scholars committed to academic excellence, whose graduates demonstrate the attributes, among others, of critical analysis, ethical conduct, civic engagement, and spirituality.

Use of Findings

The findings have been used as indicators of institutional effectiveness for our regional accreditor and our board of trustees. They also form the basis for annual performance objectives for deans, academic departments, and academic administrators. They will be a centerpiece in an upcoming review of the college's mission statement.

Impact of Using the Findings

The Mission KPI Summary, having been presented to the college community at a collegewide convocation, to the board of trustees, and to the Middle States Commission on Higher Education, provides an important single-source report card on Iona's success in achieving its mission. As a comprehensive assessment tool, it provides various stakeholders with a public accounting of performance in all areas of the college's operations.

Success Factors

Iona's mission statement is known to all students and employees and is prominently displayed in every campus building. The use and public reporting of the Mission KPI Summary (see Exhibit 14.1) have been successful in reinforcing the centrality of the mission in all that we do and in highlighting the importance of assessment and public accountability to internal stakeholders. In addition, the comprehensive and public reporting of Mission KPI allows students, faculty, staff, and administrators alike to share in Iona's accomplishments and continuing challenges. Mission KPI results are shown in Table 14.1.

EXHIBIT 14.1. EXECUTIVE SUMMARY.
MISSION KPI REPORT

KPI 1–6. Diversity

These six KPIs demonstrate our achievement of the mission's call to being a diverse community of learners and scholars. The data for KPIs 1–4 are pretty straightforward. KPIs 5 and 6 show two different and important data elements.

In each box is a dual figure, such as 2.63/2.57. This reflects the responses of our graduating seniors on the NSSE survey (2.63) compared with the national average for all Carnegie classification masters institutions (2.57). The numbers are from responses on a 4-point Likert scale. With respect to these two diversity questions, Iona's students had a more favorable response than the national average. In addition, the chart shows the progression at Iona from 2004 to 2007, indicating that our students respond more favorably now than they did three years ago.

KPI 7–9. Academic Excellence

KPI 7 assumes that the achievement of national accreditation for our academic programs reflects the external analysis of our faculty quality and accomplishments, the integrity of our syllabi, and the quality and demonstrated learning outcomes of our students. We are seeking ten accreditations and currently have (or are candidates for) seven.

KPIs are generally accepted measures of institutional accountability.

KPI 10–13. Academic Components

KPIs 10–12 are drawn from the NSSE survey and, following the pattern described above under diversity, measure the specific academic outcomes of independent thinking, skilled decision making, and technological adaptability. KPI 13 is a demonstration of a commitment to lifelong learning as measured by graduate school attendance.

KPI 14–21. Personal Attributes of Graduates

All drawn from the NSSE survey as indicators of values and ethics, service and civic engagement, spiritual development, physical development, and social development. The data show a comparison to national averages as well as Iona's improvement from 2004 to 2007. KPI 15 shows Iona students' growth from the freshman year (2004) to the senior year.

KPI 22–25. Internships and Career Counseling

Data drawn from the annual Senior Survey. Data for KPI 24 will begin to be collected and reported in the 2007–08 academic year.

TABLE 14.1. IONA COLLEGE—MISSION KPI RESULTS: COMPARISON AND TRENDS 2004–2007.

Mission Element: " ... a diverse community of learners and scholars ... "				
Key Performance Indicator	2005	2006	2007	
1. Diversity of Faculty (% women / % non-white) (IR)	36/9	35/10	35/10	0
2. Diversity of Undergraduate Student Body (% women / % non-white) (IR)	54/23	54/25	55/25	+
3. Diversity of Graduate Student Body (% women / % non-white) (IR)	59/18	64/19	66/25	+
4. International Diversity of Student Body (% non USA) (IR)	2	2	2	0
	2004*	2007*	2010*	
5. Iona contributed to understanding people of other ethnic/racial backgrounds (NSSE 11l) (IC / Peers)	2.63/2.57	2.68/2.64		+
6. Institution encourages contact among students from different backgrounds (NSSE 10.c) (IC / Peers)	2.55/2.40	2.56/2.47		+
Mission Element: " ... dedicated to academic excellence ... [and] intellectual inquiry ... achieved by ... dedicated teaching, ... creative research and scholarship ... "				
Key Performance Indicator	2005	2006	2007	
7. % of target academic accreditations attained (IR)	50%	60%	70%	+
8. 4-year graduation rate (IR)	40%	42%	47%	+
9. 6-year graduation rate (IR)	53%	56%	57%	+
Mission Element: "Iona College graduates will be sought after because they will be: Skilled decision makers ... independent thinkers ... Lifelong learners ... Adaptable to new information and technologies ... "				
Key Performance Indicator	2004*	2007*	2010*	
10. Participated in course-based, in-depth analysis (NSSE 2b) (IC / Peers)	3.39/3.28	3.28/3.21		−

TABLE 14.1. *(continued)*

Mission Element: "Iona College graduates will be sought after because they will be: Skilled decision makers ... independent thinkers ... Lifelong learners ... Adaptable to new information and technologies ... "			
Key Performance Indicator	2004*	2007*	2010*
11. Applied concepts to practical problems & new situations (NSSE 2e) (IC /Peer)	3.27/3.23	3.25/3.18	+
12. Developed skills in computing technologies (NSSE 10g) (IC / Peers)	3.13/3.13	3.54/3.44	+
	2005	2006	2007
13. % of this year's graduates entering graduate programs (SS 3)	66%	75%	76% +
Mission Element: "Iona College graduates will be sought after because they will be: ethical ... decision makers ... motivated to leadership, service and civic responsibility ... individuals who integrate the spiritual, intellectual, civic, emotional and physical dimensions of their lives"			
Key Performance Indicator	2004*	2007*	2010*
14. Development of a personal code of values and ethics (NSSE 11n) (IC / Peers)	2.72/2.71	2.87/2.66	+
15. Development of a personal code of values and ethics (NSSE 11n) (Δ Fr. To Sr.)		2.71/2.87	+
16. Participation in service activities while at Iona (NSSE 7b)	.48/.57	.60/.54	–
17. Extent to which Iona has fostered a deeper sense of spirituality (NSSE 11p)	2.21/2.00	2.32/1.91	+[1]
18. Participated in physical fitness development while at Iona (NSSE 6b)	2.17/2.46	2.76/2.54	+[1]
19. Experienced institutional support to help student thrive socially (NSSE 10e)	2.23/2.10	2.40/2.14	+[1]
20. Extent to which institution fostered interest in welfare of community (NSSE 11o)	2.40/2.41	2.59/2.40	+[1]
21. Institution contributed to student voting in local and national elections (NSSE 11i)	1.97/1.84	2.15/2.06	+

(continued)

TABLE 14.1. *(continued)*

Mission Element: "Iona will achieve these goals by . . . internships . . . [and] intensive career counseling . . . "				
Key Performance Indicator	2005	2006	2007	
22. % of graduates who completed internships (SS)	45%	67%	69%	+
23. % reporting internship helped with preparation for employment (SS)	–	93%	90%	–
24. % of students receiving Career Development Services (GL)	n.a.	n.a.	n.a.	
25. % of students seeking employment with job offers at graduation (SS)	64%	73%	77%	+

*administration dates of NSSE; 1 significant difference from NSSE peers

Data Sources: *IR* = Iona College Office or Institutional Research Reports (KPI 1,2,3,4,7,8,9), *NSSE(xx)*=National Survey of Student Engagement (question #), *SS* = Iona College Senior Survey, *GL* = Gael Link (Career Development Tracking Software). Will begin reporting in 2007–08

Key Performance Indicators of Institutional Inputs: 1, 2, 3, 4, 19, 20, 23, 24

Key Performance Indicators of Student Outcomes: 5, 6, 7, 8, 9, 10, 11, 12, 13, 14, 15, 16, 17, 18, 21, 22, 25

KPI #7 - Accreditations Sought (* = acquired)

AACSB* - Business

AAMFT* (candidacy 2006) - Marriage and Family Therapy

ABET* - Computer Science

ACEJMC* Mass Communication

ACJS - Criminal Justice

ACS - Chemistry

AHUPA - Health Care Administration

CSWE* - Social Work

NASP* (candidacy 2007) - Psychology

NCATE* - Education

Linking Learning Outcomes Assessment with Program Review and Strategic Planning for a Higher-Stakes Planning Enterprise

Kim K. Bender, Colorado State University

◆ ◆ ◆

Look for an online planning platform for learning outcomes assessment that is integrated with an established program review process. Discussion of student learning in program review meetings increased from 10 percent of the meeting time in 2002 to 35 percent in 2007.

Background and Purpose(s) of Assessment

Sustaining learning assessment after reaccreditation: After Colorado State University (CSU) successfully attained reaccreditation in spring 2004, the director of assessment and the Office of the Provost's administrators developed a strategy to sustain the annual student learning outcomes assessment process. Because CSU is a highly decentralized institution with extensive research activity, we anticipated that faculty would not engage in learning assessment activity and reporting if a routine self-evaluation process were not strengthened and integrated with existing planning and evaluation policy, such as that associated with program review and special accreditation.

Planning and self-evaluation integration: Initially, our online planning platform for accomplishing learning outcomes assessment existed as a compartmentalized activity, separate from other university quality monitoring actions. It also did not generate system output reports for faculty showing what learning assessment looked like at CSU. The university needed to intensify the high-stakes value of doing the planning and self-evaluation so that the strengths and weaknesses of student performance could be determined routinely at the program level.

Visibility and viability of annual assessment process: The university worked to develop higher visibility of the Plan for Researching Improvement and Supporting Mission (PRISM) system (see Bender & Siller, 2006), establishing viability and portability in order to gain faculty confidence in the process. The assessment director has made several presentations at national assessment conferences since 2003, and in 2005 CSU entered a collaborative assessment project with the University of Nebraska-Lincoln (UNL) (see Resource A, p. 283).

Assessment Method(s) and Year(s) of Implementation

A home-grown database and software. CSU staff developed their own programming code and database system to provide an online planning infrastructure for faculty to use in forming and sustaining program-level assessment plans. The institution could have purchased software, but administrators believed that part of establishing a faculty culture of ownership and valuing systematic improvement in student learning relied on a campus administration commitment to generate homegrown resources. The homegrown method has become the faculty's system as they continuously modify its capacity and functionality.

Annual learning assessment integrates to program review. Program review for the institution is now completely online. The self-study documents follow a uniform template design as determined by department and institutional needs. The intent is to have faculty begin viewing student learning in the same way as they see outcomes for faculty research and service. The database areas for annual assessment and program review are linked so that external program review teams can view a department's assessment planning activity over a six-year period. Implemented in spring 2006, this feature has been functioning for three planning cycles.

Program review structurally linked to strategic planning. All the program review self-studies contain an action planning section where departments articulate their goals, strategies, barriers, and self-evaluation methods. The online database requires departments to complete a checkbox exercise that links each action plan goal to the CSU strategic planning goals and metrics. Aggregated data from this activity reveal which parts of the strategic plan are receiving strong planning activity and which parts are receiving little or no planning activity.

Interinstitutional collaboration. The CSU and UNL collaboration is realized in three ways: (1) sharing of the same database structure and functions expands the testing population for identifying problems, (2) collaborative presentations at national assessment conferences demonstrate external utility, and (3) regular interinstitutional staff meetings communicate weaknesses and direct improvements.

Required Resources

Colorado is a low-funding state for higher education, encouraging CSU to have the lowest administrative costs among its peers. For this reason, substantial emphasis was placed on modernizing planning and self-evaluation to produce savings in human labor. The PRISM continuous improvement system shares one server that is centrally maintained and uses university software licenses, including ColdFusion.

Each department designates at least one individual to enter assessment data in the online database once each fall. Each member of the university peer-review committee responsible for evaluating the quality of assessment planning annually spends about fifteen hours on these service obligations.

Findings

Integration of planning expanded. CSU faculty created 169 academic assessment plans and student affairs maintains 32 unit plans. As of 2005, all PRISM academic learning outcomes (512) were embedded in the online program review self-studies. By 2006, action plan goals for program review were linked structurally to university strategic planning goals within the PRISM database.

A coherent infrastructure affects faculty dialogue. About 90 percent of the university peer-review committee's feedback to departments regarding program review is now recorded in the online database for continuity of planning and accreditation needs. Departments respond to these comments, forming a documented dialogue among faculty about improving student learning as well as faculty research and service. Because the university uses a standard template structure, all departments now provide significantly more commentary on their self-evaluations of student learning. Over a six-year period, this focused attention generated a dramatic increase in the number of action plan goals directed to improving self-evaluation of student learning. Discussion of student learning in formal program review meetings, once dominated solely by research and faculty resource issues, has risen from 10 percent of meeting time in 2002 to roughly 35 percent in 2007.

Program participation increases over time. In 2002, only about 8 percent of academic programs practiced systematic direct learning assessment. In 2008, one of the eight colleges has realized a 100-percent reported participation rate in direct assessment for spring, other colleges are now performing at a 60-percent program participation rate, and a minority of colleges experience a low program participation rate. As programs approach the time for completing a program review self-study, participation in learning outcomes assessment increases significantly. Sharp increases in action plan goals dedicated to developing better program assessment activities have occurred over the last three years, where none had existed before.

Use of Findings

Changing evaluation guidelines to affect faculty behavior. Because the CSU system is based on the philosophy that creation of good processes generates good outcomes, the findings that the institution pays attention to are process oriented. For example, finding that program review self-studies presented sparse discussion of curriculum and student learning evaluation, the online program review self-study template design was expanded in the student learning sections and an exemplary practice was embedded. Because this information is now available to departments years in advance of scheduled reviews, faculty members are aware of institutional expectations well before self-study preparation begins.

Transparent to the public. The documentation and tracking of learning outcomes research is not kept secret. The PRISM design includes a feature that shares annual learning assessment plans with students and the public. Employers are given assessment information related to internships and learning outcomes so that they can see if these match their workplace needs. Reports of student learning improvements appear on this site, categorized by type, with volume indicated.

Impact of Using the Findings

Organizational learning environment accelerates improvement. With its online planning and self-evaluation platform, PRISM forms an organizational learning environment that enables all campus community members to learn from each other about strategies that deliver performance. Each template section (for example, student learning planning) of a program review self-study includes a good departmental example. The structure of review forms a captive audience of department faculty and external faculty reviewers who open these best practices to learn what information belongs in each section. In this way the best departments pull others up.

Self-evaluation structure changes faculty culture. Evidence of changes in faculty culture, valuing continuous improvement of student learning, is growing at a fast rate.

- CSU's new program proposals now include requirements for descriptions of how student learning will be assessed and how the program will demonstrate self-evaluation of learning to the institution.
- Departments are adding PRISM learning assessment descriptions to their special accreditation self-studies.
- External-to-the-university program review team reports more frequently mention a department's good use of the PRISM infrastructure.
- The College of Liberal Arts has placed program assessment plans, findings of student learning, and improvements on its Web site.
- Grant-funding proposals from faculty that relate to instructional design are including descriptions of PRISM as the means used to measure and document gains in student learning.

Improvement synergies result from institutional collaboration. Collaboration between CSU and UNL keeps both institutions positioned to make continuous improvement in the overall campus infrastructure for program planning and self-evaluation in student learning. There is little opportunity to become complacent or settled as changing needs and technological innovations drive synergies of advancement at both institutions. Currently both universities have a core of staff programmers meeting once per week to redesign database capacity and functionality.

Success Factors

Focus on the learning research process. The emphasis at CSU is for departments to demonstrate the intensity and depth of their self-evaluation of student learning instead of demonstrating value-added gains in student learning. We learned that faculty are not impressed with the value-added approach, preferring learning research that informs the design of the curriculum so that it strengthens student learning.

Make learning assessment a higher-stakes activity. Developing an online self-study template that includes a student learning section similar in length and intensity to faculty research and service sends a powerful message of institutional commitment to instructional excellence. In addition, continually placing learning alongside research and service in this way leads to a common recognition of all three activities.

Provide continual exposure to learning assessment. Including annual learning assessment and planning integration in the new strategic planning metrics has provided additional exposure. This has added another layer of peer-review scrutiny about the success of student learning as the strategic planning metrics are reviewed each year for progress by committees of faculty and administrators. Continual exposure is crucial for developing a faculty culture favorable to learning research.

Relevant Institutional Web Sites Pertaining to This Assessment Practice

To view assessment plans, use "view all resources" and select "public site":

http://improvement.colostate.edu

To demonstrate planning functions by department, log-in with *demo* as username and password:

http://assessment.colostate.edu

Building a Context for Sustainable Assessment

Jackie Snell, San Jose State University

◆ ◆ ◆

Look for multiple approaches to building sustainable assessment, including appointing assessment facilitators in each college, providing faculty development experiences, and conferring awards for good practice as well as recognition of assessment as service in the promotion and tenure process.

Background and Purpose(s) of Assessment

Building a system of meaningful student learning assessment at the program level, as contrasted with simply grading at the course level, requires a well-planned infrastructure. Simply responding to periodic accreditation pressures for assessment is more likely to create resentment than meaningful assessment. Creating a culture of assessment is a dynamic process of building community over a number of years.

Assessment Method(s) and Year(s) of Implementation

Faculty and administrators at San Jose State University have developed a number of building blocks to encourage a culture of assessment of student learning. None of these alone can create sustainable assessment.

Mentors and evangelists. Two assessment facilitators from each college are designated by the dean of the college. One is a faculty member who is knowledgeable about and a believer in assessment. The other is an associate dean of the college, an appointment that demonstrates the commitment of administration. Assessment facilitators are available for collegewide presentations and for consultation with departments.

Faculty development. The university makes funds available for guest speakers and assessment materials for department assessment retreats. Money can even be

NOTE: The author would like to acknowledge the support of the University of Nebraska at Lincoln (UNL), more specifically its assessment leadership staff, Dr. Jessica L. Jonson and Jeremy Penn, who direct UNL's robust continuous improvement process and facilitate the collaborative assessment partnership between UNL and Colorado State University. The generosity and support of Carolyn Bender generated the opportunity to create the featured improvement system.

used for food, an important community-building lubricant! Retreats supplement workshops sponsored by the Center for Faculty Development.

Recognition: The provost recognizes good work in assessment by an individual or group from each college. Certificates recognizing various forms of faculty achievement are awarded at an annual spring forum.

Retention, tenure, and promotion. Program assessment is recognized as service to the department, college, or university for the purpose of retention, tenure, and promotion.

Reporting mechanisms. Assessment facilitators, with support from the director of assessment, collect assessment reports annually. Until a culture of assessment was established, these were semester reports. These reports become an appendix to, and are discussed in, a self-study for program planning.

Integration with existing accountability. Assessment of student learning has become an essential part of program planning. Each program submits a self-study once every five years that includes a development plan for the subsequent five years. The plan includes not just how many faculty the department wants to hire, but also changes to the curriculum, addition or subtraction of programs, and improvements in student learning outcomes. New program planning guidelines were introduced at our university in spring 2007. We are now in the midst of integrating assessment of student learning into program planning. Assessment of overall general education goals, in addition to assessment of area student learning objectives, started the design phase in academic year 2007–08 and will be finalized in 2008–09.

Dissemination. Each assessment facilitator is responsible for identifying exemplary practices within the college. These are discussed among the facilitators and provide examples for discussion back in the colleges. Each college designs its own assessment reporting and dissemination method, but most colleges have an assessment council or committee, in addition to a curriculum committee.

Each year the provost recognizes best practices in each college via Provost Assessment Awards. Awards are presented at the Spring Forum, which has a different theme each year. The most recent theme was the "Scholarship of Teaching and Learning."

Annual assessment reports are posted on the assessment Web site and must be signed by the dean of the college before submission. They constitute an important part of program planning self-studies, which are read by the dean and associate dean of the respective colleges, by the AVPs of undergraduate and graduate studies, the vice provost, the director of assessment, the Program Planning Committee chair, and at least one external reviewer.

Required Resources

Our university has over 30,000 students and offers more than 134 bachelor's and master's degrees. To help develop and implement assessment of student learning in this number of programs, we have one full-time (faculty) director of assessment, one class release per semester for one faculty member from each college (plus some time from a college-level administrator), one or two workshops each semester offered by a faculty development office, a budget for department or college assessment retreats, and a Web presence as part of the Undergraduate Studies Web site.

Findings and Their Use

Because of a push to get to the point of collecting data in time for an accreditation visit, we have found that many departments were focused on collection of data, and some were not reflecting on the meaning of the data nor putting the results to any use. Because of this, reporting forms have been redesigned to focus more on student learning and program development.

In 2006 administrators were in the position of having required herculean efforts to jump-start the assessment process, with many departments having designed program learning objectives and having collected data on most of them. The faculty was overworked. In order to turn the corner to *sustainable* assessment, departments were asked to align their assessment efforts with the five-year program planning cycle. Under the new plan, data for most student learning objectives should be collected and reflected on at least once each program planning cycle, with follow-up data collected only for student learning outcomes that suggested changes in curriculum or pedagogy.

In spite of these problems, quite a few programs had progressed to implementing changes based on assessment of student learning. A common finding in both general education and degree programs is that students need more practice and feedback in written and oral communication. Some programs are finding creative ways to increase writing practice and feedback in spite of continually increasing class size and pressure on faculty to publish and provide service. For example, communications studies faculty are undertaking a complete redesign of their program specifically in response to these challenges.

Faculty in sociology created a combination multiple-choice and essay exam for the capstone course and found that students performed better on the essay portion. Poor performance on the objective portion of the exam was attributed to the need for precise knowledge of the differences between two theories. This led to a major change in pedagogy, focusing on class discussions of where two sociologists disagree with a more analytic framework.

Political science faculty developed a common rubric for the final essay in the capstone course. Based on the results of assessment, the department faculty made major changes to two of the prerequisite courses.

Impact of Using the Findings

Gradually, faculty members are coming to accept assessment of student learning and even embrace it. Those programs that have professional accreditation, in addition to university accreditation, generally have been learning about and practicing assessment longer than programs that are only concerned with university accreditation. The longer department faculty have had to figure out how assessment works for them, the more likely they are to embrace it.

Success Factors

Continuity, integration, and multiple approaches have helped our approach to assessment succeed.

Continuity refers to establishing a sustainable schedule with assessment activities planned for every semester. Only a big push just before the accreditation visit makes assessment both ineffective and very painful.

Integration refers to integrating student learning assessment across various accreditation agency requirements. Assessment facilitators, Center for Faculty Development staff, and the assessment director all work with departments to develop one assessment plan that will satisfy all relevant accreditations for that program. In addition, assessment of student learning is becoming an important and integral part of program planning and review.

Multiple approaches refers to using a variety of ways to bring attention and rewards to assessment activities, such as assessment retreats, assessment facilitators, assessment awards, and program planning. Multiple approaches refers to providing a variety of avenues for learning about assessment; it also refers to encouraging departments to develop assessment methods that suit both their program and research style. Historians are not going to be comfortable with the same assessment plan that will interest engineers.

Relevant Institutional Web Sites Pertaining to This Assessment Practice

www.sjsu.edu/ugs/assessment/
www.sjsu.edu/ugs/programplanning/

INSTITUTIONAL PROFILES BY INSTITUTION

Profiles used in their entirety are noted in bold.

Number	Institution	Author(s)	Web Site(s)
1	Agnes Scott College	Laura Palucki-Blake, Megan Drinkwater, Karen Gilbert, Emily Gwynn, Michelle Hall, Katherine McGuire, Madeline Zavodny	http://www.agnesscott.edu/academics/assessment/templates.aspx http://www.agnesscott.edu/academics/assessment
2	**Alverno College**	**Kathy Lake, Judith Reisetter Hart, William H. Rickards, Glen Rogers**	**http://www.alverno.edu/for_educators/publications.html** **http://www.alverno.edu/for_educators/publications.html**
3	**American Council on Education and Consortium of Colleges and Universities**	**Jill Wisniewski, Christa Olson**	**http://www.acenet.edu/programs/international/assessmentguide**
4	Aristotle University Thessaloniki Greece	Antigoni Papadimitriou	http://www.econ.auth.gr/index.php?lang=el&rm=1&mm=13&stid=53
5	Avila University	Sue King, David Wissmann	http://www.avila.edu/Faculty/PDFs/TnLOct06.pdf http://www.avila.edu
6	Babson College, Wellesley, MA	Diane Chase, Dennis Ceru, Heidi Neck	www.babson.edu/assessment

7	Bellevue University	Pat Artz	http://www.weaveonline.com/ https://www.weaveonline.net/subscriber/bellevue/
8	Binghamton University, State University of New York	Sean McKitrick	http://www.apa.org/ed/graduate/distance_ed.pdf http://www.learnerassociates.net/debook/evaluate.pdf
9		Sean McKitrick, Chris Knickerbocker	http://assessment.binghamton.edu.
10	Brigham Young University	Gerrit Gong, Danny R. Olsen	http://learningoutcomes.byu.edu https://learningoutcomes.buy.edu/docs/lovideo/ELO.swf
11		Ronald Terry, Kristie Seawright, Larry Seawright	http://home.byu.edu/webapp/assess/ http://home.byu.edu/webapp/assess/content/page/academic_review/index.html
12		Pat Esplin, Stefinee Pinnegar	http://academy.byu.edu
13	California State University	Robert J. Chierico	none
14	California State University Fullerton	Sabrina Sanders	http://fullertontitans.cstv.com/athleteservices/home.html
15	California State University, Dominguez Hills	Shirley Lal, Mary J. Cruise	http://www.csudh.edu/sloa/

(continued)

Number	Institution	Author(s)	Web Site(s)
16	**California State University, Sacramento**	**Vickii Castillon, Lori Varlotta**	**http://saweb.csus.edu/students/ assessment.aspx** **http://www.csus.edu/student/ VPSAPresentation2.8.07.ppt**
17	Capella University	Jeffrey D. Grann, Laurie Hinze	http://media.capella.edu/interactivemedia/ accreditation/Player/gs_multicombo_ OuterWrapper.asp http://presidentsforum.excelsior.edu/ projects/transparency.html
18	Central University of Technology, Free State; Indiana University–Purdue University Indianapolis	Hesta Friedrich-Nel, Joyce MacKinnon	http://www.cut.ac.za/academics/faculties/ healthtechnology/assessmentdiscussions
19	Cleveland State University	Rosemary E. Sutton; Marius Boboc	http://www.csuohio.edu/offices/assessment/
20	Coker College	David Eubanks	http://www.coker.edu/assessment http://highered.blogspot.com
21	College of Mount St. Joseph, Cincinnati, OH	Mary Kay Fleming	http://inside.msj.edu/academics/assessment/

22	**College of Saint Benedict and Saint John's University**	**Philip I. Kramer**	**http://www.csbsju.edu/cac/webassessmentgrid.aspx http://www.csbsju.edu/assessment/**
23	College of William and Mary	Susan Lovegren Bosworth	http://web.wm.edu/wmoa/
24	**Colorado State University**	**Kim K. Bender**	**http://improvement.colostate.edu (use "view all resources" and select "public site" to view assessment plans) http://assessment.colostate.edu (demonstrate planning functions using department log-in with demo as username and password)**
25	Columbus State University, Columbus, Georgia	J. William Hortman, Joyce Hickson, Gina L. Sheeks, Thomas P. Loughman	http://sacs.colstate.edu/qep/CSUQEPcdversion1-23-2006.pdf
26	Council for the Advancement of Standards in Higher Education	Phyllis Mable	http://www.cas.edu
27	D'Youville College	Bonnie Fox Garrity	
28	**DePaul University**	**Katherine A. Cermak, Jodi Cressman, Midge Wilson**	**http://las.depaul.edu/lsp/public_html/index.html http://condor.depaul.edu/~tla/**

(continued)

Number	Institution	Author(s)	Web Site(s)
29	Fairfield University	Curtis Naser	http://eidos.fairfield.edu/eidos.cfm
30	**Ferris State University**	**Roxanne Cullen, Michael Harris**	
31	**Florida Agricultural and Mechanical University (FAMU)**	**Uche O. Ohia**	**http://www.famu.edu/assessment** **http://www.famu.edu/Assessment/ UserFiles/File/ge.pdf** **http://www.famousassessment.com/** **http://www.famu.edu/index.cfm?a= Assessment**
32	Florida Atlantic University	Marcy Krugel	http://www.collegeofbusiness.fau.edu/ gradcomm/
33	Frostburg State University	Jay Hegeman, Spencer Deakin	http://www.frostburg.edu/academic/orie/ AlcoholEdu.html
34	George Mason University	Mary Zamon	https://assessment.gmu.edu/ StudentLearningCompetencies/Critical/html http://ctac.gmu.edu/
35	**Hocking College**	**Judith Maxson, Bonnie Allen Smith**	**www.hocking.edu/assessment_center** **http://www.hocking.cc.oh.us/ SuccessSkills/** **http://portfolio.hocking.edu**

36	Illinois State University	Mardell Wilson, Matthew B. Fuller	http://www.provost.ilstu.edu/resources/assessment.shtml http://www.assessment.ilstu.edu/program/ http://www.americandemocracy.ilstu.edu/CivicEngagementProjects/ http://www.focus.ilstu.edu/
37	Indiana University	Susan D. Johnson, Victor M.H. Borden, Susan Sciame-Giesecke	http://www.indiana.edu/~idsa/confl13007.shtml
38	Indiana Wesleyan University	Cynthia Tweedell	http://www.indwes.edu/assessment/non_traditional_program.htm http://www.indwes.edu/assessment/CAPS_Grids/mba.pdf
39	Iona College	Warren Rosenberg	
40	Indiana University–Purdue University Indianapolis	Enrica J. Ardemagni, Lisa McGuire, and Patricia Wittberg, Kathy Lay, Patti Clayton, David Strong	http://csl.iupui.edu/index.html
41	James Madison University	Lynn Cameron	http://www.lib.jmu.edu/gold/ http://www.jmu.edu/gened/info_lit_general.html

(continued)

Number	Institution	Author(s)	Web Site(s)
42	**Johnson & Wales University Graduate School**	**Joanne M. Crossman**	**http://www.jwu.edu/grad/resources.htm** **http://www.jwu.edu/grad/index.htm**
43	Kean University	Carol J. Williams	http://caroljwilliams.net http://www.icsd.info
44	**Kennesaw State University**	**Thomas P. Pusateri**	**www.kennesaw.edu/cetl/aol** **www.kennesaw.edu/cetl/cpr**
45		Michelle D. Emerson	http://www.kennesaw.edu/cetl/aol/index.html
46	Kent State University Stark Campus	Paul Abraham, Janice Kover	http://www.personal.kent.edu/~jkover/KSUstarkDM.pdf
47	Long Island University	Loretta Knapp, Margaret F. Boorstein	http://www.wmich.edu/cas/pdf/assessment_geosciences.pdf http://www.wcer.wisc.edu/archive/nise/Related_links/
48	**Medgar Evers College of The City University of New York**	**Gale Gibson-Ballah, Douglas Walcerz**	**http://www.trueoutcomes.com/** **http://www.centerdigitaled.com/conference.php?confid=263&past=1**
49	**Miami Dade College**	**Joanne Bashford, S. Sean Madison, Lenore Rodicio**	**http://www.mdc.edu/learningoutcomes**

50	**Miami University**	**Jennifer Blue, Beverley A. P. Taylor, Jan M. Yarrison-Rice, Herbert Jaeger**	**http://www.units.muohio.edu/led/Assessment/Assessment_Basics/Sample_Rubrics/Scientific_Inquiry.pdf** http://www.cas.muohio.edu/physicsweb
51	Miami University, Oxford Ohio	Beverley Taylor, Jerry K. Stonewater, Andrea Bakker	http://www.units.muohio.edu/led/Assessment/index.htm
52		Raymond Witte, Susan Mosley-Howard, Aimin Wang, Ray Terrell	
53	**Moravian College**	**Robert T. Brill**	**http://home.moravian.edu/users/psych/mertb01/**
54	National Technical Institute for the Deaf at Rochester Institute of Technology	Joseph Bochner, Marianne Gustafson	http://www.ets.org http://wwwact.org/compass http://www.ntid.rit.edu/VPandDean/soa/pages/archive/displayplan.php?year=2006&program=critthink http://www.ntid.rit.edu/vpanddean/soa/pages/archive/NTIDCriticalThinkingEvaluationRubric.pdf
55	**North Carolina State University**	**Patti H. Clayton, Sarah Ash, Jessica Katz Jameson**	**www.ncsu.edu/curricular_engagement**

(*continued*)

Number	Institution	Author(s)	Web Site(s)
56		**Kim Outing, Karen Hauschild**	**http://www.ncsu.edu/fyc/info/ assessments/** **http://www.ncsu.edu/fyc/prospective/ village/index.html**
57	Northampton Community College	Jim Benner, Carolyn Bortz, Pamela Bradley	http://www.northampton.edu/ctl/ teachingresources/Course+Outline.htm
58	**Northeastern Illinois University**	**Angeles L. Eames**	**http://www.edu/~neassess/pdf/ GenEd_Assessment_Plan_FINAL_ APPROVED.pdf**
59		Barbara Cosentino, Angeles L. Eames	http://www.neiu.edu/~deptpoff/students/ on-campus_interv/index.htm
60	Northern Arizona University	Cynthia Conn	http://coe.nau.edu/aci/resources/#workshops
61		Thomas Paradis	www.nau.edu/assessment
62	Ohio Board of Regents/Virginia Tech	John Muffo	www.enge.vt.edu
63	Ohio University	Joni Y. Wadley, Michael Williford	http://www.ohiou.edu/instres/student/fresh_ exp.html, http://www.ohio.edu/univcollege/ fye/
64	**Oklahoma State University**	**Pam Bowers**	**http://uat.okstate.edu/assessment/ index.html**

65	Pace University	**Linda Anstendig, Sarah Burns Feyl**	**http://www.pace.edu/corecurriculum http://www.pace.edu/eportfolio**
66		Barbara Pennipede, Joseph C. Morreale	
67		Sandra Flank, Susan Feather Gannon	http://www.pace.edu/page.cfm?doc_id=25480
68		Karen DeSantis and Sarah Burns-Feyl	http://www.pace.edu/page.cfm?doc_id=31813
69		Allen Stix, Andreea Cotoranu	
70	Paul Smith's College	Gail Gibson Sheffield	
71	Portland State University	Kathi A. Ketcheson, Sukhwant S. Jhaj, Rowanna L. Carpenter	http://www.oirp.pdx.edu. http://www.pdx.edu/unst/
72	Research Centre in Education–University of Minho (Portugal)	Natascha van Hattum-Janssen	http://www.cied.uminho.pt/Default.aspx?lang=en-US
73	Rowan University	Kenneth R. Albone, Lorin Basden Arnold, Harriet Benedivez, Joy Cypher, Julie Haynes, Clara Popa, Maria Simone	www.rowan.edu/colleges/communication/old_site_6_11_07/albone/2003_Public_Speaking_Assessment_Report.doc

(continued)

Number	Institution	Author(s)	Web Site(s)
74	St. Cloud State University	James Sherohman, Elaine Ackerman, Wendy Bjorklund, Lisa Foss, Sandra Johnson, Joseph Melcher	www.stcloudstate.edu/assessment
75	St. Lawrence University	Kim Mooney, Christine Zimmerman	http://www.stlawu.edu/assessment/mission.html
76		Sondra Smith	http://www.infotech.stlawu.edu http://www.stlawu.edu
77	**St. Louis Community College**	**John J. Cosgrove, Lawrence J. McDoniel**	**http://www.stlcc.edu/Faculty_and_Staff_Resources/Assessment/** **http://collegeweb.stlcc.edu/assessment/**
78	**St. Mary's College of Maryland**	**Ben Click, Linda Coughlin, Brian O'Sullivan, Lois Stover, Elizabeth Nutt Williams**	**http://www.smcm.edu/about_corecurriculum.html**
79	St. Norbert College	Robert A. Rutter	www.snc.edu/oie
80	**San Diego State University**	**Marilee Bresciani**	**http://interwork.sdsu.edu/student_affairs/index.html** **http://interwork.sdsu.edu/student_affairs/current_students/Reflective_Learning.html**

81	**San Jose State University**	**Jackie Snell**	
82		Jeanne Linsdell, Thalia Anagnos	https://testing.sjsu.edu/twst.html http://www.engr.sjsu.edu/~tanagnos/ENGR100W/exit.htm
83		Nancie Fimbel, Asbjorn Osland, Marlene E. Turner, William Zachary	
84		Amy Strage, Julie Sliva Spitzer	http://www.calstate.edu/ITL/exchanges/research/1217_Strage_etal.html
85	Savannah College of Art and Design	Laura Ng, Tom Gattis	
86	Southern Illinois University Edwardsville	Andy Pomerantz , Victoria G. Scott	http://www.siue.edu/ELTI/ http://www.siue.edu/assessment/
87	**Texas Christian University**	**Catherine Wehlburg, Edward McNertney**	**http://www.core.tcu.edu/**
88	The College of Wooster	Theresa Ford, John G. Neuhoff	http://www.wooster.edu/assessment
89		Nancy C. Grace, Sarah Murnen	http://www.wooster.edu/teagle.
90	**The Community College of Baltimore County**	**Rose Mince, Lynne Mason**	**http://ccbcmd.edu/loa/genedindex.html**

(continued)

Number	Institution	Author(s)	Web Site(s)
91	The Ohio State University College of Pharmacy	Katherine A. Kelley, James W. McAuley	http://www.pharmacy.ohio-state.edu/academics/assessment/index.cfm
92	The Pennsylvania State University	Andrea Dowhower, Philip Burlingame	http://www.sa.psu.edu/sara/pulse.shtml
93	The University of Akron	Steven C. Myers, Michael A. Nelson, Richard W. Stratton	www.uakron.edu/econ/
94	The University of Akron Wayne College	Paulette Popovich, Tim Vierheller, Patsy Malavite	http://www.wayne.uakron.edu/assessmentpresentations/
95	Tompkins Cortland Community College, Dryden, New York	Jeanne A. Cameron	http://faculty.academyart.edu/resources/rubrics.asp
96	Truman State University	David A. Hoffman	http://conduct.truman.edu/ http://conduct.truman.edu/stats.asp
97	Tufts University	Rachel Jin Bee Tan, Dawn Geronimo Terkla, Stephanie Topping	http://activecitizen.tufts.edu/?pid=19
98	United States Military Academy	Thomas P. Judd, Bruce Keith	http://www.dean.usma.edu/support/aad/EFAOCW.pdf

	Institution	Names	URL
99		Greg Graves, Alex Heidenberg	
100	**University of Alabama**		**http://www.sa.ua.edu/assessment/**
101		**A. Katherine Busby Robert A. Smallwood, Judith Ouimet**	**http://assessment.ua.edu/CLASSE/Overview.htm**
102	University of Central Florida	Julia Pet-Armacost, Robert L. Armacost	http://www.oeas.ucf.edu/ http://www.uaps.ucf.edu/presentations.html
103	**University of Hawaii at Manoa**	**Joan Harms**	**http://studentaffairs.manoa.hawaii.edu/downloads/reports/manoa_ovcaa_student_indicators_satisfactionSS_2002.pdf http://studentaffairs.manoa.hawaii.edu/downloads/reports/OSA_Performance_Indicators_01-07.pdf**
104		Nancy Stockert	http://www.acha.org/
105	University of Houston—Main Campus	Libby Barlow	(We expect our SACS web site to be available after the reaffirmation of accreditation is complete in 2008.)
106	University of Kentucky, Lexington	Heidi H. Ewen	http://itc.uky.edu/~gmswan3/openportfolioGT/password.php http://www.mc.uky.edu/gerontology

(continued)

Number	Institution	Author(s)	Web Site(s)
107	**University of Maryland**	**Greig M. Stewart**	**http://www.scholars.umd.edu/execdir/assessment.cfm**
108	University of Missouri	Tim Parshall, John Spencer	http://provost.missouri.edu/assessment/programassessment.html
109	**University of Nebraska College of Medicine**	**Hugh A. Stoddard**	**http://webmedia.unmc.edu/medicine/kdybdall/webpage/ProfessionalismRatingForm2007.pdf**
110	University of Nebraska-Lincoln	Jeremy Penn, Jessica Jonson	http://www.unl.edu/ous/pearl/pearl.shtml http://www.unl.edu/ous/faculty_resources/assessment.shtml
111	University of North Carolina at Greensboro	Erin Bentrim-Tapio	www.uncg.edu/saf/assessment
112	University of North Dakota	Anne Kelsch, Joan Hawthorne	http://www.und.nodak.edu/dept/datacol/assessment/GenEd/index.htm
113	**University of Northern Iowa**	**Barry J. Wilson**	**http://www.uni.edu/coe/epf/Assess http://www.uni.edu/assessment/**
114	University of Portland	Marlene Moore	http://www.up.edu/tl/default.aspx?cid=5545&pid=1196&gd=yes http://www.up.edu/tl/default.aspx?cid=6390&pid=1195

115	**University of South Florida**	**Teresa Flateby**	**http://usf.edu/assessment**
116	University of the Free State, Bloemfontein, South Africa	SP (Fanus) van Tonder	
117	University of Western Australia	Zarrin Seema Siddiqui	
118	University of Wisconsin–Milwaukee	Gesele Durham, Ruth E. Williams	http://www4.uwm.edu/acad_aff/access/ http://www4.uwm.edu/access_success/index.cfm
119	University of Wisconsin, Parkside	Gerald Greenfield	http://www.uwp.edu/departments/teaching.center/)
120	Virginia Tech	Steve Culver, Ray Van Dyke	www.aap.vt.edu
121	Viterbo University	Theresa R. Moore, Mary Hassinger	http://www.viterbo.edu/academic/titleiii/
122	**Walden University**	**Jordan Orzoff, Paula Peinovich, Eric Riedel**	**http://inside.waldenu.edu/c/Student_Faculty/StudentFaculty_4276.htm** **http://inside.waldenu.edu/c/Student_Faculty/StudentFaculty_4278.htm**
123	Waubonsee Community College	Stacey Randall	http://www.top.waubonsee.edu http://www.top.waubonsee.edu

(continued)

Number	Institution	Author(s)	Web Site(s)
124	Wayne State University	Richard Slaughter	http://www.cphs.wayne.edu/assessment.php http://www.guglielmino734.com/2002lpa.htm
125	Western Governors University	Diane Longhurst Johnson	http://www.wgu.edu
126	**Widener University**	**Brigitte Valesey**	**www.widener.edu/tasl/assessment.asp**
127		**Joseph Hargadon, Karen Leppel**	
128		**Emily C. Richardson**	**http://www.widener.edu/uc**
129	**William Paterson University**	**Sharmila Pixy Ferris, Anne Ciliberti**	**http://www.ala.org/ala/acrl/ acrlstandards/ informationliteracycompetency.cfm**
130	Winthrop University	Daniel A. Weinstein; Beverly Schneller	http://www.winthrop.edu/effectiveness/ http://www.millersville.edu/english/ http://cs.millersville.edu/

INSTITUTIONAL PROFILES BY CATEGORY

Profiles used in their entirety are noted in bold.

Academic Majors (undergraduate)

Jennifer Blue, Beverley A. P. Taylor, Jan M. Yarrison-Rice, Herbert Jaeger, **Miami University**

Robert T. Brill, **Moravian College**

Diane Chase, Dennis Ceru, Heidi Neck, Babson College, Wellesley, MA

Cynthia Conn, Northern Arizona University

Allen Stix, Andreea Cotoranu, Pace University

Michelle D. Emerson, Kennesaw State University

Katherine A. Kelley, James W. McAuley, The Ohio State University College of Pharmacy

Kathy Lake, Judith Reisetter Hart, William H. Rickards, Glen Rogers, **Alverno College**

Shirley Lal, Mary J. Cruise, California State University, Dominguez Hills

John Muffo, Ohio Board of Regents/Virginia Tech

Curt Naser, Fairfield University

Laura Ng, Tom Gattis, Savannah College of Art and Design

Jeremy Penn, Jessica Jonson, University of Nebraska-Lincoln

Steven C. Myers, Michael A. Nelson, Richard W. Stratton, University of Akron

Richard Slaughter, Wayne State University

Amy Strage, Julie Sliva Spitzer, San Jose State University

Richard W. Stratton, Mike Nelson

Natascha van Hattum-Janssen, Research Centre in Education–University of Minho (Portugal)

Daniel A. Weinstein, Beverly Schneller, Winthrop University

Antigoni Papadimitriou, Aristotle University Thessaloniki Greece

Barry J. Wilson, University of Northern Iowa

Gerald Greenfield, University of Wisconsin, Parkside

Jeanne Cameron, Tompkins Cortland Community College, Dryden, New York

Jim Benner, Carolyn Bortz, Pamela Bradley, Northampton Community College

James Sherohman, Elaine Ackerman, Wendy Bjorklund, Lisa Foss, Sandra Johnson, Joseph Melcher, St. Cloud State University

Gerrit Gong, Danny R. Olsen, Brigham Young University

Thomas P. Pusateri, Kennesaw State University

Judith Maxson, Bonnie Allen Smith, Hocking College

Katherine A. Cermak, Jodi Cressman, Midge Wilson, DePaul University

Kim K. Bender, Colorado State University

Jackie Snell, San Jose State University

Mardell Wilson and Matthew B. Fuller, Illinois State University

Linda Anstendig, Sarah Burns Feyl, Pace University

Nancy C. Grace, Sarah Murnen, the College of Wooster

Greg Graves, Alex Heidenberg, United States Military Academy

Carol J. Williams, Kean University

Robert A. Rutter, St. Norbert College

Uche O. Ohia, Florida Agricultural and Mechanical University (FAMU)

Thomas Paradis, Northern Arizona University

Paulette Popovich, Tim Vierheller, Patsy Malavite, University of Akron Wayne College

Student Engagement: Civic Engagement/Service Learning and International Learning Experiences

Jill Wisniewski, Christa Olson, American Council on Education and Consortium of Colleges and Universities

Robert A. Smallwood, Judith Ouimet, University of Alabama

Joan Harms, University of Hawaii at Manoa

Patti H. Clayton, Sarah Ash, Jessica Katz Jameson, North Carolina State University

Rachel Jin Bee Tan, Dawn Geronimo Terkla, Stephanie Topping, Tufts University

Enrica J. Ardemagni, Lisa McGuire, and Patricia Wittberg, Kathy Lay, Patti Clayton, David Strong, Indiana University–Purdue University Indianapolis

Carol J. Williams, Kean University

Mardell Wilson and Matt Fuller, Illinois State University

Classroom Assessment

Carol J. Williams, Kean University

Curt Naser, Fairfield University

Jennifer Blue, Beverley A. P. Taylor, Jan M. Yarrison-Rice, Herbert Jaeger, Miami University

Diane Chase, Dennis Ceru, Heidi Neck, Babson College

Allen Stix, Andreea Cotoranu, Pace University

Sandra Flank, Susan Feather Gannon, Pace University

Theresa Ford, John G. Neuhoff, the College of Wooster

Hesta Friedrich-Nel, Joyce MacKinnon, Central University of Technology, Free State; Indiana University–Purdue University Indianapolis

Bonnie Fox Garrity, D'Youville College

Joseph Hargadon, Karen Leppel, Widener University

Diane Longhurst Johnson, Western Governors University

Kenneth R. Albone, Lorin Basden Arnold, Harriet Benedivez, Joy Cypher, Julie Haynes, Clara Popa, Maria Simone, Rowan University

Joseph Bochner, Marianne Gustafson, National Technical Institute for the Deaf at Rochester Institute of Technology

Antigoni Papadimitriou, Aristotle University, Thessaloniki, Greece

Robert A. Smallwood, Judith Ouimet, University of Alabama

Enrica J. Ardemagni, Lisa McGuire, Patricia Wittberg, Kathy Lay, Patti Clayton, David Strong, Indiana University–Purdue University Indianapolis

Greg Graves, Alex Heidenberg, United States Military Academy

Marcy Krugel, Florida Atlantic University

Jeanne Linsdell, Thalia Anagnos, San Jose State University

Beverley Taylor, Jerry K. Stonewater, Andrea Bakker, Miami University, Oxford, Ohio

Carol J. Williams, Kean University

Mary Zamon, George Mason University

Susan Lovegren Bosworth, College of William and Mary

David Eubanks, Coker College

Sue King, David Wissmann, Avila University

Curt Naser, Fairfield University

Gail Gibson Sheffield, Paul Smith's College

Emily C. Richardson, Widener University

Mardell Wilson, Matthew B. Fuller, Illinois State University

Community Colleges

Jim Benner, Carolyn Bortz, Pamela Bradley, Northampton Community College

John J. Cosgrove, Lawrence J. McDoniel, St. Louis Community College

Judith Maxson, Bonnie Allen Smith, Hocking College

Jeanne A. Cameron, Tompkins Cortland Community College, Dryden, New York

Rose Mince, Lynne Mason, The Community College of Baltimore County

Stacey Randall , Waubonsee Community College

Joanne Bashford, S. Sean Madison, Lenore Rodicio, Miami Dade College

Paulette Popovich, Tim Vierheller, Patsy Malavite, University of Akron Wayne College

Faculty and Staff Development

Jim Benner, Carolyn Bortz, Pamela Bradley, Northampton Community College

Diane Longhurst Johnson, Western Governors University

Natascha van Hattum-Janssen, Research Centre in Education–University of Minho, Portugal

Roxanne Cullen, Michael Harris, Ferris State University

Loretta Knapp, Margaret F. Boorstein, Long Island University

Philip I. Kramer, College of Saint Benedict and Saint John's University

Theresa R. Moore, Mary Hassinger, Viterbo University

Marlene Moore, University of Portland

Andy Pomerantz, Victoria G. Scott, Southern Illinois University Edwardsville

Brigitte Valesey, Widener University, Texas Christian University

SP (Fanus) van Tonder, University of the Free State, Bloemfontein, South Africa

Catherine Wehlburg, Edward McNertney, Texas Christian University

Barry J. Wilson, University of Northern Iowa

Ben Click, Linda Coughlin, Brian O'Sullivan, Lois Stover, Elizabeth Nutt Williams, St. Mary's College of Maryland

Jeanne A. Cameron, Tompkins Cortland Community College, Dryden, New York

Rose Mince, Lynne Mason, the Community College of Baltimore County

Judith Maxson, Bonnie Allen Smith, Hocking College

Cynthia Tweedell, Indiana Wesleyan University

Jim Benner, Carolyn Bortz, Pamela Bradley, Northampton Community College

Patti H. Clayton, Sarah Ash, Jessica Katz Jameson, North Carolina State University

Gerrit Gong, Danny R. Olsen, Brigham Young University

Teresa Flateby, University of South Florida

Sharmila Pixy Ferris, Anne Ciliberti, William Paterson University

Uche O. Ohia, Florida Agricultural and Mechanical University (FAMU)

Ronald Terry, Kristie Seawright, Larry Seawright, Brigham Young University

Katherine A. Cermak, Jodi Cressman, Midge Wilson, DePaul University

Jackie Snell, San Jose State University

Linda Anstendig, Sarah Burns Feyl, Pace University

Nancy C. Grace, Sarah Murnen, the College of Wooster

Joseph Bochner, Marianne Gustafson, National Technical Institute for the Deaf at Rochester Institute of Technology

Mary Zamon, George Mason University

Susan Lovegren Bosworth, College of William and Mary

Loretta Knapp, Margaret F. Boorstein, Long Island University

Mardell Wilson and Matthew B. Fuller, Illinois State University

J. William Hortman, Joyce Hickson, Gina L. Sheeks, Thomas P. Loughman, Columbus State University, Columbus, Georgia

First Year Experiences

Kathi A. Ketcheson, Sukhwant S. Jhaj, Rowanna L. Carpenter, Portland State University

Kim Outing, Karen Hauschild, North Carolina State University

Joni Wadley, Michael Williford, Ohio University

Jill Wisniewski, Christa Olson, American Council on Education and Consortium of Colleges and Universities

Loretta Knapp, Margaret F. Boorstein, Long Island University

Linda Anstendig, Sarah Burns Feyl, Pace University

Pat Artz, Bellevue University

Ben Click, Linda Coughlin, Brian O'Sullivan, Lois Stover, Elizabeth Nutt Williams, St. Mary's College of Maryland

Karen DeSantis, Sarah Burns-Feyl, Pace University

Gesele Durham, Ruth E. Williams, University of Wisconsin–Milwaukee

Pat Esplin, Stefinee Pinnegar, Brigham Young University

Mary Kay Fleming, College of Mount St. Joseph

Gale Gibson-Ballah, Douglas Walcerz, Medgar Evers College of the City University of New York

Gerald Greenfield, University of Wisconsin, Parkside

Judith Maxson, Bonnie Allen Smith, Hocking College

Joan Harms, University of Hawaii at Manoa

Jay Hegeman, Spencer Deakin, Frostburg State University

Greig M. Stewart, University of Maryland

Angeles L. Eames, Northeastern Illinois University

Kathi A. Ketcheson, Sukhwant S. Jhaj, Rowanna L. Carpenter, Portland State University

Paul Abraham, Janice Kover, Kent State University Stark Campus

Joseph Bochner, Marianne Gustafson, National Technical Institute for the Deaf at Rochester Institute of Technology

Robert J. Chierico, California State University

Lynn Cameron, James Madison University

Mary Kay Fleming, College of Mount St. Joseph

General Education

Carol J. Williams, Kean University

Curt Naser, Fairfield University

Kenneth R. Albone, Lorin Basden Arnold, Harriet Benedivez, Joy Cypher, Julie Haynes, Clara Popa, Maria Simone, Rowan University

Joseph Bochner, Marianne Gustafson, National Technical Institute for the Deaf at Rochester Institute of Technology

Loretta Knapp, Margaret F. Boorstein, Long Island University

Mary Kay Fleming, College of Mount St. Joseph

Jeanne A. Cameron, Tompkins Cortland Community College, Dryden, New York

Rose Mince, Lynne Mason, The Community College of Baltimore County

Stacey Randall, Waubonsee Community College

Judith Maxson, Bonnie Allen Smith, Hocking College

Jordan Orzoff, Paula Peinovich, Eric Riedel, Walden University

Joanne M. Crossman, Johnson & Wales University Graduate School

Hugh A. Stoddard, University of Nebraska College of Medicine

Zarrin Seema Siddiqui, University of Western Australia

Andrea Dowhower, Philip Burlingame, The Pennsylvania State University

Jim Benner, Carolyn Bortz, Pamela Bradley, Northampton Community College

Sabrina Sanders, California State University Fullerton

James Sherohman, Elaine Ackerman, Wendy Bjorklund, Lisa Foss, Sandra Johnson, Joseph Melcher, St. Cloud State University

Erin Bentrim-Tapio, University of North Carolina at Greensboro

Joanne Bashford, S. Sean Madison, Lenore Rodicio, Miami Dade College

Thomas P. Pusateri, Kennesaw State University

Patti H. Clayton, Sarah Ash, Jessica Katz Jameson, North Carolina State University

Teresa Flateby, University of South Florida

Sharmila Pixy Ferris, Anne Ciliberti, William Paterson University

Angeles L. Eames, Northeastern Illinois University

Pam Bowers, Oklahoma State University

Katherine A. Cermak, Jodi Cressman, Midge Wilson, DePaul University

Linda Anstendig, Sarah Burns Feyl, Pace University

Warren Rosenberg, Iona College

Kathi A. Ketcheson, Sukhwant S. Jhaj, Rowanna L. Carpenter, Portland State University

Paul Abraham, Janice Kover, Kent State University Stark Campus

Kenneth R. Albone, Lorin Basden Arnold, Harriet Benedivez, Joy Cypher, Julie Haynes, Clara Popa, Maria Simone, Rowan University

Robert J. Chierico, California State University

Nancy C. Grace, Sarah Murnen, the College of Wooster

Thomas P. Judd, Bruce Keith, United States Military Academy

Mary Kay Fleming, College of Mount St. Joseph

Marcy Krugel, Florida Atlantic University

Jeanne Linsdell, Thalia Anagnos, San Jose State University

Kim Mooney, Christine Zimmerman, St. Lawrence University

Beverley Taylor, Jerry K. Stonewater, Andrea Bakker, Miami University, Oxford, Ohio

Mary Zamon, George Mason University

Susan Lovegren Bosworth, College of William and Mary

Jeanne A. Cameron, Tompkins Cortland Community College, Dryden, New York

David Eubanks, Coker College

Anne Kelsch and Joan Hawthorne, University of North Dakota

Sue King, David Wissmann, Avila University

Loretta Knapp, Margaret F. Boorstein, Long Island University

Gail Gibson Sheffield, Paul Smith's College

Emily C. Richardson, Widener University

Robert A. Rutter, St. Norbert College

Paulette Popovich, Tim Vierheller, Patsy Malavite, University of Akron Wayne College

J. William Hortman, Joyce Hickson, Gina L. Sheeks, Thomas P. Loughman, Columbus State University, Columbus, Georgia

Graduate Programs

Cynthia Tweedell, Indiana Wesleyan University

Heidi H. Ewen, University of Kentucky, Lexington

Hugh A. Stoddard, University of Nebraska College of Medicine

Joanne M. Crossman, Johnson & Wales University Graduate School

Jordan Orzoff, Paula Peinovich, Eric Riedel, Walden University

Marcy Krugel, Florida Atlantic University

Marilee Bresciani, San Diego State University

Tim Parshall, John Spencer, University of Missouri

Zarrin Seema Siddiqui, University of Western Australia

Diane Chase, Dennis Ceru, Heidi Neck, Babson College

Sandra Flank, Susan Feather Gannon, Pace University

Ronald Terry, Kristie Seawright, Larry Seawright, Brigham Young University

Kim K. Bender, Colorado State University

Institutional Effectiveness

Libby Barlow, University of Houston

Laura Palucki-Blake, Megan Drinkwater, Karen Gilbert, Emily Gwynn, Michelle Hall, Katherine McGuire, Madeline Zavodny, Agnes Scott College

Loretta Knapp, Margaret F. Boorstein, Long Island University

Robert A. Rutter, St. Norbert College

Paulette Popovich, Tim Vierheller, Patsy Malavite, University of Akron Wayne College

Nancy C. Grace, Sarah Murnen, the College of Wooster

Joseph Bochner, Marianne Gustafson, National Technical Institute for the Deaf at Rochester Institute of Technology

Barbara Pennipede, Joseph C. Morreale, Pace University

Thomas Paradis, Northern Arizona University

Kathi A. Ketcheson, Sukhwant S. Jhaj, Rowanna L. Carpenter, Portland State University

David Eubanks, Coker College

Uche O. Ohia, Florida Agricultural and Mechanical University (FAMU)

Steve Culver, Ray Van Dyke, Virginia Tech

William Hortman, Joyce Hickson, Gina L. Sheeks, Thomas P. Loughman, Columbus State University, Columbus, Georgia

Julia Pet-Armacost, University of Central Florida

Sondra Smith, St. Lawrence University

Rosemary E. Sutton, Marius Boboc, Cleveland State University

Kim Mooney, Christine Zimmerman, St. Lawrence University

Gerrit Gong, Danny R. Olsen, Brigham Young University

Nancie Fimbel, Asbjorn Osland, Marlene E. Turner, William Zachary, San Jose State University

Raymond Witte, Susan Mosley-Howard, Aimin Wang, Ray Terrell, Miami University, Oxford, Ohio

Program Review

Jeanne A. Cameron, Tompkins Cortland Community College, Dryden, New York

Rose Mince, Lynne Mason, The Community College of Baltimore County

Stacey Randall , Waubonsee Community College

Jim Benner, Carolyn Bortz, Pamela Bradley, Northampton Community College

Susan D. Johnson, Victor M. H. Borden, Susan Sciame-Giesecke, Indiana University

Greig M. Stewart, University of Maryland

Kim K. Bender, Colorado State University

Ronald Terry, Kristie Seawright, Larry Seawright, Brigham Young University

Mardell Wilson and Matthew B. Fuller, Illinois State University

Libby Barlow, University of Houston–Main Campus

Student Affairs

Andrea Dowhower, Philip Burlingame, The Pennsylvania State University

Barbara Cosentino, Angeles L. Eames, Northeastern Illinois University

David A. Hoffman, Truman State University

Erin Bentrim-Tapio, University of North Carolina at Greensboro

James Sherohman, Elaine Ackerman, Wendy Bjorklund, Lisa Foss, Sandra Johnson, Joseph Melcher, St. Cloud State University

Jay Hegeman, Spencer Deakin, Frostburg State University

Joan Harms, University of Hawaii at Manoa

Nancy Stockert, University of Hawaii at Manoa

Phyllis Mable, Council for the Advancement of Standards in Higher Education

Sabrina Sanders, California State University Fullerton

Sean McKitrick, Chris Knickerbocker, Binghamton University, State University of New York

Vickii Castillon, Lori Varlotta, California State University, Sacramento

Greig M. Stewart, University of Maryland

A. Katherine Busby, University of Alabama

Warren Rosenberg, Iona College

Technology

Jeffrey D. Grann, Laurie Hinze, Capella University

Jill Wisniewski, Christa Olson, American Council on Education and Consortium of Colleges and Universities

Carol J. Williams, Kean University

Curt Naser, Fairfield University

Jeremy Penn, Jessica Jonson, University of Nebraska-Lincoln

Steven C. Myers, Michael A. Nelson, Richard W. Stratton, University of Akron

Natascha van Hattum-Janssen, Research Centre in Education–University of Minho, Portugal

Linda Anstendig, Sarah Burns Feyl, Pace University

Pat Artz, Bellevue University

Gale Gibson-Ballah, Douglas Walcerz, Medgar Evers College of The City University of New York

Heidi H. Ewen, University of Kentucky, Lexington

Philip I. Kramer, College of Saint Benedict and Saint John's University

Gerrit Gong, Danny R. Olsen, Brigham Young University

Hugh A. Stoddard, University of Nebraska College of Medicine

Sondra Smith, St. Lawrence University

Thomas P. Pusateri, Kennesaw State University

Kim K. Bender, Colorado State University

Linda Anstendig, Sarah Burns Feyl, Pace University

Teresa Flateby, University of South Florida

Jeffrey D. Grann, Laurie Hinze, Capella University

PROFILED INSTITUTIONS BY CARNEGIE CLASSIFICATION

Doctoral and Research

Private

Brigham Young University; Provo, Utah

DePaul University; Chicago, Illinois

Pace University; New York, New York

Tufts University; Medford, Massachusetts

Texas Christian University; Fort Worth, Texas

Walden University; Minneapolis, Minnesota

Widener University; Chester, Pennsylvania

Public

Colorado State University; Fort Collins, Colorado

Florida Agricultural and Mechanical University; Tallahassee, Florida

Illinois State University; Normal, Illinois

Indiana University; Bloomington, Indiana

Miami University; Oxford, Ohio

North Carolina State University; Raleigh, North Carolina

Oklahoma State University–Main Campus; Stillwater, Oklahoma

Pennsylvania State University; University Park, Pennsylvania

San Diego State University; San Diego, California

SUNY at Binghamton; Binghamton, New York

University of Akron; Akron, Ohio

University of Alabama; Tuscaloosa, Alabama

University of Hawaii at Manoa; Honolulu, Hawaii

University of Maryland–College Park; College Park, Maryland

University of South Florida; Tampa, Florida

Master's

Private

Alverno College; Milwaukee, Wisconsin

Bellevue University; Bellevue, Nebraska

Iona College; New Rochelle, New York

Johnson & Wales University; Providence, Rhode Island

Public

California State University-Sacramento; Sacramento, California

Ferris State University; Big Rapids, Michigan

Kennesaw State University; Kennesaw, Georgia

Northeastern Illinois University; Chicago, Illinois

San Jose State University; San Jose, California

Truman State University; Kirksville, Missouri

University of Northern Iowa; Cedar Falls, Iowa

William Paterson University of New Jersey; Wayne, New Jersey

Special/medical

University of Nebraska Medical Center; Omaha, Nebraska

Baccalaureate

Private

College of Saint Benedict; St. Joseph, Minnesota, and Saint John's
University; Collegeville, Minnesota

Moravian College and Theological Seminary; Bethlehem, Pennsylvania

Public

CUNY Medgar Evers College; Brooklyn, New York

St. Mary's College of Maryland; St. Mary's City, Maryland

United States Military Academy; West Point, New York

Associate

Public

Hocking College; Nelsonville, Ohio

Miami Dade College; Miami, Florida

St. Louis Community College; St. Louis, Missouri

The Community College of Baltimore County; Baltimore, Maryland

Tompkins Cortland Community College; Dryden, New York

Organization

American Council on Education and Consortium of Colleges and Universities

CONTRIBUTORS OF PROFILES INCLUDED IN THEIR ENTIRETY

Linda Anstendig, associate dean and professor of English, Pace University

Patrick Artz, associate professor, Bellevue University

Sarah Ash, associate professor, Department of Food Bioprocessing, and Nutrition Sciences, North Carolina State University

Joanne Bashford, associate provost for institutional effectiveness, Miami Dade College

Kim K. Bender, director of assessment, Colorado State University

Jennifer Blue, assistant professor of physics, Miami University

Victor M. H. Borden, associate vice president, Indiana University

Pam Bowers, former director, University Assessment and Testing, Oklahoma State University, and currently associate vice president for Planning, Assessment and Innovation at University of South Carolina

Marilee Bresciani, associate professor, Administration, Rehabilitation, and Postsecondary Education (ARPE), San Diego State University

Robert T. Brill, associate professor of psychology, Moravian College

Philip Burlingame, associate vice president for student affairs, The Pennsylvania State University

A. Katherine Busby, director of assessment and planning, University of Alabama

Jeanne A. Cameron, professor of sociology, Tompkins Cortland Community College

Vickii Castillon, student affairs assessment coordinator, California State University, Sacramento

Katherine A. Cermak, associate director, Office for Teaching, Learning and Assessment, DePaul University

Anne Ciliberti, director of library services, William Paterson University

Patti H. Clayton, director, Center for Excellence in Curricular Engagement, North Carolina State University

Ben Click, professor, English, St. Mary's College of Maryland

John J. Cosgrove, director, Institutional Research, Planning, and Assessment, St. Louis Community College

Linda Coughlin, associate provost, St. Mary's College of Maryland

Jodi Cressman, director, Office for Teaching, Learning and Assessment, DePaul University

Joanne M. Crossman, professor, Johnson & Wales University Graduate School

Roxanne Cullen, professor of English, Ferris State University

Andrea Dowhower, interim assistant vice president for Student Affairs and director of Student Affairs Research and Assessment, The Pennsylvania State University

Angeles L. Eames, executive director, Assessment and Program Review, Northeastern Illinois University

Sharmila Pixy Ferris, professor, Department of Communication, and director, Center for Teaching Excellence, William Paterson University

Sarah Burns Feyl, assistant university librarian for instructional services, Pace University

Donna M. Fish, dean, School of Liberal Arts, Excelsior College

Teresa Flateby, director of assessment, University of South Florida

Matthew B. Fuller, assistant director, University Assessment, Illinois State University

Gale E. Gibson, dean and professor, College of Freshman Studies, Medgar Evers College of the City University of New York

Gerrit W. Gong, assistant to the president for planning and assessment, Brigham Young University

Joan Y. Harms, specialist in research and assessment, University of Hawaii at Manoa

Michael Harris, provost and vice president for academic affairs, Kettering University

Judith Reisetter Hart, director, Institute for Educational Outreach, Alverno College

Karen B. Hauschild, associate director, First Year College, North Carolina State University

David A. Hoffman, assistant dean of student affairs and director, Office of Citizenship and Community Standards, Truman State University

Herbert Jaeger, professor of physics, Miami University

Jessica Katz Jameson, associate professor, North Carolina State University

Susan D. Johnson, former research analyst, University Planning, Institutional Research and Accountability, Indiana University, and currently program officer, Lumina Foundation for Education

Thomas P. Judd, assistant dean for academic assessment and assistant professor, United States Military Academy

Bruce Keith, professor of sociology and associate dean for academic affairs, United States Military Academy

Thomas F. Kowalik, director of continuing education and outreach, Binghamton University, SUNY

Philip I. Kramer, director of academic assessment and assistant professor, College of Saint Benedict and Saint John's University

Kathy Lake, associate vice president for academic affairs and professor of education, Alverno College

S. Sean Madison, district director, Learning Outcomes Assessment, Miami Dade College

Lynne A. Mason, associate professor, The Community College of Baltimore County

Judith A. Maxson, provost and senior vice-president, Academic Affairs, Hocking College

Lawrence J. McDoniel, professor of English, St. Louis Community College

Sean A. McKitrick, assistant provost for curriculum, instruction and assessment, Binghamton University (SUNY)

Edward M. McNertney, director, Core Curriculum, Texas Christian University

Rosalie V. Mince, dean of instruction for curriculum and assessment, The Community College of Baltimore County

Steven C. Myers, associate professor, The University of Akron

Michael A. Nelson, professor and chair, The University of Akron

Uche O. Ohia, director of university assessment, Florida Agricultural and Mechanical University (FAMU)

Danny R. Olsen, director, Institutional Assessment and Analysis, Brigham Young University

Christa Olson, associate director, Center for International Initiatives, American Council on Education

Jordan H. Orzoff, director of outcomes assessment and interprofessional education research, Western University of Health Sciences

Brian O'Sullivan, assistant professor of English and writing center director, St. Mary's College of Maryland

Judith A. Ouimet, senior research associate, Center for Evaluation and Education Policy, Indiana University Bloomington

Kim B. Outing, assistant director for assessment, First Year College, North Carolina State University

Paula E. Peinovich, managing partner, Right Sourcing Associates

Thomas P. Pusateri, associate director for scholarship of teaching and learning, and professor of psychology, Center for Excellence in Teaching and Learning, Kennesaw State University

William H. Rickards, senior research associate, Alverno College

Eric Riedel, executive director, Office of Institutional Research and Assessment, Walden University

Lenore Polo Rodicio, chairperson, Natural and Social Sciences, Miami Dade College, InterAmerican Campus

Glen Rogers, senior research associate, Alverno College

Warren Rosenberg, provost and vice president for academic affairs, Iona College

Susan Sciame-Giesecke, dean, School of Arts and Sciences, Indiana University Kokomo

Kristie K. Seawright, associate, Planning and Assessment, Brigham Young University

Larry L. Seawright, associate director, Center for Teaching and Learning, Brigham Young University

Robert A. Smallwood, assistant to the provost for assessment, University of Alabama

Bonnie Allen Smith, coordinator, Assessment of Student Academic Achievement, Hocking College

Jackie Snell, director of assessment, professor of marketing, San Jose State University

Greig Stewart, executive director, College Park Scholars, University of Maryland

Hugh A. Stoddard, assistant dean for medical education, director of curriculum development, University of Nebraska College of Medicine

Lois Thomas Stover, chair and professor, University of Maryland Baltimore County

Richard W. Stratton, associate professor of economics, The University of Akron

Rachel Jin Bee Tan, chief psychometrician, Schroeder Measurement Technologies, Inc.

Beverley A. P. Taylor, professor of physics, Miami University

Dawn Geronimo Terkla, associate provost, Institutional Research, Assessment and Evaluation, Tufts University

Ronald E. Terry, professor, Technology and Engineering Education, Brigham Young University

Stephanie L. Topping, assistant director, Institutional Research and Evaluation, Tufts University

Brigitte G. Valesey, assistant provost for teaching, learning and assessment, Widener University

Lori E. Varlotta, vice president for student affairs, California State University, Sacramento

Douglas Walcerz, vice president, TrueOutcomes, A Cengage Learning Company

Catherine M. Wehlburg, executive director, Office for Assessment and Quality Enhancement, Texas Christian University

Elizabeth Nutt Williams, dean of the core curriculum and first year experience, St. Mary's College of Maryland

Barry J. Wilson, college of education director of assessment, University of Northern Iowa

Mardell A. Wilson, assistant provost, Illinois State University

Midge Wilson, associate dean, College of Liberal Arts and Sciences, and liberal studies program director, DePaul University

Jill Wisniewski, program associate, Center for International Initiatives, American Council on Education

Jan M. Yarrison-Rice, professor of physics, Miami University

REFERENCES

Accreditation Council for Graduate Medical Education. *Common Program Requirements: General Competencies*. 2007. Accessed March 31, 2008, at www.acgme.org/outcome/comp/ GeneralCompetenciesStandards21307.pdf.

Aloi, S. L., Green, A. S., & Jones, E. A. "Creating a Culture of Assessment within West Virginia University's Student Affairs Division." *Assessment Update*, 2007, *19*(2), 7–9.

American Board of Internal Medicine Foundation, American College of Physicians, European Federation of Internal Medicine. "Medical Professionalism in the New Millennium: A Physician Charter." *Annals of Internal Medicine*, 2002, *136*(3), 243–6.

American College Personnel Association. *The Student Learning Imperative: Implications for Student Affairs*. Washington, D.C.: American College Personnel Association, 1994.

American Philosophical Association. *Critical Thinking: A Statement of Expert Consensus for Purposes of Educational Assessment and Instruction ("The Delphi Report")*. ERIC Document Reproduction No. ED 315 423. Newark, DE: American Philosophical Association, 1990.

American Productivity and Quality Center. *Benchmarking Best Practices in Assessing Learning Outcomes: Final Report*. Houston, TX: American Productivity and Quality Center, 1998.

Angelo, T. A., "Reassessing (and Defining) Assessment." *The AAHE Bulletin, 48*(2), November 1995, 7–9.

Association of American Colleges and Universities. *Global Learning for the New Century*. Washington, D.C.: Association of American Colleges and Universities, 2007.

Association of College and Research Libraries. *Information Literacy Competency Standards for Higher Education*. Chicago: ACRL, 2000. Available from www.ala.org/ala/mgrps/divs/acrl/ standards/informationliteracycompetency.cfm.

Bain, K. *What the Best College Teachers Do*. Cambridge, MA: Harvard University Press, 2004.

Banta, T. W. "Can Assessment for Accountability Complement Assessment for Improvement?" *Peer Review*, 2007, *9*(2), 9–12.

Banta, T. W., & Associates. *Making a Difference: Outcomes of a Decade of Assessment in Higher Education*. San Francisco: Jossey-Bass, 1993.

Banta, T. W., & Associates. *Building a Scholarship of Assessment*. San Francisco: Jossey Bass, 2002.

Banta, T. W., Lund, J. P., Black, K. E., & Oblander, F. W. *Assessment in Practice: Putting Principles to Work on College Campuses*. San Francisco: Jossey-Bass, 1996.

Bender, K. K., & Siller, T. J. "How an Engineering College Uses a University's Quality Enhancement System to Generate and Manage Evidence for Multiple Accreditation and Accountability Bodies." *Quality in Higher Education*, 2006, *12*(2), 175–191.

Bloom, B. S. (Ed.). *Taxonomy of Educational Objectives: The Classification of Educational Goals, Handbook 1: Cognitive Domain*. New York: McKay, 1956.

Boyer, E. L. "The Scholarship of Engagement." *Journal of Public Service & Outreach*, 1996, *1*(1).

Bresciani, M. J. *Outcomes-Based Academic and Co-Curricular Program Review*. Sterling, VA: Stylus, 2006.

Brigham Young University. "Mission Statement." Nov. 4, 1981. Available from http://unicomm.byu.edu/president/missionstatement.aspx.

Carnegie Foundation for the Advancement of Teaching. *Knowledge Media Lab*. (Originally launched March 2004). Retrieved January 28, 2009, from KEEP Toolkit Web site: http://www.cfkeep.org/static/index.html.

Checkoway, B. "Renewing the Civic Mission of the American Research University." *Journal of Higher Education*, 2001, *72*(1), 125–147.

Clayton, P. H., & Ash, S. L. "Shifts in Perspective: Capitalizing on the Counter-Normative Nature of Service-Learning." *Michigan Journal of Community Service Learning*, 2004, *11*(1), 59–70.

Diamond, R. M. *Designing and Assessing Courses and Curricula: A Practical Guide. Third Edition*. San Francisco: Jossey-Bass, 2008.

Diller, K. R., & Phelps, S. F. "Learning Outcomes, Portfolios, and Rubrics, Oh My! Authentic Assessment of an Information Literacy Program." *Libraries and the Academy*, 2008, *8*(1), 75–89.

Dolinsky, B., Matthews, R. S., Greenfield, G. M., Curtis-Tweed, P., & Evenbeck, S. E. "Assessment Is Essential for Implementing Successful First-Year Experience Programs." *Assessment Update*, 2007, *19*(6), 9–11.

Flateby, T. L., & Metzger, E. "Writing Assessment Instrument for Higher Order Thinking Skills." *Assessment Update*, 1999, *11*(2), 6–7.

Flateby, T. L., & Metzger, E. "Instructional Implications of the Cognitive Level and Quality of Writing Assessment." *Assessment Update*, 2001, *13*(1), 4–5.

Ginsburg, S., Regehr, G., Hatala, R., McNaughton, N., Frohna, A., & Hodges, B. "Context, Conflict, and Resolution: A New Conceptual Framework for Evaluating Professionalism." *Academic Medicine* 2000, *75*(10), S6–S11.

Goldberger, M. L., Maher, B. A., & Flattau, P. E. *Research-Doctorate Programs in the United States: Continuity and Change*. Washington, D.C.: National Academies Press, 1995.

Golde, C. M., & Pribbenow, D. A. "Understanding Faculty Involvement in Residential Learning Communities." *Journal of College Student Development*, 2000, *41*(1), 27–40.

Greene, J. C., Caracelli, V. J., & Graham, W. F. "Toward a Conceptual Framework for Mixed-Method Evaluation Designs." *Educational Evaluation and Policy Analysis*, 1989, *11*(3), 255–274.

Hairston, M., Ruskiewicz, J., & Friend, C. *The Scott Foresman Handbook for Writers*. New York: Longman/Addison-Wesley, 1999.

Hansen, W. L. "What Knowledge Is Most Worth Knowing—For Economics Majors?" *American Economic Review*, 1986, *76*(2), 149–152.

Hansen, W. L. "Expected Proficiencies for Undergraduate Economics Majors." *Journal of Economic Education*, 2001, *32*(3), 231–242.

Harkavy, I. "Foreword." In S. L. Percy, N. L. Zimpher, & M. J. Brukardt (Eds.), *Creating a New Kind of University: Institutionalizing Community-University Engagement*. Bolton, MA: Anker, 2006.

Hill, J. "Developing a Culture of Assessment: Insights from Theory and Experience." *Journal of Political Science Education*, 2005, *1*(1), 29–37.

Hodges, J., et al. *Harbrace College Handbook*. Fort Worth, TX: HB College Publishers, 1998.

Howard, J. *Academic Service Learning: A Counter Normative Pedagogy*. In R. Rhoads & J. Howard (Eds.), New Directions in Teaching and Learning, no. 73. San Francisco, CA: Jossey-Bass, 1998.

Hutchings, P. "Principles of Good Practice for Assessing Student Learning." *Assessment Update*, 1993, *5*(1), 6–7.

Ibarra, H., & Lineback, K. "What's Your Story?" *Harvard Business Review*, 2005, *83*(1), 64–71.

Illinois Board of Higher Education. (2004, December). The Illinois Commitment. Retrieved March 31, 2008, from www.ibhe.org/Board/agendas/2004/December/IllinoisCommitment04.pdf.

Illinois Board of Higher Education Faculty Advisory Committee. (2003, May 2). IBHE FAC. Retrieved March 31, 2008, from www.ibhefac.org/HTMLobj-679/Minutes_May03v3.rtf.

Jones, E. A. *Transforming the Curriculum: Preparing Students for a Changing World*. ASHE-ERIC Higher Education Report, 2002, 29(3). San Francisco: Jossey-Bass.

Jones, E. A., Voorhees, R. A., & Paulson, K. *Defining and Assessing Competency-Based Initiatives*. Washington, D.C.: United States Department of Education and the National Postsecondary Education Cooperative, 2002.

Kuh, G. D., Kinzie, J., Buckley, J. A., Bridges, B. K., & Hayek, J. C. *Piecing Together the Student Success Puzzle: Research, Propositions, and Recommendations*. ASHE Higher Education Report, 2007, 32(5). San Francisco: Jossey-Bass.

Kuh, G. D., Kinzie, J., Schuh, J. H., Whitt, E. J., & Associates. *Student Success in College: Creating Conditions That Matter*. San Francisco: Jossey-Bass, 2005.

Lalli, J. S., Browder, D. M., Mace, F. C., & Brown, D. K. "Teacher Use of Descriptive Analysis Data to Implement Interventions to Decrease Students' Problem Behaviors." *Journal of Applied Behavior Analysis*, 1993, *26*(2), 227–238.

Liaison Committee on Medical Education. "Functions and Structure of a Medical School: Standards for Accreditation of Medical Education Programs Leading to the M.D. Degree." 2007. Accessed March 31, 2008, at www.lcme.org/functions2007jun.pdf.

Licklider, B. L., Schnelker, D. L., & Fulton, C. "Revisioning Faculty Development for Changing Times: The Foundation and Framework." *Journal of Staff, Program, and Organizational Development*, 1997, *15*(3), 121–133.

Lopez, C. L. (2004). "A Decade of Assessing Student Learning: What We Have Learned, and What Is Next." In P. Hernon & R. E. Dugan (Eds.), *Outcomes Assessment in Higher Education: Views and Perspectives*. Santa Barbara, CA: Libraries Unlimited, 29–71.

Lunsford, A., & Connors, R. *The St. Martin's Handbook*. New York: St. Martin's Press, 1992.

Maki, P. L. (2004). *Assessing for Learning: Building a Sustainable Commitment across the Institution*. Sterling, VA: Stylus, 2004.

Malandra, G. H. "Accountability and Learning Assessment in the Future of Higher Education." *On The Horizon*, 2008, *16*(2), 57–71.

March, A. "Multilayered Inquiry for Program Reviews." In A. Driscoll & D. Cordero de Noriega (Eds.), *Taking Ownership of Accreditation: Assessment Process That Promote Institutional Improvement and Faculty Engagement*. Sterling, VA: Stylus, 2006.

Millett, C. M., Payne, D. G., Dwyer, C. A., Stickler, L. M., & Alexiou, J. J. *A Culture of Evidence: An Evidence-Centered Approach to Accountability for Student Learning Outcomes*. Princeton, NJ: Educational Testing Service, 2008.

National Board of Medical Examiners. Embedding professionalism in medical education: Assessment as a tool for implementation. 2002. Accessed March 31, 2008, at http://ci.nbme .org/professionalism/default.asp.

National Study of Living-Learning Programs. Retrieved December 6, 2007, from www .livelearnstudy.net/.

Nesheim, B. E., Guentzel, M. J., Kellogg, A. H., McDonald, W. M., Wells, C. A., & Whitt, E. J. "Outcomes for Students of Student Affairs-Academic Affairs Partnership Programs." *Journal of College Student Development*, 2007, *48*(4), 435–454.

New York State Department of Education. Principles and Operational Criteria for Good Practice Indicators in Higher Education, 2007. Accessed January 30, 2009, at http://www.highered.nysed.gov/ocue/ded/practice.html.

Ostriker, J. P., & Kuh, C. V. (Eds.). *Assessing Research-Doctorate Programs: A Methodology Study*. Washington, D.C.: National Academies Press, 2003.

Palomba, C. A., & Banta, T. W. *Assessment Essentials: Planning, Implementing, and Improving Assessment in Higher Education*. San Francisco: Jossey-Bass, 1999.

Pascarella, E. T., & Terenzini, P. T. *How College Affects Students: Findings and Insights from Twenty Years of Research*. San Francisco: Jossey Bass, 1991.

Pascarella, E. T., & Terenzini, P. T. *How College Affects Students, Volume 2: A Third Decade of Research*. San Francisco: Jossey-Bass, 2005.

Paul, R., & Elder, L. *The Miniature Guide to Critical Thinking*. Santa Rosa, CA.: The Foundation for Critical Thinking, 2001. Available from www.criticalthinking.org.

Peterson, M. W., Einarson, M. K., Augustine, H. C., & Vaughan, D. S. *Institutional Support for Student Assessment: Methodology and Results of a National Survey*. Stanford, CA: National Center for Postsecondary Improvement, 1999.

Peterson, M. W., & Vaughan, D. S. "Promoting Academic Improvement: Organizational and Administrative Dynamics That Support Student Assessment." In T. Banta (Ed.), *Building a Scholarship of Assessment*. San Francisco: Jossey Bass, 2002.

Phelan S., Obenshain S. S., & Galey W. R. "Evaluation of the Non-Cognitive Traits of Medical Students." *Academic Medicine*, 1993, *68*(10), 799–803.

Schrader, P. G., & Brown, S. W. "Evaluating the First Year Experience: Students' Knowledge, Attitudes, and Behaviors." *Journal of Advanced Academics*, 2008, *19*(2), 310–343.

Seybert, J. *Assessing Student Learning Outcomes*. New Directions for Community Colleges, no. 117. Jossey-Bass: San Francisco, 2002.

State Higher Education Executive Officers. *Accountability for Better Results: A National Imperative*. Boulder, CO: State Higher Education Executive Officers, 2005.

Suskie, L. *Assessing Student Learning: A Common Sense Guide*. Bolton, MA: Anker, 2004.

Troxel, W. G., & Cutright, M. *Exploring the Evidence: Initiatives in the First College Year*. Columbia, SC: National Resource Center on the First-Year Experience and Students in Transition, 2008.

United States Department of Education. *A Test of Leadership: Charting the Future of U.S. Higher Education*. Washington, D.C.: United States Department of Education, 2006.

Walvoord, B. E. *Assessment Clear and Simple*. San Francisco: Jossey-Bass, 2004.

Widener University (2006, October). *Self-Study Report for Re-Accreditation by the Middle States Commission on Higher Education*. Chester, PA: Author.

INDEX

Page references followed by *fig* indicate an illustrated figure; followed by *t* indicate a table; followed by *e* indicate an exhibit.